Outspeak

Narrating Identities That Matter

Sean P. O'Connell

State University of New York Press

Published by
State University of New York Press, Albany

Printed in the United States of America

For information, address State University of New York Press,
90 State Street, Suite 700, Albany, NY 12207

Production by Kristin Milavec
Marketing by Anne M. Valentine

Library of Congress Cataloging-in-Publication Data

O'Connell, Sean P., 1958–
    Outspeak : narrating identities that matter / Sean P. O'Connell.
        p.   cm.
    Includes bibliographical references and index.
    ISBN 0-7914-4737-5 (hc : alk. paper)—ISBN 0-7914-4738-3
        (pbk. : alk. paper)
    1. Gay men—Identity.   2. Lesbians—Identity.   3. Gender identity—
Philosophy.   4. Identity (Psychology).   I. Title.
HQ76.036 2000
306.76'62—dc21

                                                                99-086459

10   9   8   7   6   5   4   3   2   1

For my Bill, whose
love and support these
past fourteen years have
meant everything to me

Contents

Acknowledgments

Without the support and encouragement of a number of people and institutions, this book could not have come about. I thank Jeremiah Coffey, Susan Cole, Ellen Feder, Honi Haber, Michael Hartwig, Morris Kaplan, Edward Stein, James Swan-Tuite, Gail Weiss, and Philip Zampini whose friendship, conversation, and comments on early drafts of this book inspired me to continue working on it despite the many responsibilities and diversions that come with being a faculty member at a small college. I thank Sharon Meagher, Wendy Farley, and Alison Leigh Brown for their careful and insightful readings of the manuscript. Their comments were pivotal to its completion and were the impetus for the addition of several important sections of the text. I thank Karsten Harries for sponsoring me as a Yale Visiting Faculty Fellow, for reading and commenting upon significant sections of this book, and for enriching my intellectual life in countless ways. I thank my many students at Albertus Magnus College who taught me the responsibilities of listening. I thank David Hoy, Jocelyn Hoy, Hubert Dreyfus, and Merold Westphal for sponsoring various grant applications and providing feedback on this project. I thank the National Endowment for the Humanities, Yale University, and Albertus Magnus College for financial support that enabled me to participate in seminars and institutes, and that gave me the most precious gift of time for writing. I thank the production staff at the State University of New York Press for their patience and care in the production of this book.

I thank Taylor & Francis/Routledge, Inc. for permission to reprint Sean P. O'Connell, "Claiming One's Identity: A Constructivist/ Narrativist Approach," originally published in *Perspectives on Embodiment,* edited by Gail Weiss and Honi Fern Haber, pages 61–78. Copyright © 1999.

Finally, I thank my family, my parents, Dennis and Evelyn O'Connell, my brother, Dennis, and my partner, William, for their unfailing patience, support, and love.

Introduction

MCI, the telecommunications firm, recently produced an advertisement for its internet service that praised the internet for opening a new age in which one could free oneself from one's gender, race, age, and appearance, thereby enabling one to become who one "truly" is. This promotion has a very "American" feel to it insofar as it promotes the image of the "self-made man," and the idea that individuals can be whatever they want so long as they take initiative and responsibility for themselves. But this idea of finding oneself by freeing oneself is actually a puzzling one, for in the last analysis, it is difficult to imagine what would be left after separating oneself from one's history and environment. Yet, the appeal of this advertisement, the dream of freedom that it promotes, is unmistakable given how the social and conceptual structures at play in identity formation in contemporary society operate to constrain and, in many cases, to oppress the subjects constituted through them or, as Judith Butler and Luce Irigaray have argued, refused them.

The dream promoted by MCI is actually the dream of a nonrepressive community, but what is interesting is how this particular advertisement makes explicit the fact that such a community can be realized only through the exclusion of difference, of multiplicity, and ultimately of the very conditions that make genuine community and meaningful life possible. To live a meaningful life requires a context, I would argue a narrative context, sufficiently rich to enable one to realize an identity, a coherent understanding of who one is and how one stands in relation to others. The danger is that the context may well consist of a way of life informed by a world-view that claims to be comprehensive, to offer only one acceptable end or goal for human thought and action.

Curiously, contemporary American culture at once makes apparent the dangers of attempting to escape all cultural contexts or of embracing world-views that claim to offer comprehensive accounts of what it means to be. Despite the existence of a predominant culture, America is a pluralist society. In "Nihilism and Black America," Cornel West makes the point that the absence of a sufficiently compelling mythic vision operative in the culture is at the core of the sense of nihilism, the sense that life is meaningless, hopeless, and loveless, that most tellingly operates in the African-American community, but is at work throughout American society.

Without a sufficiently rich context, there can be no meaningful life. At the same time, the plurality of world-views operative within American society makes apparent the dangers attendant upon adopting a world-view. Many of the world-views that are operative claim to be comprehensive and thereby seek to exclude not only other world-views, but also those who adhere to them. Additionally, these various world-views mark differences that work to exclude and to oppress those who are constituted through them. Finally, the very plurality of world-views tends to set the individual adrift, to constitute the atomized individual who is forced to choose between the various alternatives, either by employing criteria that are already informed by some determinate vision, or by pretending to an objectivity that is impossible.

My aim in this book is to explore the possibilities for realizing a relation between society, community, individual, and world-view, or mythic vision, that can at once recognize the value and necessity of context for constituting a meaningful life and provide resources for addressing the various possibilities for oppression and exclusion that are entailed thereby. My access to this large question is through work currently being done in gender theory. This choice of access is undoubtedly rooted in my own quest for constructing a meaningful life as someone who, through much struggle, has come to identify himself as a gay man. However, as should be evident, the issues at stake should concern everyone in contemporary American society, in particular those who experience themselves as marginalized in this society. Hopefully, the theoretical tale that I weave in what follows will serve as a useful touchstone for anyone wrestling with these issues.

In turning to gender theory, what is initially striking is that many gender theorists, following Michel Foucault, are suspicious of any world-view that claims to disclose the meaning of being, as well as of the various hermeneutics of suspicion, which attempt to disclose a reality underlying articulated world-views. There are a number of reasons for this. Most pointedly, fundamental to gender theory as liberatory praxis, is the recognition that gender identity can be used as the tool of oppression. Foucault's work supports the claim that gender identity is constructed and in the service of power relations, thereby enabling a restructuring of the semantic field so that traditional categories and ways of framing questions dissolve. But, as Judith Butler points out in *Bodies That Matter*, Foucault leaves largely unthematized the fact that the construction of gender identity requires a foreclosure of other possibilities, possibilities whose potential to make a claim upon us is fundamental to the economy of social transformation. Foucault's work does not take up the power of possibility, of the absent, the unnamed and perhaps unnamable, to make a claim upon us so that even in the realization of our most ambitious projects, we feel the pain of absence, of what might have been had we taken another course. An appeal to the possible has the potential to be a valuable resource for those seeking strategies for disrupting the power relations at work in contemporary society, and in particular for those concerned about oppressive gender formations. But if it is to serve as such, it is necessary to weave a tale about the nature or character of world-views as both lived and articulated that can meet Foucault's reservations regarding them. I believe that the resources for doing this are to be found by mining the hermeneutical projects of Heidegger, Ricoeur, and Gadamer. In so doing, it will be possible not only to rethink but to reconstitute the relations between world-view, society, self, and community in a way that will at once promote the constitution of a meaningful life and provide resources for addressing the exclusionary and oppressive possibilities that are woven into the very fabric of contexts of meaning.

Chapter 1, "Coping with Chaos in Pluralist America: Between Gender Oppression and the Foreclosure of Meaning," introduces the problematic, examines and assesses Foucault's work as it has been employed in gay and lesbian studies, and argues that we turn to Heidegger, Gadamer, and Ricoeur to develop an approach to gender theory as praxis built on the insights of Judith Butler. The chapter begins with an exploration of the significance that participation in a community with a shared life secured through shared belief systems, practices, and a common language grounded in a shared world-view has for the self-understanding of many people. It then raises the question of whether or not the quest for meaning might itself be suspect, and turns to a consideration of the difficulties attendant upon the claim that discourses articulating the world-views of individuals and of particular communities located within a pluralist society have disclosive power. In particular, it takes up the tale that Foucault tells of how the belief that reality has a deep meaning can operate in webs of power relations to constitute personal and social identities, and to generate knowledges that carry within them the seeds of oppression. This discussion highlights the fact that Foucault's work implies that gender identity is constructed and in the service of power relations, and explores why this is of interest to those working in gay and lesbian studies. While emphasizing Foucault's contribution to gender studies, the discussion concludes, by drawing upon the work of Judith Butler and Luce Irigaray, that his description of the ontogenetic function of discourse does not go far enough. Foucault effectively challenges any attempts at grounding the meaning of life and personal identity through appeal to some transcendent reality understood as "how things are," or "ought to be." But he does not take advantage of the fact that his work leaves open the possibility that world-views might make a claim upon us as articulations of possibilities for being in the world. What this means and its significance for gay and lesbian political praxis are the concerns of the last part of the chapter. This last section takes up the hermeneutical projects of Heidegger, Gadamer, and Ricoeur to show how the articulations of world-views might be so visioned as to serve as viable resources for disrupting the power relations at work in contemporary gender and sexual formations.

Chapter 2, "Hearing Gay Voices: Toward Building Community in a Pluralist Society," develops an alternative to Foucault's account of politics as war continued by other means, an alternative that shows how individuals can reasonably commit themselves to specific social agendas informed by determinate world-views and at the same time seek dialogue with individuals who maintain different and often competing world-views. The chapter opens with a reflection on the difficulties of constituting a meaningful life in a pluralist society. Such a society offers us a number of competing world-views, each of which dictates how we should make sense of our lives. Picking up on the thesis developed in the first chapter, chapter 2 shows how it is possible to mitigate these difficulties by reading people's accounts of who they are as testimony to possibilities for being in the world, as opposed to exhaustive, absolute accounts of reality. John McNeill's *The Church and the Homosexual* and Arthur Evans's *The God of Ecstasy* serve as focal points for developing this thesis. The two works share a common goal of developing a positive vision of what it means to be gay by engaging particular world-views and their foundational myths, but differ in respect to the mythic visions they address. McNeill develops an interpretation of the Judeo-Christian tradition that can accommodate a positive vision and role in the community for gays and lesbians. Evans steps out of the Judeo-Christian tradition and turns to a discussion of the worship of Dionysus in early Greek culture to develop an account of what it means to be gay in a world that is free from the influence of the predominant patriarchal paradigm operative in contemporary Western culture. By viewing these works as testimony to possibilities for being in the world, it becomes possible to avoid the usual dangers attendant upon absolutist accounts of reality. At the same time, such viewing provides a basis for maintaining that these works can sustain meaningful action and can thus make a claim to be heard. The argument also draws upon Gabriel Marcel's account of testimony and Paul Ricoeur's discussion of the disclosive power of myths. It takes seriously the Heideggerian claim "that what we understand first in a discourse is not another person, but a 'project,' that is, the outline of a new way of being in the world." It shows how it is possible to read testimony as the insight into being that is afforded by the individual's unique situation. As Ricoeur notes, one's situation constitutes one's opening onto being, one's access to being, in terms of which one gains insight, insight characterized by Ricoeur as an event of truth. Such a view promotes recognition of the limitations of one's own testimony, leaves ample room for suspicion, and encourages listening to what others have to say. Exploring these implications in some detail makes clear the possibility of genuine commitment on the part of the individual and the desirability of a society which does not merely tolerate the presence of a plurality of world-views, but encourages critical and engaged dialogue between those sustained by different visions of reality. In short, it shows the possibility and the desirability of a certain sort of dialogical community. In the course of this discussion, I shall address a number of difficulties, the most obvious being that such a community, which has the goal of promoting dialogue, must itself be informed by a single mythic vision or world-view. In addition, I shall distance myself from Jurgen Habermas's and Seyla Benhabib's respective theories of communicative ethics and the sorts of conversations that they envision to be possible and desirable between people holding differing world-views in a pluralist society. The chapter concludes with a consideration of how adopting the models of community and dialogue developed in it would impact the work of those engaged in gender studies as praxis.

Chapter 3, "Claiming One's Identity: A Constructivist/Narrativist Approach," explores the process of bodily materialization whereby individual and community identity formation is realized. This chapter attempts a synthesis of key insights from Judith Butler, Jacques Lacan, and the narrative theories of Paul Ricoeur and David Carr. The synthesis suggests that a creative tension can be maintained, in the life of the individual and the community, between stable identities that are performatively realized in bodily materializations and the possibilities for subjectivity foreclosed by these very realizations. The chapter opens with a brief discussion of Eve Kosofsky Sedgwick's contention that, despite the apparent opposition between appeals to nature and to nurture to account for sexual orientation, both are alike in their privileging of heterosexuality. The suggestion is made that by thematizing the constructed character of sexuality, we will accomplish three things:

1. We will meet Kosofsky Sedgwick's concern by marking the artificiality of making sexual identity and

orientation the pivotal axis for determining personal identity.

2. We will provide a space for maintaining that sexual orientation and identity, although constructed, are nonetheless real, thereby opening an avenue for honoring the attestations of those maintaining such identities as gay, lesbian, or bisexual.

3. We will show that recognizing the sense in which these identities are real carries with it important implications for approaching life in the community and for engaging in political praxis.

In brief, the assertion is made that many who identify themselves as gay, lesbian, or bisexual see such identifications as responses to something in themselves that they had to integrate into their identities if they were to be true to themselves. A constructivist approach to sexual identity and orientation must be able to honor such attestations while avoiding the dangers that Kosofsky Sedgwick's work makes apparent. The chapter shows that it is possible to develop such an account of the constructed character of sexual identity and orientation by drawing on the work of Judith Butler and Paul Ricoeur. Ricoeur's description of cultural language supports the view that articulations of sexuality and sexual identity, while culturally informed, can nonetheless have disclosive power. Butler's work, particularly her discussion of Lacan, lends support to Ricoeur's position because it arrives at a similar conclusion by a different route. In addition, it deepens the discussion by explicitly looking at sexual identity formation and by addressing the particular dangers attaching to all articulations of sexual identity. Engaging Butler's discussion of the latter makes clear that dismissing professions of sexual identity as misguided or mistaken because such identities are "mere constructions" constitutes a form of violence against those who claim them, while refusing to problematize those very identities leads to still other forms of violence. It is in this context that Ricoeur's account of identity as narratively configured, supported by Heidegger's discussion of gift, makes a second contribution to the discussion. Ricoeur's description of personal identity as a narrative formation affords a way of thinking about claims to sexual identity which honors Butler's concerns by making it possible to think about attestations of sexual identity as at once legitimate and subject to the sort of contestation essential to liberatory praxis. In short, the last part of the chapter addresses three questions:

1. How can we respect the claims of subjects regarding their gender identity?

2. How can we challenge those very claims when they fail to recognize their own contingency, their status as conditioned possibilities?

3. How can we exploit the contingency of gender identity formation for liberatory praxis?

The first three chapters depend upon an account of the disclosive and constructive power of discourse and narrative to support the possibility for the formation of individual and social identities that can sustain meaningful life and action while at the same time disturbing the dangers of dogmatism, totalitarianism, and authoritarianism. The last two chapters, "Speaking What Has Yet to Be Said: The Call for Giving Voice to Responsive Narratives and to Hearing beyond Them" and "Controlling Stories/Conflicting Narratives," argue that realizing such a project requires one to move beyond merely listening to others or merely questioning oneself and others. Taking into account the reality of power differentials that serve to constrain and to silence opens a space for such listening and questioning, but it is not enough if the other has no language to speak what needs to be said. These chapters explore the obligations that accrue from this recognition, the obstacles encountered in meeting them, and how they might be met. They take as their focal point the peculiar challenges facing gays and lesbians seeking to construct a meaningful life narrative in a heterosexist society. Chapter 4 opens by pressing the claim that our understandings of who we are and how we stand in relation to the world and to others is narratively configured. This is important for three reasons:

1. It sets the conditions for meaningful discourse;

2. It shows how the very process of narrative understanding contributes to the production of the abject,

which is essential for discovering not only new stories, but new *kinds* of stories by ... attending to what remains undisclosed but present as undisclosed in the narratives through which individuals have become who they are;

3. It makes it possible to recognize that the story that one tells *about* the character of narrative understanding can provide those who identify themselves as gay, lesbian, or bisexual with clues for engaging in meaningful political praxis and constituting a meaningful life.

From a somewhat different angle, recognizing that one's understanding is narratively configured militates against dogmatism and provides impetus for not being at home in one's own narrative universe. It thereby opens a space for meaningful dialogue, understood as dialogue that engages the other in his or her otherness. At the same time, it creates a space for considering how the narrative structure of human understanding poses obstacles to dialogue with the other as other and to the formation of genuine community. A detailed description of the narrative structure of human understanding, one that draws heavily upon the work of Jean-Francois Lyotard, sets the stage for articulating and addressing two sets of obstacles. The first set of obstacles stems from one of the implications of this description, namely that, while human beings can make sense of their lives narratively, they cannot do so in such a way that conflicting narrative possibilities can be dismissed, though these possibilities might well be refused. In other words, when and if one comes to reflect critically upon the narrative universe informing one's existence, and on conflicting narratives, one cannot decide between them in some objective way, nor can one establish criteria for social discourse and praxis that could forestall all objections to any claims to legitimacy these criteria might make. Recognizing this carries with it the advantage of making one sensitive to the inevitable coloring that one's deliberations take on, given the language employed. But this advantage contains a danger: to use the language of Gadamer, one cannot escape all prejudices (prejudgments). It is a prejudice to think that such escape would even be desirable, for it would amount to foreclosing all possibilities. But it does mean continually putting at risk the other, reading the other to the other's disadvantage. It therefore poses serious challenges with respect to justice and to the constitution of meaning for those seeking to live meaningful, satisfying lives in a pluralist society. This constitutes the first set of difficulties. The second set pertains to the structure of narrative itself and is of particular concern to gays and lesbians. Judith Roof's *Come As You Are* raises the question: What if the very structure of narrative itself carries within it the tendency to exclude and to marginalize? Might there be something about the logic of narrative structure that contributes not only to conflicts between people, but to the exclusion and silencing of those who cannot be accommodated within the narrative? More specifically, if the narrative structure that we have been taught, regardless of the specific narratives that we construct, conspires with a heterosexist logic, then the very course of all narrative possibilities will be irremediably confined in such a way that the place at the table for gays and lesbians cannot be that of dialogical partner. The stories that gays and lesbians could tell would have to be hopeless ones, or ones that would allow them to take solace in the fact that they were fighting the good fight by trying to mimic the heterosexual in a homosexual key, even if they could not possibly succeed.

The first set of difficulties is addressed by taking up Lyotard's claim in *The Postmodern Condition* that "to speak is to fight." In brief, chapter 4 maintains that if one's interest is in the marginalized and the forgotten, it is good to recognize both the fertile power of Lyotard's metaphor, the extent to which it guards one against totalizing narratives, and to attune one's ear to other possibilities, such as those opened when Emmanuel Levinas proclaims, "the face speaks," a claim that does not preclude the possibilities opened by Lyotard's metaphor, but that nonetheless invites one to hear something quite different. One must move beyond an agonistic view of narrative discourse if one is to attend to the other as other, and more significantly, if one is to meet one's obligation to respond to the demands of the other to be heard when the other has no voice and no language. The discussion concludes with some provisional suggestions about what it might mean for someone who finds herself or himself identified as lesbian or gay in the discourses at play in mainstream American society, to assume responsibility for the other in the construction of one's narratives.

Chapter 5 takes up Roof's concerns regarding the mutual imbrication of narrative and heterosexist logic. Roof rightly maintains
that it is neither possible nor desirable to abandon narrative understanding. But when narrative and heterosexist logic form an alliance that affords only oppressive and oppressing life-stories, those
of us who have come to understand ourselves as lesbian, gay, or bisexual by virtue of the narratives available to us, must discover
some way of negotiating these contexts. While Roof is justly pes-
simistic about succeeding in breaking what she sees as a virtually
inevitable alliance of narrative and heterosexist logic, the argument
of this chapter is that it is possible to weave a tale of narrative that
encourages the telling of tales as a liberatory strategy. Analyses of
the "coming out" episode of *Ellen* and the Bruce Willis film, *The
Fifth Element*, are used to illustrate and support Roof's contention
that there is a hegemonic heterosexual narrative at work in Western culture today, and that "our understandings of narrative are
both gendered and heterosexually inflected," such that our conception of narrative and the heterosexual narrative create a synergy
that is hard to resist, one that is oppressive to gays and lesbians.
But the chapter suggests that it is nonetheless possible to find a
way to work within the interplay of sedimentation and innovation
that Ricoeur characterizes as constituting a living tradition in
order to fulfill our responsibilities to ourselves and others to challenge and to be challenged by the stories that we tell. A first step in
this direction would be to recognize those stories that roughly follow the narrative arc that meets traditional Western expectations
regarding what counts as a satisfying story, but do not work either
to privilege heterosexuality or marginalize gays and lesbians. Precisely because they draw upon narrative expectations, these stories
are followable, carry with them a sense of probability, cannot be
simply dismissed as they engage the values and concerns at play in
the hegemonic narrative, and open alternative possibilities for
being in the world, even if they are initially thought to be impossible. Chapter 5 illustrates the potential of such a strategy by looking
at John Boswell's Christian story of salvation, *Same-Sex Unions,* at
Martha Nussbaum's Platonic love story, "Love and the Individual,"
and at Henning Bech's story of modernity, *when men meet.*

As this introduction suggests, I have enlisted the work of many
creative thinkers to explore the terrain outlined here. This poses a
number of dangers, such as misconstruing their views, writing a

text that is inaccessible, and losing sight of the issues that are at stake. I doubt that it is possible to completely avoid any of these dangers, but believe that the journey that I have taken in writing this book has helped to somewhat mitigate the last two. Despite the theoretical issues addressed in this book, it was not merely an academic exercise, and it is not intended to be merely of academic interest. As someone who was raised a devout Catholic and who attended a Catholic seminary, I found it difficult to apply the label "gay" to myself. When I finally did so, it was a liberating experience. At the same time, I came to recognize the power of this label to constrain, marginalize, and serve as the instrument of oppression. Through the years, I have seen and felt its power to silence, promote, and shape discourse. I began this book with the naïve hope that it would encourage straight people to listen carefully to what gays and lesbians have to say about themselves, to give credence to their testimony. Writing it has led me to an abiding appreciation for the significance of this testimony, combined with a sobering recognition of its limitations, of the power of such testimony to actually contribute to hegemonic discourse. I have also learned about the power of silence to testify to what cannot be spoken in the language that is at hand, and of the imperative to speak, to speak against the silencing of voices whose speech can speak, despite language and because of language, what must be said. Hopefully, this book will contribute to a better speaking and to a better listening.

COPING WITH CHAOS IN PLURALIST AMERICA
Between Gender Oppression and the Foreclosure of Meaning

Man does not decide whether and how beings appear, whether and how God and the gods or history and nature come forward into the light of Being, come to presence and depart. The advent of beings lies in the destiny of Being. But for man, it is ever a question of finding what is fitting in his essence, which corresponds to such destiny . . . Man is the shepherd of Being.

—Martin Heidegger, *Basic Writings*

—*mm*—

The setting is a class of fifteen students in an introductory social and political philosophy class. It is the end of the semester in a small Catholic college. The topic is gay and lesbian civil rights; four students are presenting various positions using a "talk show format." Two presenters have just given arguments favoring civil rights protections for gays and lesbians. The third begins developing an argument for the contrary position using natural law, when one of the students in the audience starts almost to cheer and make arm gestures in support of what is being said. This student is a clean-cut, white, nineteen-year-old male who plays sports, gets good grades, and typically does not question authority. Why this passion from someone who is usually unassuming, well-mannered, and interested in pleasing his teachers? His behavior seems out of character, especially in a classroom with only fifteen students in it. I cannot resist, so I turn and ask why he cares about this so much. The class laughs, and the student does not seem to mind the question. But he is surprised. He stumbles for an answer. Eventually, he says that the world is peopled with vipers, and that we have to draw the line somewhere. Actually, this reply does not surprise me, but I do not trust myself with a response and, after all, there is a panel of students who have the floor. The third presenter resumes his argument, and I give him a run for his money in the question-and-answer session.

Despite the many theories on the subject, the most puzzling thing to me is my student's insistence on drawing the line at sexual orientation. What is not quite so puzzling is his desire to "draw the line" somewhere, and it is this desire that I want to address. It is an old story that people typically understand themselves and their lives in the context of a community, and that communal membership is framed in terms of those who belong and those who do not. Communal life is secured through belief systems, practices, and a common language, all of which are grounded in a shared world-view with its attendant set of commitments. Most pernicious to communal identity, and to the sense of meaning that it provides for its members, is not external attack but self-doubt, the suspicion that the vision of life underpinning communal practices is off the mark. I think an argument could be made that, at a deep level, there is a shared vision of life, a shared language operative in American society. If actions are symptomatic, conspicuous consumption is not the unique province of pubescent adolescents and yuppies. From my own experience, staid academics, "radical deconstructionists," Marxists, and guppies all like to shop. Is buying Judith Butler's latest book or a nose ring really so different when what is at stake is status? Still, I do not want to lose contact with my student's statement. There is discomfort. American society is a pluralist society; perhaps this is enough to generate space for self-doubt. Or perhaps, the vision of things that underpins shopping, whether it is expressed or unexpressed, is just not enough, not enough to give this student the order, meaning, protection, and sense of belonging for which he yearns. And the yearning itself is real, not isolated to one person. Ironically, this very longing animates many of the queers this student would find so abhorrent. In his introduction to the Vintage edition of *The Culture of Desire,* Frank Browning expresses his own ambivalence for what he calls "culture making," and suggests that, for "gays" at least, making culture is a self-conscious act of will, one that involves continual remaking. But he ends with the following revealing remark:

> If, however, we are free to find our own culture through nothing more than the force of collective self-assertion, through naming and renaming, forming and reforming ourselves until memory has no possibility of meaning, it may also be that we are condemned to dwell in the solitude of our self-invention, in which the culture of desire turns out to be nothing more than the loneliest of American longings, the simple desire for culture.[1]

This desire for culture, what I take ultimately to be a desire for community, has as its night side a deep-seated anxiety that life, in particular my individual life, is not and cannot be in any ultimate sense meaningful. I think that Cornel West best captures this sense of anxiety in his characterization of nihilism as the greatest threat facing the African-American community:

> The proper starting point for the crucial debate about the prospects for black America is the nihilism that increasingly pervades black communities. *Nihilism is to be understood here not as a philosophic doctrine that there are no rational grounds for legitimate standards or authority; it is, far more, the lived experience of coping with a life of horrifying meaninglessness, hopelessness, and (most important) lovelessness.* This usually results in a numbing detachment from others and a self-destructive disposition toward the world. Life without meaning, hope, and love breeds a coldhearted, mean-spirited outlook that destroys both the individual and others.[2]

Although West does not concern himself here with philosophical attempts to surmount some form of cosmic nihilism, what is nonetheless at issue is the realization of a context in which one can engage in a meaningful life. Is it not this context that my student, gays and lesbians, queers, African Americans, and fundamentalist evangelicals all seek? One might wish to avoid the meaningfulness/meaninglessness dyad, and indeed, if one can no longer affirm that life is meaningful in some nonarbitrary sense, there may even be incentive to investigate the possibility of some other framework for approaching living. But the point here is that the question is existentially meaningful to Americans and will not be lightly abandoned.

And yet, as someone who took a long time to call himself a gay male and who found the experience marvelously liberating, I nevertheless have to wonder. Despite the extent to which the question of meaning has become critical for many in contemporary western society, for those who have found themselves cast in the role of the abject, the search for meaning has become peculiarly problematic because it always seems to involve arbitrary and painful exclusions, not to mention claustrophobic identity formations. From a more theoretical perspective, those working in the hermeneutical tradition informed by Heidegger, and gender theorists following the lead of Foucault, offer ample space for articulating misgivings about both the question and the search for meaning.

Focusing first on such thinkers as Heidegger, Gadamer, and Ricoeur, who share in common the conviction that Being is disclosed in myth, symbol, and poetry, we discover reservations regarding the existence of a transcendental meaning of Being that serves as the telos of human thinking and action. Heidegger, Ricoeur, and Gadamer all agree that the situatedness of human beings makes the Hegelian project of the realization of Absolute Spirit impossible. Truth is an event of the disclosure of Being, a disclosure that allows for provisional meanings, provisional meaningfulness, and provisional projects that can never be definitively grounded. To appeal to an absolute meaning of Being is to abstract from the concrete context and to fail to realize the possible meanings that the unique situation affords. The meaning of Being is realized in the process of disclosure, not in some conclusion to the process. Accordingly, to seek "the" meaning of Being and to locate "the" meaning of one's life is to miss the eventful character of one's life and its situatedness.

A second area of concern is that the question of the meaning of life has traditionally led to a focus on the self as a fixed entity with an established identity. In *Being and Time,* Heidegger maintains that the subject-object dichotomy is derivative from Dasein's being-in-the-world.[3] When it is made fundamental, the question of Being is forgotten. The subject is made into a presence-at-hand, an object, and as such its possibilities for Being are concealed. On the other hand, the realization of authentic Dasein, the realization of an authentic Self, is a task to be achieved, and one that is presumably only finished with death.

Michel Foucault and gender theorists following his lead, such as Jana Sawicki, share the preceding reservations regarding both the determinate meaning of Being and an essentialist approach to the self. Yet the reasons for their reservations are different. Gadamer and Ricoeur, following Heidegger, have cultivated perspectives that operate under the sign of hope that Being speaks, that Being "makes itself understood *as* language."[4] Gadamer and Ricoeur alike share Heidegger's conviction that "Language is the house of Being."[5] It is because Being speaks that life is meaningful. Correspondingly, it is possible to go astray, and it is possible that Being is not gracious. Ricoeur, in fact, characterizes hope as hope in spite of evil that there is meaning to be found in the movement of history.[6] Foucault, on the other hand, makes no such appeal to the disclosure of Being. While Foucault falls roughly in the tradition of what Ricoeur has called the hermeneutics of suspicion, a hermeneutics that seeks to discover a hidden reality operative under appearances, he aspires to move beyond that tradition by claiming that there is no "deep reality" at work.[7] He argues that the notion of a "deep meaning" or "hidden reality" is itself a social construction, and, by extension, he claims that Ricoeur's and Gadamer's views regarding the disclosure of Being in discourse, provoking a hermeneutics of the given, are wrong-headed.

While Heidegger, Gadamer, and Ricoeur flag the difficulties surrounding the question of, and the quest for, meaning, it is Foucault and those indebted to him who fully recognize the depth and range of the difficulties, especially as they touch on the lives and identities of marginalized subjects. As we shall see, Foucault is able to weave a tale of the search for meaning which initiates the search itself into the service of power relations, the constitution of personal and social identities, and the generation of knowledges that carry within them the seeds of oppression. In other words, Foucault's work traces how my student's search for meaning has the potential for playing into the constitution of a world generated through constraining power relations. On the other hand, it is not so clear that Foucault's tale answers the felt need of my student or could ever act as a palliative to his drive for meaning. It is impossible to discredit this felt need, any more than it is possible to prove that it has some legitimate ground. It is equally unlikely that this felt need can be obliterated.

By offering an approach to the question of meaning that is grounded in the work of Heidegger, Gadamer, and Ricoeur and that takes as its point of departure the dangers inherent in the quest for meaning signaled by Foucault, I believe that it is possible to weave a new tale for my student. It will answer his felt need for meaning while opening a path for him to walk and talk with the other as other, not as the other through whom he establishes his identity, or the other as silenced exile. Conversely, I believe that this new tale will offer resources to gender theorists (and to queer philosophy teachers—and what philosophy teachers are not) that will enable them to challenge the founding of a meaningful world and the constitution of an identity through the sort of oppressive formation perpetrated by (or through, or on?) my student. To set the stage for this, I will begin by exploring the Foucauldian landscape from the perspective of why many gender theorists have found it appealing.

Power Relations: Foucault

Though I argued in the preceding section that Foucault distances himself from a hermeneutics of suspicion, it is clear from his work that he is greatly influenced by that master of suspicion, Friedrich Nietzsche. Like Nietzsche, Foucault is deeply concerned about power and its exercise; like Nietzsche, he is suspicious of claims to objective knowledge and to valid theory and sees in them the exercise of power;[8] like Nietzsche, he calls into question the givenness of the individual and instead sees the subject as constituted through the exercise of power.[9]

Allan McGill argues that, in Foucault's earlier work, even up to and including *The Order of Things,* there is a nostalgic note sounded on behalf of a deep structure of things.[10] In the *Archeology of Knowledge,* this note disappears, and Foucault takes the position that there is only interpretation; there is no deep reality that is revealed through interpretation, no originary facts or objects which are not themselves the products of discourse.[11] In an essay entitled, "Nietzsche, Marx, Freud," Foucault argues that Marx's, Nietzsche's, and Freud's respective hermeneutics of suspicion did not reach below surface appearances to reveal a core reality or firm foundation or objective truth. Rather, their interpretations showed that the objects of their interpretations were themselves interpretations.[12] In the 1970s, with his *History of Sexuality,* Foucault not only claims that discourse does not reveal. . . . or conceal some "deep truth," but that discourse itself has an ontogenetic function; it constructs worlds. Conversely, by recognizing its ontogenetic function, one can set against a given discourse a competing one, for no discourse can secure absolute legitimation.[13]

Refusal to simply appropriate a hermeneutics of suspicion leads to a number of interesting questions, such as:

1. If discourse is not guided by a reality that lies outside of itself, how is it that worlds are founded in discourse?

2. Why is it that discourses change, that new worlds arise, that there is history?

3. What impetus could there be for discursive innovation?

In the 1970s and 1980s, Foucault develops a discourse on power that answers these questions. While recognizing that the traditional juridico-discursive model of power as repressive does describe one form of power, he argues that a model of power as productive, productive of knowledges, of social order, of subjects, is a viable alternative that incorporates an account of how repressive forms of power are possible.[14] Foucault does not attempt to develop a new, and presumably truer, description of power than the one found in the repressive hypothesis. Rather, he deploys an alternative account of power as part of a strategy to undermine the notion of power as a cause that transcends and accounts for events and things.[15] If this account is to succeed, it must destabilize transhistorical accounts of the nature of the world and of the self, destabilize itself as a transhistorical account, and nonetheless make a claim on us.

Foucault develops his account of power as productive by juxta-posing it with the juridico-discursive model of power that is opera-tive in much traditional Western political theory.[16] In the latter model, power is viewed as repressive. It is in the possession of an in-dividual, individuals, or a class, and is exercised through prohibi-tions enforced by sanctions. Typically, "Power represses nature, the instincts, a class, individuals."[17] Much of Western political theory has concerned itself with determining the conditions that must obtain for there to be legitimate authority and what the limits of sovereign power ought to be. Such concerns presuppose the juridico-discursive model, and they assume that there are certain power relations that can be legitimated.[18] In the first of two lectures delivered in 1976, Foucault expresses dissatisfaction with the repressive hypothesis in its juridico-discursive form, maintaining that it is inadequate to the task of describing power relations at work in modern penal institu-tions, psychiatry, and infantile sexuality.[19] In an interview published as "Truth and Power," he claims that an account of power as purely repressive and coercive cannot adequately explain how power com-mands obedience. "What makes power hold good, what makes it ac-cepted, is simply the fact that it doesn't only weigh on us as a force that says no, but that it traverses and produces things, it induces pleasure, forms knowledge, produces discourse."[20]

In contrast to the repressive hypothesis, Foucault argues that power can be considered not as the possession of an individual or class, but as operative in and through relations between individuals. In this view, one begins the analysis of power with the local exercise of power. It is this exercise that gives rise to the identity of subjects related in power, and to the development of institutions, govern-mental forms, etc.[21] Most significantly, power relations produce knowledges which in turn sustain and generate power relations. In short, Foucault maintains that the social body is produced through "manifold relations of power which permeate, characterize and con-stitute the social body," and which themselves cannot "be estab-lished, consolidated nor implemented without the production, accu-mulation, circulation and functioning of a discourse. There can be no possible exercise of power without a certain economy of discourses of truth which operates through and on the basis of this associa-tion."[22] It makes no sense to Foucault to think of power, knowledge, discourse, and subjects independently of one another in this view of power relations. Power circulates between subjects who are themselves constituted as such through the interplay of force relations, and power and knowledge are joined together and generate one another through discourses which serve as their condition, and at times, as the arena for their contestation.[23]

In *The History of Sexuality, Vol. I,* Foucault makes a case for a productive model of power by showing that the discourse on sexuality developed in the eighteenth and nineteenth centuries did not work primarily as an instrument for the repression of sex, but rather as a discourse that introduced the very concept of sex as an essence, something with which one must be concerned.[24] How to deal with sex became a problem, a concern that enabled the development of strategies of control, intervention, and surveillance of people's lives. This discourse on sex underpinned practices such as the monitoring of populations with respect to birthrate, age of marriage, etc.,[25] and produced certain sorts of subjects (the hysterical woman, the masturbating child, the Malthusian couple, the perverse adult)[26] whose identities were determined by their sexuality and whose modes of behavior were to be studied and ultimately brought under control.[27] The following passage illustrates the relations between power, discourse, knowledge, and the subject that Foucault seeks to explore in the work:

> Not a collective curiosity or sensibility; not a new mentality; but power mechanisms that functioned in such a way that discourse on sex . . . became essential. Toward the beginning of the eighteenth century, there emerged a political, economic, and technical incitement to talk about sex. . . . one had to speak of sex; one had to speak publicly and in a manner that was not determined by the division between licit and illicit, . . . one had to speak of it as of a thing to be not simply condemned or tolerated but managed, inserted into systems of utility, regulated for the greater good of all, made to function according to an optimum. Sex was not something one simply judged; it was a thing one administered. It was in the nature of a public potential; it called for management procedures; it had to be taken charge of by analytical discourses. In the eighteenth century, sex became a "police matter—in the full and strict sense given the term at the time:

not the repression of disorder, but an ordered maximization of collective and individual forces.[28]

The History of Sexuality begins with the observation that the twentieth century accuses its immediate past of having repressed sexuality and insists that this repression stop. The twentieth century says that we must speak about sexuality and make its truth known if we are to become fully realized human beings. This seeming departure of the twentieth century from its past, marked by its claim that the past "sinned" against sexuality, in fact conceals an underlying unity between the last few centuries and the present.[29] They all have constructed "sexuality" as a defining aspect, perhaps the most significant defining aspect, of the human person. Far from a simple repression of sexuality in the eighteenth and nineteenth centuries, discourses about sexuality multiplied as sexuality became a locus of control.[30]

A first survey . . . seems to indicate that since the end of the sixteenth century, the "putting into discourse of sex," far from undergoing a process of restriction, on the contrary has been subjected to a mechanism of increasing incitement; that the techniques of power exercised over sex have not obeyed a principle of rigorous selection, but rather one of dissemination and implantation of polymorphous sexualities; and that the will to knowledge has not come to a halt in the fact of a taboo that must not be lifted, but has persisted in constituting—despite many mistakes, of course—a science of sexuality.[31]

Foucault equates this multiplication of discourses with the multiplication of "sexualities."[32] The nineteenth century saw the founding of "homosexuality" and "heterosexuality" as such. Disciplines such as psychiatry came to the fore, defining people according to their sexual identities, charting the course that people must follow if they wanted to be "healthy." These disciplines guided "private" institutions such as the family in the establishment of appropriate relations between its members, and "public" institutions such as schools about the regulations that should be enacted and enforced to make sure that sexuality is properly managed. What is important to note here is that the exercise of disciplinary power generated the identities of people according to their sexuality; generated power through the activities of subjects themselves even as individual subjects became powerless in the sense that everyone was tied to an ideal of normalization; and generated knowledge and discourse that both constituted sexuality and established controlled conditions for speaking about it.[33]

While twentieth-century rhetoric suggests that there has been a shift in attitude regarding sexuality—from seeing it as a powerful force to be suppressed to seeing it as something that people must integrate into their lives for self-realization—Foucault argues that this shift is not really so radical. It has in fact only served to solidify the concept of sexuality and sexuality's importance as the focal point for the realization of ideals of personal and societal identity. It has continued the longstanding imperative in the West to speak the truth about sex, and in so doing has continued the production of a truth in the service of power and domination, not of freedom.[34]

That we live in a sexually obsessed society should not be a controversial claim. But the extent to which this obsession contributes to our identity formation and the relations of power and domination in which we operate is worth considering. In twentieth-century America, we identify ourselves according to our sexuality; we strive to realize ourselves as sexual beings of certain sorts; we go to experts, read books, and seek advice in order to navigate the course to sexual fulfillment and social acceptance. We consider that the state and society have a stake in our sexuality. The family is thematized as a place where healthy sexuality is formed, and it accordingly becomes a focal point for the exercise of power.[35] (Should we consider the talk about "family values" in recent presidential campaigns with ominous foreboding?) Clearly, my student's passionate concern regarding matters homosexual becomes intelligible in this context. What is important to note here is that people are engaged in their own regulation. They place themselves under the authority of others in order to learn the truth about themselves, to become free, healthy, self-actualized individuals, but in so doing, they actually become the subjects of domination.[36] As Jana Sawicki notes, "Disciplinary power is exercised on the body and soul of individuals. It increases the power of individuals at the same time as it renders them more docile (for instance, basic training in the military)."[37] Power is generated between persons even as they are brought under control, managed, and manipulated; their efforts to internalize an ideal, or ideals, of normalization ultimately require submission and conformity.

Given Foucault's account of power as productive of order that ultimately oppresses, the question for those working in gender studies is what courses of action ought to be taken in order to overturn the systems of domination that have grown up around and through the discourse on sexuality. How can we circumvent the congealing of stagnant identities and the tyranny of normalization implied by increasing concerns regarding "ideal sex"? In a certain sense, the answer is simple. Foucault understandably takes as a fundamental project the subversion of those knowledges that are at once in service to power in the creation and maintenance of order and are the products of that order. One must disrupt, explode from within, the discourses that have made possible and have served to legitimate the present state of affairs. One must destabilize, delegitimize discourse so that other possibilities might emerge. But this is not sufficient. The establishment of new discourses, new relations, new knowledges, and new subjects can only lead to the establishment of a new order of domination, one that serves its own perpetuation. The only antidote would seem to be ongoing revolution. Allan Megill characterizes the situation as follows:

> . . . order itself is brought before the bar. It is brought before the bar because every order is necessarily extant—even if only in thought—and hence participates in the corruption of all that is present . . . thought "cannot help but liberate and enslave" (MC, pp. 339/328). Putting a plausible gloss on this we may suggest that thought liberates, then (as it becomes part of new, oppressive order) serves to enslave. Given the enslaving tendencies of all thought, all interpretation, all discourse, and all language, one is infinitely justified in opposing these orders. One does this not in the name of a better order, but because opposition is the only choice, aside from absolute passivity, that one has. Foucault thus opts for a peculiar brand of permanent revolution—permanent because it seeks to realize no image of an ideal society.[38]

Naturally, the call for ongoing revolution has an appeal to gender theorists dissatisfied with the extant order. However, revolutionaries not only act out of dissatisfaction with the present state of affairs but in light of a vision of what they take to be a better alternative. This leads us to consider why Foucault's work has attracted the attention of those working in gender studies since most, presumably, are committed to an agenda that includes an alternative vision.

One reason for the interest in Foucault's work is that it implies that gender identity is constructed and in the service of power relations. This enables a restructuring of the semantic field so that traditional categories and ways of framing questions dissolve. Building on Foucault's claim that subjects are constituted according to the very power relations that regulate them, Judith Butler makes the case in *Gender Trouble* that the subject of feminist theory, "woman," is the production of juridical systems of power that claim only to represent, not to produce, "woman." When feminist theory accepts the category "woman" (even when it contests gender profiles as socially constructed), it tends to concern itself with the question of how women might be more fully represented in language and politics. But if it is the case that the very production of gendered subjects occurs "along a differential axis of domination or to produce subjects who are presumed to be masculine," such endeavors are inevitably doomed to failure.[39] When feminists appeal to political systems for the emancipation of women, their appeals come too late, for behind their backs, the category "woman" has been produced to facilitate the domination of those assigned to it. Feminist critique that accepts the foundationalist suppositions of representative politics "presumes, fixes, and constrains the very 'subjects' that it hopes to represent and liberate."[40] If one were to delegitimate the discourse in which "woman" is constituted by displaying its constructed character, this would create a space for the elimination of the sort of domination that women experience, though it would also mark a radical transformation of feminist theory.

More fundamentally, Butler argues that the categories, "man" and "woman," as well as many of the attempts to disrupt those categories mounted by gender theory, suppose that subjects have an ontological status independent of the political orders in which they find themselves. Such a view is necessary to social contract theory, for it "guarantees a presocial ontology of persons who freely consent to be governed and, thereby, constitute the legitimacy of the social contract."[41] Undermining this essentialist supposition undermines the power relations that it supports. Butler makes a case that the self-identical status of the person is not ontologically grounded. Rather, it is instituted through regulatory practices. She argues for the potential of parodic discourses operating within the field of gendered identity to destabilize these regulatory practices by discrediting the notion of a presocial sexed subject and subverting the juridical structures of language and politics that constitute the current field of power.[42] Specifically, she maintains that the regulatory practices currently at work in society incorporate gender in the establishment of coherent identity formation and that the deployment of persistent gender identities that transgress the norms of cultural intelligibility "provide critical opportunities to expose the limits and regulatory aims of that domain of intelligibility and, hence, . . . open up within the very terms of that matrix of intelligibility rival and subversive matrices of gender disorder."[43] With respect to feminist theory, Butler shows the limitations of essentialist suppositions even when they are put in the service of subverting hegemonic constructions of gender identity. She argues that a metaphysics of substance underpins "the production and naturalization of the category of sex itself,"[44] and thereby, I presume, supports efforts to establish a discourse on sex and a social order that can be legitimated.[45] Butler suggests that all efforts to appeal to a "better order of things" to incite social change harbor the seeds of domination and oppression.[46]

A second reason for interest in Foucault derives from the fact that, in feminist and gay and lesbian movements, tensions have arisen because of a refusal to recognize difference and a tendency to reduce identity to one determining factor in the name of solidarity. Judith Butler asks, "Is unity necessary for effective political action?"[47] The establishment of a common identity as the ground for political action can actually result in exclusionary practices that thwart provisional unities that might effectively accomplish commonly recognized objectives. In *Feminist Theory from Margin to Center,* bel hooks explores how African-American women, lesbians, women from various socioeconomic backgrounds, and men have been alienated from the "women's movement" through the identification of "woman" with upper-middle-class white women and their (supposedly homogeneous) agenda. One example of this is the emphasis that was placed upon work as a means to personal fulfillment, self-actualization, and power early in the contemporary feminist movement. hooks notes:

> As workers, poor and working class women know from their experiences that work was neither personally fulfilling nor liberatory—that it was for the most part exploitative and dehumanizing. They were suspicious of bourgeois women's assertion that women would be liberated via work and they were also threatened. They were threatened because they knew that new jobs would not be created for those masses of white women seeking to enter the work force and they feared that they and men of their classes would lose jobs.[48]

This passage is interesting because it not only shows the importance of recognizing difference if one is to develop solidarity, but it also illustrates that the male/female dichotomy is not an absolute determinant of identity. One might well consider one's racial or socioeconomic identity to be defining. Moreover, it suggests how the agenda of a particular group might actually be incorporated into predominating power relations. For certain sectors of women to adopt traditionally exploitative roles is not meaningful social change from the perspective of many. By destabilizing the subject, Foucault's position recognizes that a web of discourses may constitute the locus of conflicting claims because of the discourses at work. Acknowledgment of constituted differences, and recognition of these differences as constituted, is useful in developing coalitions across differences while encouraging sensitivity as to how those differences are at play in individuals' lives with respect to situation and perspective.

Thirdly, Foucault's stance encourages recognition of the dangers implicit in all "positions." In *Epistemology of the Closet,* Eve Kosofsky Sedgwick offers a critique of the essentialist/constructivist debate regarding the constitution of homosexuality that ought to give us pause in light of the preceding discussion. Sedgwick has reservations about both constructivist and essentialist positions because she recognizes the potential of each to be used in the service of oppression in specifically constituted historical circumstances. With respect to the advocates of constructivist approaches, Sedgwick notes that feminists have looked to the malleability of culture as a promise of the possibility that oppression can be ended, and that many working in gay studies have eagerly embraced that same promise. But in a constructivist view, there is no basis for contesting the claim that those who have the power to shape society have the right to do as they wish. Sedgwick forcefully suggests that, in the historical context in which we stand, "it is so difficult to intervene in the seemingly natural trajectory that begins by identifying a place of cultural malleability; continues by inventing an ethical or therapeutic mandate for cultural manipulation; and ends in the overarching, hygienic Western fantasy of a world without any more homosexuals in it."[49] Conversely, the essentialist view militates against the pretensions of social engineering, but, according to Sedgwick, supports our homophobic society in equally ominous projects of genetic engineering.[50] Indeed, her analysis shows the pertinence to gender studies of Foucault's suspicion of all "positions." Says Foucault:

> My point is not that everything is bad, but that everything is dangerous, which is not exactly the same as bad. If everything is dangerous, then we always have something to do. So my position leads not to apathy but to a hyper- and pessimistic activism. I think that the ethico-political choice we have to make every day is to determine which is the main danger.[51]

Finally, Foucault's work recognizes that we are situated beings. Our struggles must operate from within the contexts that give rise to them in order to disrupt those contexts. Like Judith Butler, Foucault in his later work presents an account of discourse as performative; it constitutes what it claims only to reveal or to represent.[52] There is no possibility of moving outside of discourse to some "true reality," for it is discourse itself that generates the representation of some hidden . . . or revealed reality. We are always already within discourse. We find ourselves in the context of an order of things established in discourse whose establishment by discourse is hidden. What counts as a liberatory practice will be determined by the way in which power relations are constituted in a particular discourse. The following passage from Sawicki's *Disciplining Foucault* regard-

ing the advisability of antipornography campaigns to combat patriarchal sexual oppression, given the current social climate, aptly illustrates this point:

> . . . a series of links have been established between the rad-
> ical feminist strategy of anti-pornography legislation and
> the New Right's efforts to censor any sexual practices that
> pose a threat to the family. This is not to suggest that the
> antipornography movement is essentially reactionary, but
> rather that at this time it may be dangerous.[53]

Despite the new avenues that Foucault's work opens for gender studies, including possible recognition of the work in gender
studies as itself a strategy for disrupting oppressive regimes, there
are those who have important reservations about it. Sawicki suggests that critics in general are concerned that the nihilistic, pes-
simistic, and relativistic aspects of Foucault's project undermine
its capacity to promote a positive political agenda.[54] There are, of
course, several ways of answering such objections. One could argue
that they arise from a desire to be able to locate a privileged account of reality that could serve as a foundation for political action, and that Foucault has shown the obstacles and dangers attending attempts to secure sure foundations. As Sawicki argues,
"Are there not good historical reasons to be suspicious of universalist history, or the search for anthropological foundations and
master schemes for social transformation?"[55] Further, one could
argue that the concrete experience of oppression in a given set of
circumstances does not need overarching theoretical justifications
to inspire revolution and the establishment of effective strategies
suitable to the concrete contexts in which they arise. And is it not
true that what counts as emancipatory at one time might well be
oppressive at another?

But it seems to me that other doubts surface regarding Foucault's "position" if we recognize that it is, after all, a *strategy*. Earlier, I said that we would have to consider what claim Foucault's account of power as productive could make on us. If we follow his
alternative account to its logical conclusions, we must see the account of power itself as a production that can lay no claim to some
sort of transcendent "truth."[56] In the delightfully topsy-turvy world

in which we find ourselves through Foucault's discourse, this logical conclusion serves to bolster rather than to undermine his "argument." The contingency of the discourse on power does function strategically to derail attempts to appeal to a deep reality laying beneath discourse or partially disclosed by it. But does the universe of discourse that Foucault has introduced work *strategically* to surmount the oppression(s) that have arisen through the relations established in the discourse on sexuality? If we consider how oppression is recognized and how projects of reform are engendered, there is a case for claiming that it does not. One could argue that it is unlikely that attempts to delegitimate discourses on sex, sexuality, and gender will have any real effect on those who have a stake in these discourses. Conversely, while Foucault's universe of discourse may raise the consciousness of those who are oppressed, it is not so certain that it can also serve as a sufficient basis not only to motivate action, but to establish communities of resistance. While the members of such communities need not share the same world-view or the same convictions, they must share some common ground, some vision and language capable of supporting effective action, even if it is only the common ground of outrage, something not so easily engendered as one might suppose. There is a pragmatic value to the appeal to a transcendent reality. It establishes the ground for committed action and the call for conversion that is necessary if there is to be genuine social change. It can also nourish hope that there will in fact be change. Indeed, it is difficult to see why one would follow Foucault in the sort of hyperactivity for social change that he advocates. If such activity results in the redeployment of power relations which result in oppression, why would one be interested in such a redeployment unless one were convinced that there were some real advantage to being the oppressor rather than the oppressed?

But it is important to recognize that the thrust of Foucault's work is to show that all systems are dangerous. The pessimism that such recognition engenders cannot and should not be eliminated. We live in contingency; what is liberatory can become oppressive. This does not, however, preclude the awareness of constraint, of foreclosure, which the system itself creates even as it generates and is generated by the round of knowledges, identities, institutions, and power relations. A system of power relations can constitute a reality whose oppressive character is born within it. In the nexus of power relations itself, subjects can be generated whose very constitution impels resistance. The difficulty is that resistance can reinscribe the very power relations that have created abject subjects/objects. The beauty of Foucault's strategy is that it disturbs this economy. Subversion can then occur not because one feels dissatisfied or looks to some ideal standard according to which the present state of things falls short, but because the reality constituted by and constituting the current web of relations devours itself from within. From a purely local reality, a concrete, lived reality, subjects can meaningfully speak about a better world. The danger arises when one fails to take account of the incalculable dangers of one's own speech. This, I think, is Foucault's point. But there are some stray threads that add to the texture of this strategic account of power relations. To the objection that one would have little reason to replace one oppressive system with another, one could reply that there is no reason to suppose that all power relations need be oppressive. In fact, the tendency to self-perpetuation in a system is what makes it most prone to oppression, and it is precisely this that Foucault attacks. Finally, what of the notion of oppression itself? It is out of tune with Foucault's project to claim that systems should be overthrown because they are oppressive, as if nonoppression itself could constitute an ideal. Is there not something oppressive about rejecting oppression, especially if oppression carries within its universe conflict and coercion? Could a nonconflictual society create beautiful spirits? But even this question, or especially this question, is too normatively loaded.

But perhaps there is a remainder, something left over, an unthematized possible thematic that Foucault's tale strategically avoids (remember that Foucault's analytics of power is, after all, a strategy, not a dogma). In *Bodies That Matter,* Judith Butler develops a nuanced account of the constitution of identity through the performative gesture. Butler makes the point that to claim that gender and sex are constructed is not to claim there is a subject that constructs gender and sex. One does not put on or take off a gender in the way that one puts on or takes off a coat. In fact, subjects do not decide on their gender; rather, gender, according to Butler, "is part of what decides the subject."[57] A key insight that Butler highlights in this text, which was left in shadow in *Gender Trouble,* is that the constructed character of gender and sex does not imply that constructs themselves can be dismissed as artificial and dispensable:

Moreover, why is it that what is constructed is understood as an artificial and dispensable character? What are we to make of constructions without which we would not be able to think, to live, to make sense at all, those which have acquired for us a kind of necessity? Are certain constructions of the body constitutive in this sense: that we could not operate without them, that without them there would be no "I" and no "we"? Thinking the body as constructed demands a rethinking of the meaning of construction itself. And if certain constructions appear constitutive, that is, have this character of being that "without which" we could not think at all, we might suggest that bodies only appear, only endure, only live within the productive constraints of certain highly regulatory schemas.[58]

But of course Butler is not implying here that there is only one possible or ideal construction. Indeed, that reiteration is necessary to secure gender and sexual bodily identity suggests that various rematerializations of the bodily self are possible. The necessity of reiteration to secure identity opens a space for recognizing the noncoincidence of one's identity and the possibilities for constituting a self that are foreclosed by the very gendered matrix of relations which determine the possibilities for selfhood in this culture. More precisely, according to Butler, "the construction of gender operates through *exclusionary* means, such that the human is not only produced over and against the inhuman, but through a set of foreclosures, radical erasures that are, strictly speaking, refused the possibility of cultural articulation."[59] In the sort of heterosexual society in which we find ourselves, the homosexual is an impossible subject, but as such, operates in the heterosexual economy as the excluded through which the possible is defined. However, precisely because reiteration is necessary to the actualization of gender identity, a space is opened for the possibility of the impossible; reiteration opens the possibility that repetition will not be of the same. What remains unthematized in Foucault is the extent to which the possibility of what appears impossible, foreclosed in a gendered matrix, can stake a claim on those who have ears to hear.

A brief turn to Luce Irigaray might be helpful here. According to Irigaray, women are represented in the schemas of Western ontology, but in a way that excludes them. There is no place for women in the available schemas. There is a remainder, an excess, a difference between women and the way that they are figured that Irigaray seeks to mark over and over within the figuration itself. Analogously, the impossible, abject subjects necessary to sustaining the reality of this heterosexual economy in which we find ourselves are not reducible to their function in that economy. Present in their flesh is the remainder, the absence in this economy, the possibility of other gender configurations, which makes reiteration necessary and subject to failure or mutation.

Left in shadow in Foucault's work is the power of possibility, of the absent, the nonexistent, the unnamed and perhaps unnamable, to draw us, fascinate us, and make a claim upon us so that even in the realization of our most ambitious projects we feel the pain of absence, of what might have been had we taken another course. My student's outburst could be understood, in light of what has been said, as an attempt to sustain his own identity, as testimony to his lived experience and to the richness and value of the relations that have informed his own life. Foucault's work effectively challenges any attempts on the part of this student to ground his life and his very identity through an appeal to some transcendent reality understood as how things "are" or "ought to be." But can more be done? Can unrealized possibility make a claim on this student? It is only when the vision of reality and the self realized in the lifeworld of this student makes a claim to being the sole possibility that it can be denounced as arbitrary. As a realized possibility, this possibility opens before us; and it is only by attending to this that we can make contact with the person, the self who, after all, has arisen out of it. By attending to the student, the person living out of a realized possibility, it is possible to awaken other possibilities, to destabilize the ground on which he stands, and on which we stand, without doing the sort of violence to his lived experience that would lead to denial and a rigid reiteration of the same. Again, simply to dismiss this student's self-understanding as somehow arbitrary would be to perpetrate a certain violence. Those of us who have experienced ourselves as standing on the margins of society and who have struggled with the question of our identities should not be willing to inflict this violence. Working out an alternative way of thinking about our professions of who we are in a way that can avoid this violence while opening us up to critical engagement and individual and social transformation is the project of these first three chapters.

But first, a different course for thinking about individual and social transformation, one that on the surface relies on the capacity of human beings for self-formation and self-transformation *without appealing to the claims of the possible*, a course that offers itself if we follow Foucault in such later works as *The Use of Pleasure* and *The Care of the Self*, deserves our attention. In these last two volumes of *The History of Sexuality*, as well as in interviews and essays, Foucault focuses on the ways in which subjects who are constituted through webs of social relations are capable of self-determination by engaging in what he calls "practices of freedom." Foucault, in fact, draws a significant distinction between "practices of freedom" and "processes of liberation."[60] While he agrees that there is a certain usefulness to the latter phrase for referring to states of domination, he suggests that the idea of liberation is problematic to the extent that it suggests a determinate, fixed subject to be liberated.[61] By taking up "practices of freedom," Foucault suggests that historically and culturally situated subjects have the capacity to engage in practices of self-constitution.

To make this more concrete, it is worth turning to Foucault's development of a genealogy of the desiring subject in the last two volumes of *The History of Sexuality*. While in his earlier works, Foucault focused on techniques of domination, in these works, he turns his attention to what he calls "techniques of the self," by which he means the techniques an individual uses to come to understand himself or herself as a subject.[62]

> In any case, it seemed to me that one could not very well analyze the formation and development of the experience of sexuality from the eighteenth century onward, without doing a historical and critical study dealing with desire and the desiring subject. In other words, without undertaking a "genealogy." This does not mean that I proposed to write a history of the successive conceptions of desire, of concupiscence, or of libido, but rather to analyze the practices by which individuals were led to focus their attention on themselves, to decipher, recognize, and acknowledge themselves as subjects of desire, bringing into play between themselves and themselves a certain relationship that allows them to discover, in desire, the truth of their being, be it natural or

fallen . . . Thus, in order to understand how the modern individual could experience himself as a subject of a "sexuality," it was essential first to determine how, for centuries,
Western man had been brought to recognize himself as a
subject of desire.[63]

By turning his attention to Greek and Roman antiquity and to the
early Christian era, Foucault shows that selves cannot be reduced
to something resembling objects that are stamped out through the
application of techniques of domination, formed through the institutions, discourses, knowledges, practices in place in their societies.
Rather, by looking at the practices of self-questioning and moral
austerity that developed around sexuality, particularly in ancient
Greece, Foucault explores the capacity of individuals to engage in
their own self-constitution, to engage in what he calls the "arts of existence," by which he means, "those intentional and voluntary actions by which men not only set themselves rules of conduct, but
also seek to transform themselves, to change themselves in their
singular being, and to make their life into an *oeuvre* that carries certain aesthetic values and meets certain stylistic criteria."[64] Foucault notes that the ancient Greeks discussed sexuality in the context of an aesthetics of existence.[65] In general, this means that for
the Greeks, ethics was understood in terms of care of the self. It involved a way of being and acting that enabled one to develop a character that appeared to oneself and to others as "good, beautiful, hon-
orable, estimable, memorable, exemplary."[66] More specifically, it
means the cultivation of freedom understood as the sort of self-mastery and self-understanding that enables one to care for oneself, to
make use of oneself and of one's faculties for one's well-being, and
ultimately, to realize in one's person that person that one wants to
be.[67] This cultivation of freedom led to thematization of sexual practices in four areas of daily life: dietetics, economics (marriage),
erotics (the relationship between men and boys), and wisdom. In
contrast to Western systems of sexual morality that focus on universal codes to be assimilated by and applied to subjects, the Greeks
were concerned with the cultivation of self-mastery and the use of
pleasure to achieve a full and satisfying life. What is interesting is
that in the ethical discourses developed by the Greeks, aimed at
Greek male citizens, the concern was with precisely those areas in

which they were at liberty, most notably, their sexual conduct.[68] This enables us to catch a glimpse of a key distinction that Foucault develops in *The Use of Pleasure* between morality understood as the rules and values recommended to individuals and the ways in which people respond to these rules and values. If the aim of the Greeks, or of Greek male citizens, was effectively to practice their liberty, then the moral literature they developed was aimed at guiding them in the accomplishment of this liberty. Ultimately, the individual had to determine what his response to such advice and recommendations would be. In short, this points to a gap or opening between the standards of conduct—the values, norms, and prescriptions that are at work in a given culture—and how people deal with them. The key point here is that through their response, people are able to engage in self-formation, to shape their own existence, by adopting various practices in various ways.[69]

A word of caution is necessary here. It must be remembered that in *The History of Sexuality,* Foucault is engaging in a genealogy of the desiring subject. In so doing, he wants to show how the fabrication of this subject is complicit in perpetrating relations of domination. In particular, Foucault is interested in showing how establishing the ideal of the free, autonomous, and self-determining self can give rise to varieties of normalizing practices, political programs, and submission to hermeneutical practices aimed at unearthing hidden contents of the self, etc., all of which can operate to create relations of domination and oppression.[70] It would be a mistake to see Foucault as trying to get at some ideal self that stands independently of social relations whose essential nature is to be autonomous and self-constituting. As Ladelle McWhorter notes, for Foucault, selves do not exist independently of historical forces but are "the networks of forces themselves."[71] Selves can be understood as events that occur and are continually reenacted by virtue of the web of power relations through which they have been constituted as subjects. However, precisely by recognizing the contingency of historically constituted selves, in part through the very sorts of genealogical investigations that Foucault undertakes, he creates a space for these historically constituted selves not to engage in projects of self-realization, but in practices of self-transformation. Hence, while Foucault does not envision the liberation of the self, he does conceive of practices of freedom, of historically constituted subjects being able to be agents capable of self-transformation by disrupting the very power relations through which they have been constituted.

Complementing what has been said, Moya Lloyd argues, in fact, that Foucault provides two strategies for engaging in self-transformation. The first is to practice a politics of refusal, which entails refusing the identities through which individuals have been constituted as subjects. The second is to promote new modes of subjectivity.[72] For our purposes, it is important to note, with respect to the first strategy, that in essays such as "What Is Enlightenment?" and in interviews such as "Practicing Criticism," Foucault understands that a central component of this strategy is to critique accepted modes of saying, thinking, and doing. This is done through an examination of the contingency of the events and circumstances that "have led us [historically] to constitute ourselves and to recognize ourselves as subjects."[73] It is through unearthing this contingency that transformation becomes possible. Because one no longer accepts these events as given, one is open to change and is thereby able to envision ways of doing, thinking, saying, and being differently.[74] The second strategy involves determining what changes are possible and desirable given the context in which one finds oneself, and determining the form that these changes should take. This is the work of ethics understood as an aesthetic practice in which one works on oneself to effect one's self-transformation in light of certain goals, "to develop and transform oneself, and to attain to a certain mode of being,"[75] As Lloyd notes, the process of self-transformation can employ a variety of exercises, "from writing the self (autobiography, diary, memoirs), through dietetics and household management, the interpretation of dreams, to the production of the self as a work of art (Baudelair the dandy)."[76] Again, what is noteworthy about these practices is that they do not constitute practices of liberation, in which determinate subjects are able to gain self-realization, but rather practices of freedom, in which historically constituted subjects are able to effect their self-transformation.

In beginning this discussion of Foucault's later work, I suggested that it offers a way of thinking about individual and social transformation that seems, on the surface, to enable us to dismiss as significant to the processes of individual and social change appeals to unrealized possibilities to make a claim on us. Is it indeed possible to dispense with such appeals? To fully answer this requires spelling out exactly what the nature or character of the claim of an unrealized possibility would be, what it would mean to say that such a claim is made, and in what sense such a claim could be said to be compelling. At present, I only want to trouble Foucault's account sufficiently to set us on the course of taking up these larger issues.

What role, if any, do unrealized possibilities play in Foucault's account? Effecting reinvention or transformation does not occur solely through recognition of the contingency of the subjectivities that are currently enacted. Recognition of contingency does not of itself elicit change. Change is more likely to occur in response to the concrete experience of conflict. Because subjects are typically constituted through, and are the sites of, multiple discourses and practices, conflict is in fact probable. One need only consider Audre Lourde's reflections concerning the multiple and conflicting demands that are placed upon her as a black, female, lesbian, mother in this society.[77] It seems virtually impossible that she should passively live out the societal expectations attending her with such an identity. But this is not enough. To effect change requires some vision of what is possible. In "The Subject and Power," Foucault maintains that we should not understand subjects as ever creating themselves ex nihilo. Rather, they engage in the practices of freedom leading to self-transformation in view of the possibilities that are open to them given the concrete circumstances in which they find themselves.[78] It seems to me that without envisioning these possibilities, engaging freely in self-transformation, much less social transformation, is not possible.

But something more is needed, something more than Foucault has given us. Engaging in the project of self-transformation requires more than experiencing conflict and envisioning possibilities. It involves recognizing that certain possibilities are worth pursuing and others should be rejected. As I hope to argue in chapter 4, it involves being answerable to others, perhaps being inevitably guilty before others, because of the possibilities that one has pursued or refused. In fact, a case could be made that Foucault's own work confirms this. What is he doing through weaving his genealogies and his later ethical and aesthetic discourses if not opening us up to the possibilities of engaging in the practices of freedom? What is he doing if not calling us to engage in the sorts of political actions, whatever they happen to be at a given time, that will promote our engagement in self-transformation? While Foucault is recognized as someone committed to emancipatory social change, he is often criticized for not providing the normative assumptions upon which such change should be founded.[79] Calling for such norms is terribly problematic. How is one to justify the norms that one uses for deciding between the establishment of one world rather than another? But does not Foucault present us with a vision that at least in some sense seeks to lay a claim on us?

Taken from a different angle, I cannot get past the conviction that taking up a given possibility for one's own requires conviction that taking up that possibility is worthwhile. But sustaining this requires opening oneself to different possibilities for discourses than those that Foucault has laid before us. Foucault eschews hermeneutical approaches to discourses when they presume that discourses either reveal or conceal a "real self," or a "true" reality. He recognizes that hermeneutical approaches to history aimed at discovering the meanings unfolding in historical development are in fact complicit in the maintenance of systems of domination. He offers as an alternative a view of history as a continuous power struggle involving attempts to replace one system of domination by another.[80] Again, he recognizes in the hermeneutics of desire, in the interpretation of individuals' dreams, fantasies, and desires, the fostering of practices leading to control and domination. In fact, Foucault's vision of discourses in general seems to be an agonistic one, in tune with Lyotard's view that to speak is to fight. But might there be a disclosive power to discourses that should be honored? Might there be the possibility that discourses can in some sense speak the truth, lending themselves to hermeneutical investigations aimed at letting the truths that these discourses make possible happen? Might it be possible to recognize that at least some discourses make a claim upon us that should be honored without supposing that all claims should be honored—that any discourse speaks "The Truth"—and without forgetting that to speak can be to fight?

Those experiencing the conflicts implicit in the power relations at work in contemporary gender and sexual formations who seek to transform them and to transform themselves must strive to make apparent the contingency of those formations, envision other possibilities, and experience certain possibilities as worthy of pursuit.

That is, they must be drawn to certain possibilities. But to advocate these possibilities responsibly and with conviction requires more; it requires that these possibilities be critically engaged, so that their claim to worthiness of pursuit can be recognized as true. But if appeals to the claims of the possible are to work strategically for those seeking to disrupt the power relations in place, it is necessary to weave a tale about the nature or character of articulated world-views, a tale that can meet Foucault's reservations regarding these articulations. Remember that Foucault questions not only the truth claims of such accounts, but also the various forms of the hermeneutics of suspicion which posit an underlying reality hidden beneath these accounts, a reality that can be discovered through analyses of one sort or another. The nature of articulated world-views must be rethought if they are to play a role in political action by giving voice to the possible. The hermeneutical projects of Heidegger, Ricoeur, and Gadamer lend themselves as resources for such a rethinking.

Truth as Dis-closure: Heidegger, Ricoeur, and Gadamer

In *Gender Trouble,* Judith Butler argues that gender attributes are performative rather than expressive of an underlying fixed essence in order to disrupt the claims to legitimacy of any criterion of "true gender" attributes and to unmask gender identity as a regulatory fiction.[81] The question that I should like to raise is whether or not the distinction, performative/expressive, is fundamental when considering discourse generally and when considering works of art, texts, etc., in particular. By disrupting this distinction, it may be possible to develop an account of how world-views understood as articulations of possible ways of being can make claims on us, while at the same time successfully engaging the difficulties that Foucault rightly poses.

Martin Heidegger's "The Origin of the Work of Art" offers a promising starting point, for in it he argues that in art, there is a disclosure of a possibility for Being, the happening of truth (aletheia), and the setting up of a world. Heidegger begins the essay by noting that the common sense view of art sees the work as having its origins in the artist. But he goes on to say that artists are such only by virtue of their art.[82] He then wonders if art and artist are not constituted by a third thing, by Art, and then, conversely, asks if Art is not Art by virtue of art and artists.[83] Through this series of reflections, Heidegger problematizes the origin of the work of art and manages to raise the question of the nature of art. He proceeds to disenfranchise traditional attempts to treat art as if it were a thing or a piece of equipment. Through consideration of Van Gogh's painting of peasant shoes as a work which reveals that the equipmental character of equipment lies in its reliability, he "stumbles on" the workly character of the work of art:

> What happens here? What is at work in the work? Van Gogh's painting is the disclosure of what the equipment, the pair of peasant shoes, *is* in truth. This entity emerges into the unconcealedness of its being. The Greeks called the unconcealedness of beings aletheia . . . If there occurs in the work a disclosure of a particular being, disclosing what and how it is, then there is here an occurring, a happening of truth at work.[84]

Heidegger is careful to distance himself from any attempt to align this account of the disclosure of being to a mimetic theory of art. Instead, he ascribes an ontogenetic function to art. By considering a distinctly nonrepresentational work, the Greek temple, he argues that the work of art ". . . opens up a world and at the same time sets this world back again on earth, which itself only thus emerges as native ground."[85] Here, performance and disclosure come together. The work acts; it sets up a world. From the perspective of those who enter into the work as a work, those whom Heidegger calls preservers, the truth of the work happens.[86] That is, the work actually acts to create a community of those who live in the disclosure of the work, who through the work share a common world: "Preserving the work does not reduce people to their private experiences, but brings them into affiliation with the truth happening in the work. Thus it grounds being for and with one another as the historical standing-out of human existence in reference to unconcealedness."[87] This act of setting up the world and setting forth the earth creates possible ways of being and engenders action through the disclosure of a possible way of being in the world.

Hans-Georg Gadamer's description of the relation of art and audience in *Truth and Method* lends support to Heidegger's account of the ontogenetic character of art. Gadamer says that if we attend to our own experiences of art, we will find that works of art make claims upon us. These works happen to us and demand that we in some sense "get them right." If works made no demand, if we experienced no claim, there would be no interpretation.[88] But to get a given work right is neither to determine the author's meaning nor to consider the work as a cultural manifestation. It is, rather, to attend to the world and to the possibilities for being that are opened up in and by the work. While this requires attention to the work's origins, it no less requires attention to the context in which the work is being heard. That is, according to Gadamer, just as the work is not indeterminate, it is not fixed. The meanings of a work are produced through its history. Each time a work is heard in a new context, an event of meaning occurs through the interaction of work and context; the work discloses and creates possibilities for being in its being heard at a given time by a given audience. Paul Ricoeur expresses a similar idea when he says that poetic and fictional narrative refer to one's being in relation to others even as it establishes this relation.[89]

When I attend a performance of *Antigone,* I am able to hear what the work has to say to me in part by attending to its origins and what it had to say to its Greek audience, but what the work means to me also depends upon my situation and concerns. It is by hearing the work in this new context that a meaning of the work comes to life and new possibilities for being are generated. It is important to recognize that this eventful rising up of meaning is not something that I decide; it is something that happens to me and compels my assent. Truth has nothing to do with correct statements about existent states of affairs or ideal orders; truth is an event that happens to consciousness and that opens up possibilities.[90] Thinking of Judith Butler in this context, we might ask if parody, through its destabilization of gender identity, does not reveal, "to those who have ears to hear," the truth that a gender identity oppresses when it is definitively stabilized and presented as the only possibility.

There are a number of parallels that one could draw between Heidegger's and Foucault's respective positions, in particular the fact that both ascribe an ontogenetic function to discourse. But each works out different possibilities for engaging discursive productions that an ontogenetic view of discourse affords. Foucault's decision to frame his account in terms of power relations heightens suspicion of all orders and of the discursive formations that are born out of and support them because of their inherent potential for coercion. Further, it leads not only to suspicion of all culturally generated discursive productions, but to a suspicion of the interpretations flowing from the various hermeneutics of suspicion. While such interpretive enterprises claim to liberate, they can themselves establish new visions of things that are coercive. On the other hand, Heidegger's account of art (and language) as performative and disclosive enables him to recognize in human works the potentiality of a bestowal, the gift of Being. Heidegger describes Being metaphorically as the space in which beings step forward into unconcealedness. This unconcealedness does not preclude the possibility of the concealedness of beings, the possibility of dissemblance and error; in fact, it is only because there is unconcealedness that recognition of the possibility of dissemblance is possible.[91] Heidegger's account does not suppose a fixed Absolute that is either revealed or concealed in discursive productions. Instead, what is revealed and concealed through such productions are possibilities for being. By adopting this stance towards discursive productions, Heidegger opens up hope that human works can disclose meaningful possibilities for human living; that human beings may have something important to say to one another; and that the discourses of various people can make claims on those who listen, can be compelling without simply coercing.

That there is reason for taking Heidegger's approach seriously surfaces through a brief consideration of Ricoeur's discussion of symbolic language and Gadamer's description of the necessary conditions for insight. Consideration of Ricoeur's and Gadamer's work will at the same time enable us to fully appreciate the hermeneutical approach being advocated here, to address the concerns raised by Foucault's position, and to establish an effective strategy for gender studies as praxis.

Ricoeur's turn to hermeneutics was occasioned by his prephilosophical conviction that human beings are intermediate beings, finite/infinite beings who find themselves always already situated in a given context, but capable of transcending their contexts by raising questions and adopting alternative perspectives. The aim at transcendence does not shield inquiry from the suspicion that it might be futile. Simply because human beings desire to know and imaginatively project themselves into other situations does not mean that they have genuine insights. But in the development of his hermeneutic phenomenology, Ricoeur argues that there is good reason to suppose that human works can only arise through the disclosure of Being. Human works say something about something to someone, and they could not do this were there no experience about which to speak. With this, Ricoeur envisions a second Copernican revolution. The subject is decentered in favor of Being as the origin of inquiry. It is because Being does indeed speak to us through human works as the expression of the experience of Being which offers hope that the meaning of Being unfolds through inquiry. Of course, the hope that inquiry is meaningful falls short of proof that it is so, but the hope remains sufficient for the wager involved in undertaking the inquiry.

Ricoeur develops support for his position first by initiating a critique of semiotic and structuralist approaches to language, such as those developed by Ferdinand de Saussure and Claude Levi-Strauss, respectively. Semiotic accounts describe language as a closed universe of signs, an approach that Ricoeur refutes: "It is because there is first something to say, because we have an experience to bring to language, that conversely, language is not only directed towards ideal meanings but also refers to what is."[92] There would be no speech act if there were no bond with reality to constitute its initiation. Without a linguistic system, there can be no articulation of meaning. But the development of a linguistic system is only for the sake of articulation of meaning.[93] Structuralist accounts of texts such as Claude Levi-Strauss's confuse the message of texts with the means by which the message is produced and thereby miss the ground for discourse; it is not possible to have discourse that is not about something.[94]

Ricoeur complements this critique with a positive account of the disclosive power of symbols, myths, and metaphors. Of particular interest is his claim that symbols embody a double intentionality that allows them to move beyond designation to manifestation. The first or literal sense of the symbol as sign is the basis for a second sense. This shift comes about through a likeness of the first intention to the second. For instance, to be physically stained is like being defiled in the realm of the sacred. Thus, stain can act as a symbol for defilement. According to Ricoeur, symbol stands on the border of bios and logos; it is the first bubbling forth of that which is prior to language, the sheer experience of life.[95] This experience cannot be definitively captured in its articulation: there is always a surplus of meaning toward which language continually strives. Here we see at play the finitude and situatedness of the human condition. One never possesses the truth. At best, one is possessed by it, is engaged in the never-ending task of understanding, interpretation, and the working out of the disclosure of Being. Still, according to Ricoeur, one gains a certain affirmation both of one's choice of symbols and myths and of one's interpretation of them if one is able to develop an interpretation that consists in a meaningful, coherent discourse on human beings and their being in the world.[96]

Of course, it is possible that myths and symbols deceive. Though Ricoeur, as well as Heidegger and Gadamer, provides significant insights while wrestling with these issues, he offers no easy panaceas; the idea that the truth of discourse consists of the possibilities it opens up does not permit the development of a "criterion of proof" for validating symbols, myths, and their interpretations. The truth of symbols and myths falls upon us; validation is lived, not proved. What is important for our purposes to note, however, is the claim that a pretheoretical being-at-home in the world is the necessary precondition for the possibility of alienation, deception, and despair. Ricoeur maintains that it is only as openness onto the world, it is only in light of an originary relation to being, that one can discover oneself as a finite openness. It is this originary relation, says Ricoeur, that commands that we live in hope that being is meaningful and that one might grow in one's understanding of the meaning of being.[97]

A cautionary note seems in order here. Foucault would no doubt be right in hearing in this discussion the echoes of the appearance/reality distinction, a distinction that he has challenged as itself a discursive production. But I believe that the focus on human finitude goes far in counterbalancing this, for what is at issue is not the disparity between a false or partial conception of reality and reality, but the interplay of disclosed and foreclosed possibilities. That human beings are finite, situated beings who can never make claims to truth as certitude in no way precludes hope that being can be meaningful, and that meaning can be disclosed through discursive productions. It is here that Hans-Georg Gadamer's account of the cultural situatedness of human beings as the ground for insight is particularly helpful, for it at once undercuts all attempts to arrive at some absolute, transtemporal, transcultural meaning of being, acknowledges the real possibilities of error and evil, and supports hope that being can be meaningful.

Of course, to claim that the situatedness of human beings grounds insight may, on first hearing, sound strange since ethnocentrism is typically grounds for suspicion, and, indeed, Gadamer would never argue that we should simply uncritically accept the veracity of cultural prejudices. What he does claim is that meaningful possibilities are conditioned and made possible by context. A first step in recognizing this is to consider perception. Following Aristotle, Gestalt psychology, and phenomenology, Gadamer maintains that perception is never "pure"; it is always invested with meaning. I do not hear "a sound," but a baby crying, an alarm, etc.[98] Gadamer would ultimately agree with Thomas Kuhn that all observation, all perception, is theory-laden; there is no perception without a paradigm.[99] Similarly, prejudice, understood as pre-judgment, is a necessary condition for conscious judgment and understanding because human beings are always already beings-in-the-world:

> The concept of the situation is characterized by the fact that one does not find himself standing over against it and therefore can have no objective knowledge of it. One stands in it, finds himself already in a situation, the clarification of which is a task never to be perfectly completed. . . . The clarification of this situation, that is, effective-historical reflection in it, is not perfectible, but this imperfectability is not due to a deficiency in reflection, rather it is ascribable to the essence of the historical being that we are. Being historical means never dissolving into self-knowledge"[100]

But the situatedness of human consciousness is not something to be purely and simply lamented. It is a prejudice to think that all prejudices are bad. Prejudice provides an orientation for inquiry and action; prejudice enables one to recognize and to challenge other prejudices; and the recognition of one's prejudices can constitute the reflective ground necessary to changing one's position by expanding one's horizons through critical engagement of others' prejudices. To be a situated being is to have available to oneself the possibilities for meaningful existence that the situation opens up. How else could Foucault and his allies have committed themselves to the strategies that they have adopted had they not operated out of such prejudices as: oppression is evil; there is an interplay between actuality and possibility; and one should engage in hyperactivity? In other words, what Gadamer recognizes is that one can never wholly escape one's situation, for one can never absolutely eliminate one's prejudices. Even the attempt to thematize one's situation necessarily involves uncritical employment of the unthematized discourse of thematization. This of itself, however, is not a reason for despair. Foucault claims that for centuries we have awaited the "word of God," and for centuries we have waited in vain.[101] Gadamer, on the other hand, suggests that we have experienced our situations as the occasions for the creation of meaningful lives. He believes that our lives are marked by events of disclosure, events of truth that are rooted in the soil of our situatedness. It is the experience of insight that grounds the hope that our insights will bear fruit in meaningful lives.

Strategically, there are three advantages to adopting this perspective on discourse drawn from Heidegger's, Gadamer's, and Ricoeur's hermeneutics. Firstly, action requires insight and conviction. Without insight, there can be no sense of oppression; without conviction, there can be no commitment to change. One acts only when one believes that the present situation is wrong and that a better state of affairs is possible. Foucault is suspicious of any position that would assign to discourse the power to "make being present," because he believes that the very configuration of discourse constitutes a difference between itself and its putative reference that cannot be bridged. I would argue that, while it is certainly the case that discourse establishes relations and founds worlds, this establishment and founding is possible only through a recognition of possibility, and it is only undertaken on the condition of a recognition of desirability. Communities are only possible because their members share common visions. Communities only change because these visions are partial and are experienced and recognized as such through the conflicts and tensions that arise in the lives of their members. This leads us to the second advantage of this position.

Heidegger, Gadamer, and Ricoeur all insist that the finitude of the human condition precludes dogmatic claims to absolute insight and utopian projects, which can so easily become tyrannical. Foucault is particularly cautious about accounts that maintain that there is a nondiscursive ground for discourse because such accounts make of the nondiscursive ground an essence, a unified whole . . . or multiplicity, that can serve as the ground for the legitimation of systems of power. But to suppose that discourse is ontologically grounded does not necessitate that Being is one or many and that this unity or multiplicity must be recapitulated in our lives. If one recognizes that disclosure is never definitive and that real historical conditions are constitutive of the real possibilities for the future, then attempts at privileging a given order of things as definitive become nonsensical. But, then, what is left? This is best answered by considering works of art. When considering works from vastly different schools, or vastly different schools of work, is it necessary to privilege one or the other with respect to "art," or to say that one or the other is "more" or "less" art? At the same time, is it not the case that both speak, that through their sheer presence they command recognition of the disclosure which is nothing beyond the world that they set up? Within a particular horizon, within a particular world that is set up through a disclosure of being, it is possible to recognize value and make choices. Between worlds, it is possible to recognize different values and the viability of different choices. But finally, it is only because possibilities for being arise that it is possible to gesture to the limits of horizons, and it is only because possibilities for being speak out against what discourse sets up that one can undertake new acts of creation, acts that can be carried out only through the constitution of communities of discourse. This leads to the third advantage of this position for gender theory as praxis.

Heidegger's, Gadamer's, and Ricoeur's accounts offer grounds for those operating from different perceptions and with different interests to consider what others have to say. Only through recognition of the limitedness of one's own perceptions, and conviction that others may have legitimate insights, will one engage in meaningful dialogue and go about the business of building community rather than forcibly promoting what one takes to be one's interests. Only those who recognize the power of discourse to reveal and conceal will allow a plurality of discourses to speak in the hope that a rich and varied terrain will disclose new possibilities, new contexts, for living life well. Stated more contentiously, it is not enough to force my student to choose between blindly clinging to his illusions as reality or embracing his illusions as illusions and seeing them dissolve into nothingness. There is a third possibility, to open our ears to the claims that sirens' songs make upon us.

HEARING GAY VOICES
Toward Building Community in a Pluralist Society

... an identity crisis may be better than certainty, no conclusion is better than mastery's illusion.

—Judith Roof, *Come As You Are*

—————

The unique challenges that pluralism poses to one's attempting to create a meaningful life are well illustrated by two conversations that have come to the fore in contemporary American society. The first is best articulated by Robert Bellah, et al.'s *Habits of the Heart,* while the second has surfaced in the various multicultural works that have proliferated during the past two decades. In *Habits of the Heart,* Bellah, et al., describe and critique the societal fabric of private and public life in America. The authors' description consists of tracing contemporary emphases on self-reliance and individualism to their historical roots, namely, expressive and utilitarian individualism. They also note that there are biblical and republican traditions at work in the culture that provide the basis for a second language in terms of which Americans can understand themselves. Still, they suggest that because of social and economic developments in the nineteenth and twentieth centuries, these traditions are no longer sufficient to serve as a basis for forming community. The result is a social crisis. Without a coherent sense of community, individuals cannot engage in the task of living meaningful lives. The question for Bellah, et al., becomes: how are we to establish adequate contexts for the development of meaningful human lives in light of the present crisis. Implicit in the authors' discussion is the assumption that authentic human life takes place in community. What the community provides is a context permeated by a world-view in terms of which individuals can understand themselves. *Habits of the Heart* makes a substantial plea for the need for a new communal understanding if Americans are to lead meaningful lives. But the reasoning of *Habits* seems inverted. In order to have community that can provide a context for meaning, it suggests, we must create something like the republican or biblical traditions that had previously sustained community. Such a claim forgets that these traditions could sustain community only because they were accepted, because they inspired belief by the community that the tradition united. What does seem to be the case is that a community will not tolerate a condition that does not provide a context for meaning. Richard John Neuhaus presses this point in *The Naked Public Square* through his disturbing discussion of the "Christian right's" attempt to establish forcibly a new context of meaning for all of American society, to seize what has become a naked public square.

There are two questions of particular interest that surface in this context. If human beings require a social context fed by a compelling world-view but find themselves confronted by competing world-views, how is it ever possible for individuals in any meaningful sense to choose their world-view, to believe genuinely in anything? This seems to be a fundamental question if Bellah, et al., are right when they contend that there is no longer a compelling vision underpinning life in America. If there is no basis, might individuals simply arbitrarily adopt an account of reality out of a felt need? The adoption of a world-view on no other grounds could easily lead to a dogmatic stance, to an unwillingness to tolerate competing visions born from an insecurity regarding one's own. Unthinking patriotism, the sort that relies on symbols that are reduced to signs of membership, provides apt illustration of such a stance. These considerations give rise to the second question. How do individuals who require a social context and a story in which they can understand themselves authentically engage in the task of accepting or rejecting a given story and a given social context as adequate to self-understanding? The significance of this question is highlighted if we take up the second conversation alluded to above.

Since the 1960s, college campuses have seen the development of such programs as African-American studies, women's studies, and gay and lesbian studies. Correspondingly, critical works in feminist literature, gay and lesbian studies, even masculine studies, have abounded. These works, while of varying quality, all testify to people's felt need for a language which they can use to understand themselves. They stand in the light of Gadamer's claim that "Being that can be understood is language."[1] But at the same time, people make choices regarding the language, or languages, that are most appropriate for self-understanding. While they initially attempt to understand themselves in terms of the language present at hand in their community, when language fails to produce what they take to be genuine self-understanding, people go in search of a new language. Here is where the interests of mainstream America as articulated in *Habits of the Heart* meet with those of individuals who feel alienated from mainstream America. Both require compelling world-views to provide the context for their lives, and both are faced with the fact that there are no operative world-views, no traditions, no accounts of reality sufficiently compelling and rich enough to supply a context of meaning for American society as a whole. This, of course, is not to say that there is no language available in American culture; there are many languages, and many that are quite rich. It is to say, rather, that the very wealth of choices poses a problem, at least for those seeking some legitimation for the choices made. It is also to say that the sense that there is no sufficiently rich common language in America is unsettling. As Paul Ricoeur notes: "What a group fears most is no longer being able to identify itself because of crises and confusions creating strain; the task is to cope with this strain."[2]

If we are to address the current crisis of meaning to which these two conversations point, we must pay attention to the relation between individuals and their attempts to articulate the meaning of their lives. It is important to recognize that such attempts do not take place in a vacuum, or from a viewpoint that transcends all world-views. Human beings are born into a context, into a society in which certain world-views are operative. Even if, in the language of Thomas Kuhn, there are a number of competing paradigms operative in our society, these paradigms are nonetheless operative. As significantly, it is important to problematize, perhaps to reconfigure, that which one seeks when one asks of language a "genuine" self-understanding. This will be a particular concern in the following chapter.

Again, Paul Ricoeur suggests that symbols and myths constitute the initial articulations of the human experience of being in the world.[3] In *The Symbolism of Evil,* he characterizes myth as the verbal expression of a form of life that seeks to be in tune with being.[4] It is by reflectively engaging myths and symbols, by thinking and acting from them, that the world-views operative in contemporary society arise. Even a rejection of given myths and symbols, or of interpretations of them, in order to constitute new myths and symbols presupposes the originally operative myths and symbols. In short, once one recognizes the finitude of the human condition, one must recognize that all inquiry, all questioning, must begin from somewhere; there is no presuppositionless starting point.[5] Recognition that inquiry is historically and culturally situated makes even more complex the task of struggling to articulate the meaning of life in the context of competing myths and competing interpretations of those myths. The suspicion arises that the decision to adopt or to reject a given myth, and a given interpretation, is somehow invalidated because it is not made from a vantage point that stands outside of all myths, all contexts. This raises the question whether it is ever possible to affirm the legitimacy of the decision to reject a particular myth in favor of an alternative. To sharpen this, we might think of Heidegger's discussion of authenticity in *Being and Time.* According to Heidegger, one is able to gain a distance from the everyday world and a certain detachment from the conceptual frameworks, or myths, that inform it by recognizing the contingency of one's existence. The fact that one need not be makes one's being an issue. How one is going to respond to the conceptual frameworks informing one's life becomes an issue. This occurs in several ways:

through the recognition that one is going to die, through anxiety, and through what Heidegger calls the silent call of conscience. This distancing is necessary for authentically making a choice regarding the way in which one is going to live. Without such distancing, one would simply fall into the roles assigned by society. But it in no way provides one with a criterion for choice. Heidegger's claim that the call of conscience is silent, for instance, points to the fact that criteria arise only with the adoption of a world-view. This leads to the heart of the initial suspicion that the choice is arbitrary. From one perspective, this makes the choice suspect. But from another, it simply places it beyond the scope of question, and hence of critique. Something more is needed.

In what follows, I will argue that any attempt to come to terms with the crisis of meaning facing contemporary American culture and the suspicion surrounding the situatedness of any inquiry aimed at the adoption of a context of meaning must recognize that the creation and interpretation of myths, the appropriation of myths, and the establishment of world-views arise as *testimony* to one's relation to the other and to oneself and articulate a possible way of being in the world. They are not best understood as attempts to provide an exhaustive, absolute account of reality. We can see what this claim entails if we first examine concrete instances of individual attempts at the development of such testimony. To this end, we will briefly examine John J. McNeill's *The Church and the Homosexual* and Arthur Evans's *The God of Ecstasy*. With this as a context for reflection, we can then turn to a more general consideration of the relation of the individual to the articulation of a world-view.

Testifying to What It Means to Be Gay: McNeill and Evans

McNeill's *The Church and the Homosexual* and Evans's *The God of Ecstasy* suggest positive visions of what it means to be gay by engaging particular world-views and mythic visions. But their respective stances are quite different. McNeill develops an interpretation of the Judeo-Christian tradition that can accommodate a positive vision and role in the community for gays and lesbians. Evans, on the other hand, takes up a discussion of the worship of Dionysus in early Greek culture in order to develop an account of what it means

to be gay that is free from the influence of the predominant patriarchal paradigm operative in contemporary Western culture. Mc-
Neill, then, operates within a tradition while trying to transform it,
while Evans moves outside of a predominant paradigm in order to
suggest another point of view.

In turning to McNeill's thesis, it is helpful to recognize that the
Judeo-Christian tradition offers various alternatives for understanding both what it means to be gay and the role that the gay person plays in the community. There are some who would simply deny
that human beings have a fixed sexual orientation. The focus is on
acts, and homosexual activity is viewed as sinful. The Catholic
Church, McNeill's denomination, has not followed this line. It has
been sensitive to the claims of the scientific community regarding
sexual orientation, and admits that homosexuality may be a result
of genetic or developmental factors.[6] But this does not negate its understanding of genital relations between homosexuals as immoral.
It views such acts as failing to meet the ideal for sexual relations,
namely, the realization of unity between spouses and procreation.
Charles Curran has developed an interesting variation of this position in "Homosexuality and Moral Theology: Methodological and
Substantive Considerations." Curran places his discussion of homosexuality in the context of an account of original sin. According to
Curran, original sin forms part of objective reality, and individual
decisions must be made in light of its reality. Homosexuality is an
objective condition falling short of the ideal, a legacy of original sin.
The homosexual is not responsible for his or her individual homosexuality, and may therefore find that the best option available is to
cultivate a monogamous homosexual relationship given the impossibility of realizing the ideal.[7]

McNeill is not satisfied with the negative accounts of homosexual relations offered by the Christian tradition nor with Curran's attempt to develop a Christian stance that "tolerates" but fails to affirm a positive role for homosexuals as such in the Christian
community. Still, NcNeill is a Christian, a Catholic Christian, unwilling simply to break with the tradition. Instead, he mines it to
develop an articulation of what it means to be gay that he can affirm as appropriate and can use as the basis for interpreting experience and engaging in action. There is a movement here in two directions. McNeill seeks an interpretation of the Judeo-Christian

vision that can accommodate what I will provisionally call here his preunderstanding of being gay, saving for the next chapter a more nuanced discussion of identity claims. Conversely, he relies upon the tradition for a language to use to articulate what it means to be gay and to establish viable possibilities for living as a gay person.

McNeill's effort reflects the Catholic concern for scriptural and traditional authority. He begins by arguing that biblical passages traditionally cited as condemnations of homosexual behavior are taken out of context and misrepresented by those who cite them. By contextualizing such passages as the Sodom and Gemorrah story, he argues that what have been viewed as condemnations of homosexuality are actually condemnations of inhospitality and pagan worship.[8] He then suggests that the Judeo-Christian tradition offers positive ground for the development of homosexual relationships that are enriching to those who participate in them. Finally, he makes a case for the role of the homosexual in modern society as one who can help reverse the tide of dehumanization attendant upon contemporary heterosexual identity images.[9]

Evans's *The God of Ecstasy* is a more ambitious work than that of McNeill. Instead of posing an alternative interpretation of a predominant tradition, it appeals to a world-view that is no longer dominant in Western culture, one that provides a perspective from which Evans can critique what he sees as the patriarchal value system at work in the culture. It is a world-view that Evans envisions as being more amenable to the accommodation of gays and lesbians than the world-views of those espousing patriarchal values. Using Euripides' play, *Bakkai,* as a point of departure, Evans develops a series of essays exploring matriarchal strains found in archaic Greek culture and the impact that the rise of patriarchal values had upon Greek culture and our own. He focuses on *Bakkai* because he sees there Euripides' reflection on the conflict between the patriarchal values of classical Greece, represented by King Pentheus, and the more archaic matriarchal values, represented by the god Dionysus. In the play, an effeminate Dionysus is spurned by the proud King Pentheus, who refuses to recognize the divinity of Dionysus. The god ultimately brings Pentheus to ruin.

Evans explores in detail the difference between matriarchal and patriarchal societies. Of particular interest is his characterization of patriarchal societies as hierarchical and dependent upon relations of domination and of "matriarchal," or women-centered societies, as generally dependent upon relations of cooperation. Patriarchal societies, he suggests, usually arise where there are limited resources and hence competition for them, while "matriarchal" societies thrive where resources are readily available. Evans maintains that Greek society underwent a transformation from being "matriarchal" to being patriarchal through invasion by nomadic tribes from the north who were suffering from a scarcity of goods. This transformation resulted in a diminution of the status of women and a curtailment of the kinds of lesbian and gay activities typical in cultures where people feel a close bond with nature.[10] According to Evans, societies that establish patterns of domination for survival promote competition between men so that they will be willing to participate in war, and break down community among women by relegating them to their husbands' households. Because the activities typically undertaken by women, such as foraging and the preliminary cultivation of plants, become less central to survival, women in such societies are reduced to second-class citizens, and behaviour that is associated with women is discouraged among men.[11]

By explaining the suppression of homosexual activity as a product of contingent material conditions, Evans offers a basis for rethinking what it means to be a gay or lesbian person. Undermining traditional taboos by reaching back to an archaic tradition, he establishes a point of departure for arguing that the present way of conceiving gay and lesbian relations is the product of an ideology that needs to be reconsidered. What is interesting about Evans's discussion is that he does not advocate a rejection of patriarchal paradigms in favor of a matriarchal paradigm rooted in the worship of Dionysus, or more generally, of nature. His aim, rather, is to supply a place for us to stand so that we might rethink the present.[12] Further, through a discussion of the ills accompanying patriarchal culture, the ills deriving from policies of domination regarding other people and the environment,[13] Evans gives to those who might not be interested in the place of gay or lesbian people in contemporary society a reason for rethinking the present.

In reflecting upon McNeill's radical reinterpretation of the Judeo-Christian tradition and Evans's mining of a world-view that is not currently predominant, it is natural to ask why one should follow either of their leads. Their arguments are rooted in interpretations of our past and of our present that we need not adopt. This returns us to our initial problem. Contemporary society offers us the opportunity to make some choices about the stance from which we are going to view the world. But how are we to engage in the process of choosing? Existentially, the choice must be taken seriously and cannot be viewed as arbitrary.

We can find a clue if we attend to McNeill's and Evans's respective projects. I would like to suggest that, if one can say that McNeill and Evans, as professedly gay men, chose their projects, one can with equal validity entertain the possibility that their projects chose them. There were traditions to hand in which McNeill and Evans could have constructed meaningful lives. McNeill, for instance, could have followed Curran's lead and seen the homosexual condition as an objective sign of original sin operative in the world. He did not choose to understand being gay in this way. It is worth considering the following account of why this is so. McNeill's reinterpretation of the Christian tradition arises because he *could* not choose to understand being gay in Curran's way. Similarly, Evans *could* not accept a world-view or a set of primary myths that grounded patriarchal values as ultimate. McNeill's and Evans's work stemmed from a recognition that the operative accounts of reality did not provide an adequate context for their appreciation of what it means to be gay. Their work is at once testimony to this awareness and the welling up of a new understanding of what it means to be a gay or lesbian person, a meaning that takes the form of establishing the conditions and the possibilities for meaningful action.

The Nature of Testimony: Disclosing and Foreclosing Possibilities for Being in the World

The suggestion before us is that we gain much if we consider McNeill's and Evan's work as testimony. Gabriel Marcel sheds light on the nature of testimony by juxtaposing it with the statement of an observation. The latter is the simple recording of a phenomenon. Observation is impersonal and is not considered to effect the phenomenon. In contrast, testimony involves the one testifying personally. In testifying, the individual makes a commitment: he or she bears witness, and does so before someone, before what Marcel calls a transcendence.[14] Further, testimony is about something, something which the individual takes to be independent from him or herself, something objectively real.

This brief sketch of testimony implies an interesting relation between the one who bears witness and the world. A witness is someone engaged in a particular mode of receptivity. Marcel asserts that modern philosophers pose two options for human beings, to be either passive onlookers uninvolved with reality, or active, free beings.[15] He objects: "By adopting this standpoint, do we not forfeit all chance of understanding the essential point of our lives—the fact that we are witnesses and that this is the expression of our mode of belonging to the world?"[16] Marcel fleshes out his proposed alternative by calling to mind our characterization of those who lead lives of devotion, those who are faithful to something or to someone, as bearing testimony by their lives.[17] Certainly, such lives are not lived in passive receptivity, nor are they lives of unreflecting acts. As testimony, they involve the act of fidelity. But such an act depends upon "a grace received," a gift. Marcel brings together act and receptivity by insisting that one can lead a life of creative receptivity:

> Receptivity covers a wide scale of gradations: at one end of it is "suffering," in the sense in which wax "suffers" the imprint of a seal; at the other end is giving—even self-giving—as when we speak of a hospitable host "receiving" his friends. This kind of "reception" is entirely different from that of a vessel which is filled with an alien substance; it is a participation in a reality, in a plenitude, and a communication of oneself.[18]

What Marcel is suggesting is that life can be lived as a response to a gift given. Such a life is an act of response, a creative act that bears testimony.

My initial inclination is to consider McNeill's and Evans's enterprises as acts of creative fidelity to a gift given. But our focus is not on their lives; it is on their works, the world-views that are proposed by their texts. Marcel's discussion of testimony contributes to the consideration of their works by suggesting that we think of them as articulations bearing the stamp of a gift given. The significance of this becomes apparent if we return for a moment to Ricoeur's account of the referential character of language and of the origin of symbol and myth.

Recognizing Testimony, Creating Dialogue, Building Community: Ricoeur

Recall from the preceding chapter that Ricoeur takes exception to structuralist approaches to language, arguing that it belongs to language "to say something about something to someone."[19] His most compelling reason for rejecting an exclusively semiotic approach is that language only exists because we are in the world and affected by it. It is this experience of being in the world that is brought to language:

> The referential function is so important that it compensates, as it were, for another characteristic of language, namely the separation of signs from things. By means of the referential function, language "pours back into the universe" (according to an expression of Gustave Guillaume) those signs which the symbolic function, at its birth, divorced from things. All discourse is, to some extent, thereby reconnected to the world. For if we do not speak of the world, of what should we speak?[20]

Ricoeur takes this claim regarding the origin of language as the basis for his argument that language fundamentally refers to what is.[21] He thus supports a hermeneutics that is not about working out the meaning of what is given, but about the disclosure and the closure of *possibilities* for meaning that it opens up through its engagement of symbol, myth, narrative, and discourse generally.

Ricoeur's position is highlighted by his discussions of symbol and myth. In his view, symbol stands on the border between bios and logos;[22] it is the initial articulation of one's response to reality, a response called forth by reality's demand for articulation. In the symbol, a world is simultaneously opened up and created. By world, Ricoeur means the horizon of existence, the other as one is aware of it in relation to oneself.[23] Through the creation of symbols, and of myths as the extensions of symbol into narrative form,[24] a horizon is both opened up and given form.

More generally, Ricoeur describes such texts as poetry and fictional narrative as events of meaning whose reference is one's being in relation to the other. In addition, he emphasizes that this relation is not established prior to the text; the text establishes it in and through its articulation.[25] Thus he adopts Heidegger's position "that what we understand first in a discourse is not another person, but a 'project,' that is, the outline of a new way of being in the world."[26]

If Ricoeur is right, it would seem that the appropriate attitude towards such works as McNeill's reading of the Christian tradition and Evans's resuscitation of the Dionysian tradition must be the kind of openness that one has when one is truly receptive to a gift given. The primary task is to enter into the work to see what it has to say about being in the world. In regard to texts, Ricoeur calls this the act of appropriation, an act in which one can distinguish three moments. Firstly, appropriation as interpretation of the text is self-interpretation. In reading the text, one seeks who one is through the claims the text makes regarding one's being in relation to others. Secondly, appropriation involves making the text one's own. Such obstacles as the cultural distance of the text must be surpassed as far as possible. Finally, appropriation involves the reenactment or actualization of the text. This consists fundamentally in the actualization of the text's semantic virtualities in the reader. Ricoeur compares this reenactment to the performance of a musical score.[27] Through the act of appropriation, one arrives at what Gadamer calls a "fusion of horizons" in which ". . . the world of the reader and the world of the text merge into one another."[28]

But at this point, we meet a difficult challenge. Might not works open up a world that establishes a distorted relation of the self to the other? Like the members of a dysfunctional family, perhaps those who appropriate these works enter into relations which fail to nourish, leaving them stunted, isolated creatures. This suspicion can take the form of a dismissal of McNeill's and Evans's works as merely ideological distortions of reality.[29]

Ricoeur suggests that one of the functions traditionally served by ideologies is the legitimation of authority. Ideologies bridge the gap between the authority's claim to legitimacy and the citizenry's belief in that claim.[30] Given this view, one indeed might wonder if *The Church and the Homosexual* and *The God of Ecstasy* are not simply fabrications placed in the service of legitimating certain kinds of actions, certain forms of life. At the personal level, they might be the tools of self-deception; in the public realm, they might be used to thwart the attacks of a hostile society. This suspicion becomes acute given McNeill's opposition to interpretations of scripture and tradition at odds with his own and Evans's challenge of the Western patriarchal tradition.[31]

The suspicion that a given testimony is false cannot be easily dismissed, nor should it be, as I will later argue. Nonetheless, recognizing that the articulation of a world-view may be testimony and acknowledging the character of language as referential, taken together, can provide a suitable basis for claiming that it is possible to reflect fruitfully upon such works as McNeill's and Evans's without focusing on the motives of their authors or making an immediate determination regarding their ideological status. To see this, it is helpful to consider Ricoeur's discussion of written texts.

In *Hermeneutics and the Human Sciences,* Ricoeur describes discourse as an event whereby language is actualized and surpassed as a mere system. What is realized in discourse is meaning. It is meaning which is the object of understanding in discourse and which endures the fleeting character of the event.[32] Ricoeur conceives of written works as discourse. The event is the creation of the work, and it can be characterized as a labor "which organizes language."[33] This introduction of the work as a result of labor is important. Through the labor of the author, the work becomes objectified. The event of meaning passes away and what remains is the witness to that movement which is at the same time the bearer of meaning. Because it has broken its moorings with the event of meaning, the text takes on a life of its own, and the meaning that it carries with it becomes independent of its author.[34]

Ricoeur likewise maintains that the work cuts its moorings from its psycho-sociological origins:

> An essential characteristic of a literary work, and of a work of art in general, is that it transcends its own psycho-sociological conditions of production and thereby opens itself to an unlimited series of readings, themselves situated in different sociocultural conditions. In short, the text must be able, from the sociological as well as the psychological

point of view, to "decontextualise" itself—in such a way that it can be "recontextualised" in a new situation—as accomplished, precisely, by the act of reading.[35]

This account of the text is important, for it claims that our attitude in approaching a text should not be to gain entrance to an alien life, as Dilthey or the Romantics might argue.[36] Rather, the text refers to a possible way of being in the world, and it is to this that we should attend.[37] Of course, this is not to say that there is no role for suspicion, but what that role is remains to be seen. To address this, we must examine more closely the claim made earlier, that inquiry is of necessity situated.

Ricoeur's recognition that the human person is always historically situated carries with it the insight that reflection must begin from somewhere, an insight that constitutes the cornerstone of the hermeneutics of finitude as it arises from the Heideggerian theme that all perception, all understanding, all experience involves mediation.[38] Gadamer expands on this in *Truth and Method,* arguing that being-in-the-world is a condition for knowledge. It is only as situated being that Dasein has knowledge of the world. The emphasis here should not be missed. Situatedness is not a hindrance to knowledge, but rather its condition.[39] Gadamer highlights this claim when he argues that pre-judgment, prejudice, is the condition for understanding. The task, he says, is not to eliminate prejudice in order to gain genuine knowledge or to arrive at the truth, but to determine "where is the ground of the legitimacy of prejudices? What distinguishes legitimate prejudices from all the countless ones which it is the undeniable task of the critical reason to overcome?"[40]

This insight regarding the situatedness of inquiry carries with it an imperative that we rethink what we seek when we seek the truth. According to Ricoeur, interpretations of the philosophical enterprise have carried with them two models of truth. Traditionally, truth has been viewed in terms of the task of unifying knowledge. This task consists in the reconciliation of speech to reality and of minds to one another.[41] "It is the task of imposing unity on the diversity of our field of knowledge and of resolving differences of opinion."[42] Understanding philosophical inquiry in terms of this task leads to an amelioration of the discord between philosophies standing in opposition to one another through an appeal to the unity of intention animating philosophical inquiry. The unity of intention legitimates a distinction between genuine inquiry as that which contributes to progress toward the desired unity and inquiry which fails to do so, and it posits the possibility of finding a law of progress which will facilitate the determination of genuine inquiry.[43] Recognition of the irremediable situatedness of inquiry requires that we recognize that such a project of truth can never be complete. But Ricoeur also finds such a project to be troubling. Firstly, it fails to recognize the unique contribution that the various philosophical approaches make with respect to the vision of the real, for it tends to reduce them to moments of one single philosophy.[44] Secondly, Ricoeur sees in such an enterprise the tendency towards a closed-mindedness that can serve as the birthplace of violence.[45] The desire for a single, unified truth can foster the claim to its possession too soon, thereby cutting off genuine inquiry, genuine openness to alternatives. The result of giving in to such temptation is authoritarianism.[46]

The second approach to the philosophical enterprise that Ricoeur considers asserts the value of philosophies in their singularity as providing individual visions of the world springing from individual, original problematics.[47] What such an approach recognizes is that there are many philosophical stances precisely because different philosophies address different questions and have their origins in unique circumstances.[48] As a result of this, various philosophical attitudes can be viewed as incommensurable rather than competing. This is important because it gives rise to a new conception of truth. No longer is truth considered the agreement of thought to some contextless, absolute reality. It is, instead, "the adequation of answers to questions, of solutions to problems."[49] As with the first account of the philosophical enterprise and its vision of truth, Ricoeur has difficulties with this account and its vision. Most important is the tendency this approach has for encouraging involvement in a given problematic to the exclusion of all others.[50]

Ricoeur does not simply dismiss the preceding two accounts of the philosophical enterprise and their suppositions regarding truth. He recognizes that both say something true:

> On the one hand, I have something to discover personally, something that no other except myself has the task of discovering. If my existence has a meaning, if it is not empty, I

have a place within being which invites me to raise a question that no one else can raise in my place. The narrowness of my condition, my information, my encounters, my reading, already outline the finished perspectives of my calling to truth. And yet, on the other hand, to search for truth means that I aspire to express something that is valid for all, that stands out on the background of my situation as something universal. I do not want to invent or to say whatever I like, but what is. From the very roots of my situation I aspire to be bound by being. Let being be thought in me—such is my wish for truth.[51]

Reflection on these two models leads Ricoeur to adopt an intersubjective definition of truth. Ricoeur recognizes that the individual is at once bound to a situation and yearns to transcend that situation in order to obtain absolute knowledge, a grasp of being that exhausts the meaning of being. Because the situation constitutes one's opening onto being, one's access to being, it provides ground for genuine insight. Similarly, the perspectives of others provide ground for insight, for an event of truth, the shining forth of being. Through communication, one can transcend one's own situation and enter into the situations of others while respecting at once their uniqueness and varied contributions to a single task. By engaging in communication with others, one can transcend one's perspective without escaping it by transforming it through a fusion of horizons. Truth, according to Ricoeur, is the expression of this fusion of horizons, hence his claim to defend an intersubjective definition of truth.[52] In this view, the appropriate aim of human life is not to have, to possess, the truth, but rather to live in its light.

At this juncture, we are in a position to address the question of the role that suspicion plays in approaching the worlds opened up by texts. Viewed negatively, its role is not to aid and abet the elimination of the testimony found in these texts by explaining it away, seeing in the world-views they construct flattering garments covering a diseased body. Rather, its role is to wean one away from the dogmatism that destroys the context of communication. In this sense, one should engage in a two-fold suspicion, a suspicion regarding one's own perspective, and a suspicion regarding the perspective of the other. But what is the character of this suspicion? It is not primarily a suspicion that one's own views or those of the other are distorted or false; rather, it is the suspicion that they are perspectival and hence limited in their capacity to let being shine forth. This formulation requires elaboration. Given what has been said, letting being shine forth means envisioning possibilities for being, an envisioning which itself is operative in the very being of possibilities. It belongs to suspicion to be a player in the field of constituting possibilities for being.

One might object that this is too limited a role for suspicion to play, and perhaps with some reason. It does seem that there are several reservations that require consideration, two of which are particularly noteworthy. Firstly, recognition that inquiry must start from somewhere, that one is historically and culturally conditioned, that the symbols and myths available to reflection are themselves culturally conditioned, is accompanied by recognition that there is a fundamental contingency at the heart of inquiry.[53] The suspicion might well arise that one's ground is so shaky as to provide no adequate foundation for the reception of insight into being. One of the favorite themes of Ricoeur's earlier works is that inquiry begins with a wager that the place from which one starts will yield insight; faith stands at the heart of inquiry. Suspicion that this faith is misplaced can never be definitively eliminated. Our earlier discussion of the referential character of language and of the origin of symbols and myths offers some ground for hope, however, that our testimony bears witness to an unfolding awareness of being. Ricoeur maintains that it is the experience of being which calls forth inquiry; texts are the result of the human experience of being, inaugurated as much by being as by human beings. Ultimately, however, this claim cannot be used to ground the adoption of any starting point. One can be mistaken. Yet, Ricoeur makes a provocative suggestion in *The Symbolism of Evil* regarding the sort of validation for one's choice that one might eventually receive:

> . . . hermeneutics, in its turn requires that the philosopher wager his belief, and that he lose or win the wager by putting the revealing power of the symbol to the test of self-understanding. In understanding himself better, the philosopher verifies, up to a certain point, the wager of his faith.[54]

Secondly, suspicion regarding motivation, recognition that a proposed world-view may conceal certain interests, even unconscious ones, might well be helpful for what it reveals. Careful reflection regarding the world opened up by a text should not preclude consideration of what it conceals, for bringing what it conceals into dialogue provides an occasion for the event of truth.

Though a careful working out of the role of suspicion is necessary, the preceding discussion regarding how we might most fruitfully approach works like McNeill's and Evans's, as contributors to an ongoing dialogue that makes possible the event of truth, enables us to address the concerns raised in the introduction to this chapter. In the introduction, we saw the difficulties that people face when there is no one, overarching, compelling world-view that serves as the context of meaning for the community. When a number of competing world-views are operative, this poses a challenge for the thoughtful person who is striving to establish a commitment to a vision of life sufficient for engaging in meaningful human activity. It also poses a challenge to the community to maintain its integrity as such. The preceding discussion suggests that these challenges are not best met by choosing what one perceives to be "the best" world-view and eliminating the rest. Such elimination results in the elimination of participants in that dialogue which is essential to the task of truth. While various accounts of reality might claim to be comprehensive, if human beings can remember their own finitude, they will not only tolerate different voices, but also will listen to them. One who chooses a world-view recognizing that the choice is not made in a vacuum, that it is a situated choice guided by interests, will be a person capable of commitment without succumbing to dogmatism. Such a person, recognizing the contingency of his or her own choices, will welcome other voices precisely for the challenges they pose to those choices. These voices will raise questions and will also provide a point of critical reflection.[55] Again, tolerance is not enough because tolerance does not entail listening. Instead, what is needed is a genuine commitment to hear what others have to say. By considering McNeill's *The Church and the Homosexual,* it becomes possible to indicate the value of such commitment. The Christian vision that McNeill develops owes both the character and the detail of its development to those interpretations of the Christian message that fail to establish a positive place for the homosexual as such. Conversely,

McNeill offers a challenge to those alternative accounts, a challenge that becomes the condition for their development, their growth.

But is it possible to have a community in which there are a number of competing world-views that are operative? The seriousness of this question becomes apparent if we reflect on Ricoeur's and Erik Erikson's accounts of the integrative function of ideology. According to Ricoeur and Erikson, an ideological system is "a coherent body of shared images, ideas, and ideals which . . . provides for the participants a coherent, if systematically simplified, over-all orientation in space and time, in means and ends . . ."[56] Without a common language, without a common world-view, the identities of the community and of the individual are threatened. However, this difficulty can be met. In *Habits of the Heart,* the authors distinguish between a first language and a number of second languages,[57] by which they mean modes of moral discourse, which are spoken in America. At least one way that a community can support the existence of more than one world-view is if its members recognize their own situatedness and share as their common task the realization of truth. This can constitute the basis for a shared first language based on a shared commitment.

What I am proposing in essence is a certain vision regarding the human condition, an ideology in the sense just discussed. Moreover, it is an ideology that, like all ideologies, promotes particular practices and attitudes, the practice of listening and an attitude of openness to new ideas. One might ask, then, if it simply joins the ranks of competing world-views. The difficulty here seems inevitable if the preceding claims regarding the situatedness of human beings and the necessity to begin inquiry from somewhere are valid. But I do not think that this is so great a difficulty as might initially be supposed. The community that adopts this view is in effect making a wager that by allowing many voices not only to be tolerated but also heard, they will more truly live in the light of truth. If this is accomplished, then voices speaking against such an approach to community must likewise be heard. The community will continually live with the possibility of its own transformation. While it may live in the conviction that any claims to realize a comprehensive account of the human condition suffers from a hubris that fails to recognize the fragility of the human condition, it will not silence those who disagree, though it may in good conscience challenge them. But there are other difficulties that realizing such a community confronts that are more formidable and that might never be able to be satisfactorily addressed, which is not to say that the project should be abandoned. These difficulties include the following:

1. the existence of real power differentials between people in social relations;

2. the refusal to recognize subordinate and marginalized groups as eligible interlocutors;

3. the absence or suppression of language adequate to enabling marginalized people to have a voice of their own;

4. the inevitable conflict generated by employing an agonistic metaphor for thinking about the relations between different mythic visions or discourses.

These difficulties will be the concern of the final two chapters. But I want to signal here that it is precisely because of such obstacles and because I view discourse as carrying the possibility of being an event of truth, the setting up of a possibility for being, that my proposal differs from universalist discourse ethics, such as that proposed by Jurgen Habermas in "Discourse Ethics: Notes on a Program of Philosophical Justification." By considering Habermas's position, it will be possible to develop my own a bit further and set the stage for considering the difficulties raised above.

Recognizing Others versus Universalizing Norms: Habermas and Benhabib

Habermas frames his defense of a universalist discourse ethics as a response to skeptical dismissals of ethical claims as emotivist, as expressing purely personal interests, or as disguised empirical claims regarding prudence or expediency. Drawing upon Strawson, and ultimately following Kant, Habermas makes the case that moral norms are such precisely because they make a claim to general validity. Further, this claim implies a cognitive dimension, that moral norms can be shown to be right; it is this that gives them their force.[58] Of course, from the fact that moral norms make these claims, one cannot draw the conclusion that they can redeem them. To do so involves a twofold process. One must first indicate the conditions to be met for a claim of normative validity. One must then show why it is reasonable to accept these conditions. Again drawing upon Kant, Habermas argues that a normative validity claim must meet the principle of universalization. He differs from Kant, however, regarding the principle of universalization itself. Whereas Kant's principle looks to the individual as a rational moral agent who determines what is moral by asking what he or she would will as a universal maxim applicable to all, Habermas argues that, "the generalizability of maxims intends something more than this, namely, that valid norms must deserve recognition by all concerned."[59] This amendment of Kant's ethics stems from Habermas's examination of the suppositions that must obtain in argumentative discourse. Drawing on the work of Karl-Otto Apel, he argues that one of these suppositions is that no claim can be accepted as valid unless objections to it can be addressed. When it comes to making a justified moral decision, then, it is necessary that everyone's objections be engaged.[60] The perspectives of all effected must be included in the decision-making process. He concludes:

> True impartiality pertains only to that standpoint from which one can generalize precisely those norms that can count on universal assent because they perceptibly embody an interest common to all affected. It is these norms that deserve intersubjective recognition. Thus the impartiality of judgment is expressed in a principle that constrains all affected to adopt the perspectives of all others in the balancing of interests. The principle of universalization is intended to compel the universal exchange of roles that G. H. Mead called "ideal role taking" or "universal discourse." Thus every valid norm has to fulfill the following condition:
>
> (U) All affected can accept the consequences and the side effects its general observance can be anticipated to have for the satisfaction of everyone's interests (and these consequences are preferred to those of known alternative possibilities for regulation).[61]

The appeal to moral norms typically occurs when there is a breakdown in consensus regarding what course of action is to be followed. When this conflict can be traced to a breakdown of consensus regarding the norm(s) themselves, then the project becomes the discursive formation of consensus. If one is to claim that a norm is morally valid, that it should be binding on the community, one must argue that it should in principle be capable of sustaining such consensus, which means that objections raised through considering the interests of those effected must be addressed. Otherwise, the norm is just a dogmatic command. One can concretely make good on this claim only if genuine discourse prevails in which competent subjects agree that the reasons for the norm's adoption are indeed acceptable. Habermas emphasizes that such discourse must be free and open, devoid of coercion by the various interlocutors.

Given the real possibility that individuals operating out of different world-views will be unable to reach consensus regarding substantive normative claims since their interpretations of the situations at hand and their formulations of the issues at stake are not necessarily commensurable, the principle of universalization provides procedural limitations regarding the adoption of norms. One cannot, for instance, adopt a norm that would destroy the conditions for genuine dialogue. In short, the principle of universalization itself offers ground for the formation of consensus among those operating out of differing world-views. Rational moral agents cannot adopt norms that distort or otherwise circumvent genuine dialogue or that run contrary to genuine consensus.

One could see how such an approach would be initially attractive to someone interested in gay and lesbian praxis. It would be possible, for instance, to argue for the overthrow of Colorado's Amendment 2 that precludes the protection of gays and lesbians from employment and housing discrimination. It is not merely that gays and lesbians would be unlikely to assent to such an amendment. Rather, the amendment would be untenable because it would create conditions that would militate against genuine dialogue, because gays and lesbians would no longer be in a context free from coercion in which they could discuss laws pertaining to themselves. But as we shall see, it is not so clear that this would indeed be the necessary outcome of adopting a Habermasean stance.

Given the concerns of the present chapter, it is not necessary to trace the complex argument that Habermas builds to support the principle of universalization as grounds for discourse ethics. But there are several features of his project that are worth noting. Firstly, in Habermas's view, the moral skeptic must recognize the principle of universalization as a precondition for argumentation. Therefore, to avoid being involved in a performative contradiction, she or he could deny the principle of universalization only by withdrawing from argumentation altogether. Such withdrawal would amount to resigning from what Habermas calls the web of shared sociocultural life, since communication is a necessary condition for community, and argumentation, understood as reasoning for coming to an understanding, is a necessary condition for communication. As one who already finds oneself in community, the skeptic cannot avoid ethical discourse without leaving community altogether by death, mental illness, or adopting a hermetic existence.[62] But secondly, it is important to note that Habermas defends the principle of universalization solely as a rule of argumentation. As such, it is not the source of substantive principles or basic norms.[63] Rather, it constitutes a necessary condition that must be met if norms or principles are to claim validity. The formal character of the principle of universalization, in Habermas's view, places it in a position to ameliorate disputes between individuals operating from competing world-views with competing visions of the good life. Because the universalization principle is a purely procedural one, it is supposed to provide objective, unprejudiced ground for intersubjective, rational dialogue. Habermas's formulation of the universalization principle carries with it a respect for the real differences between individuals and groups engaged in moral discourse; hence, the insistence that dialogue is essential to the concrete application of the universalization principle. However, adoption of this principle supposes a standard of justification of moral principles that transcends the valuations deriving from visions of the good life instanciated in concrete world-views. Finally, in line with the preceding remarks, Habermas markedly distinguishes between practical issues and issues of the good life, normative and evaluative statements, norms and cultural values, the just and the good. According to Habermas, it is impossible for participants in a form of life to distance themselves and "take a hypothetical attitude toward the forms of life and the personal life history that have shaped their own identity."[64] Hence, with respect to evaluative questions regarding the good life and cultural values, it is impossible to develop a universalist, rational discourse. However, according to Habermas, with respect to norms and normative systems, it is possible to adopt a hypothetical attitude and employ the universalization principle in order to establish valid norms:

> We are now in a position to define the scope of application of a deontological ethics: it covers only practical questions that can be debated rationally, i.e., those that hold out the prospect of consensus. It deals not with value preferences but with the normative validity of norms of action.[65]

Here we see that Habermas's discourse ethics is at odds with the claims made earlier in this essay regarding the fundamental situatedness of all inquiry and deliberation. It appeals to a postconventional standpoint as the place of ethical discourse, while in my view, there simply is no such standpoint. I have argued for the viability and value of dialogue in a pluralist society born out of an awareness of human finitude that gives rise to a discourse community committed to the search for truth and willing to entertain respective visions of reality as testimony. This does not appeal to a postconventional stance with respect to moral and political judgment. Rather, it looks to what I can only call a conversion to a position which Paul Ricoeur expresses in terms of hope, hope that Being speaks, that expressions of the meaning of life in myths and symbols open genuine possibilities for being in the world whose claims upon us we should consider (though not accept at face value) given our own finitude. Thus, my approach avoids the tendency, found in Habermas's account, to posit a field of public discourse which does not rely upon a comprehensive vision of life and which takes precedence over "conventional" discourses from the moral point of view. By reflecting upon Seyla Benhabib's perspicacious reformulation of Habermas's discourse ethics, I will suggest why I think that this is the wiser course.

Benhabib develops an account of discourse ethics that incorporates, in her words, "a procedural reformulation of the universalizability principle along the model of a moral conversation in which the capacity to reverse perspectives, that is, the willingness to reason from the others' point of view, and the sensitivity to hear their voice is paramount."[66] According to Benhabib, moral discourse is to be understood in terms of a conversation between parties who are willing to think from one another's point of view, and to communicate genuinely with one another in order to think from each other's standpoint, so that they might arrive at an agreement. Only such a conversational model can fulfill the intent of the universalization principle, to establish moral maxims that all can recognize as binding.[67] In characterizing what makes moral judgments valid, Benhabib shifts the focus from consensus, which emphasizes the general recognition of a common interest, to the process of coming to agreement by which consensus is attained.[68] When parties come to an agreement, it is not necessarily because they recognize a common interest, but it does suppose they have engaged in a process of moral conversation that is open and fair. Benhabib targets the importance of the process of coming to agreement in the validation of moral judgment, and emphasizes that genuine agreement is born of conversation in which the parties take into account each other's perspectives. She is thus able to argue that one cannot consider the other in moral discourse only as the "generalized other," the other only in so far as she or he is like oneself, deserving of the same rights and having the same obligations as oneself. One must also consider the other as a concrete other, as an other with a specific life history and vision of life and its meaning.[69] Given this, Benhabib is not as quick as Habermas to draw a distinction between the public sphere, where justice is the primary concern and individuals must reason together to determine their rights and obligations, and the private sphere, to which evaluative questions pertaining to the good life are relegated. Thus, Benhabib develops an account of discourse ethics that makes space for a full-blooded conversation between full-blooded, concrete human beings that does not artificially distinguish between questions of the good life and the moral sphere.[70]

Benhabib further veers from Habermas when she argues that the principles of universal respect and egalitarian reciprocity that are fundamental to discourse ethics are not derived through some form of transcendental deduction but rather "are our philosophical clarification of the constituents of the moral point of view from within the normative hermeneutic horizon of modernity."[71] In short, although arguments can be made to support these principles, they are not ones that can logically compel acceptance by those not operating out of the horizon of modernity. As Benhabib notes in the course of exploring one such argument, even if it were logically necessary that one respect one's conversation partners in order to be a competent conversation partner in a fair conversation, it does not follow that one need adhere to the principle of universal respect. One might simply deny that certain individuals qualify as competent potential participants in the conversation.

To exacerbate this, Benhabib makes apparent the situatedness of universal discourse ethics in a passage that, on careful reading, does not preclude the omission of certain individuals from the dialogue:

> What distinguishes "modern" from "premodern" ethical theories is the assumption that the moral community is coextensive with all beings capable of speech and action, and potentially with all of humanity. In this sense, communicative ethics sets up a model of moral conversation among members of a modern ethical community for whom the theological and ontological bases of inequality among humans has been radically placed into question.[72]

But Benhabib does not believe that this admission regarding the situatedness of universal discourse ethics within the horizon of modernity turns it from a universalist ethics into a dogmatic one that automatically privileges certain modern values. Within the moral conversation itself, it is possible to challenge the principles of universal moral respect and egalitarian reciprocity. So long as individuals seek to show that their moral stances are valid and are not willing simply to resort to unjustified force, they must be willing to engage in discourse and abide by the necessary conditions for genuine discourse. But it is possible for them to challenge these conditions or their applicability within the discourse itself. Hence, those who are homophobic, racist, and sexist can seek to exclude certain individuals from the moral conversation, but to do so, they must show why the bases on which they wish to restrict them are appropriate.[73]

Benhabib goes on to argue that disqualifying certain groups from ethical discourse is virtually impossible since those seeking to discriminate typically want to "show" those against whom they are discriminating that they are justified, but this involves admitting the targets of discrimination to the conversation. Here, I must confess to finding Benhabib's procedure somewhat mystifying. In her view, the desire to persuade those who are being left out of the moral conversation that they should be subject to discrimination is incoherent on the part of those who are building the argument.[74] But it seems to me that individuals practicing racism, sexism, and homophobia, while they may seek to "persuade" ethnic groups, lesbians, and gays to assent to their subjugation, do not feel the need to treat them as genuine discourse partners. Much energy is usually given to explaining to themselves and to others "of their own kind" why the group under discussion does not deserve consultation and why the mode of address appropriate to them is at best paternalistic, at worst, manipulative. Why else is so much energy given to discounting the speech of women and to characterizing the homosexual as mentally unstable? The goal cannot be to appeal to women and homosexuals as equal partners in discourse.

Consideration of Colorado's Amendment 2 at this juncture is instructive. The rhetoric used in support of this amendment is that gays and lesbians should not be entitled to "special rights." This rhetoric makes use of opposition to affirmative action policies and plays on racist sensibilities in certain quarters of American society. But at a deeper level, one could argue that unwillingness to support laws that would protect gays and lesbians from discrimination is not rooted in denial that gays and lesbians experience discrimination. Rather, it lies in the fact that such laws are viewed as requiring people to acknowledge gays and lesbians as dialogue partners, as full members of the community, as people who have the requisite discursive capacity to be included in a rational discourse. Undoubtedly, this is not the only construction that one could place on it. Continued insistence that homosexuality is a "lifestyle," a "choice," would suggest an attempt to isolate homosexual acts for normative consideration in a dialogue between people who do and do not happen to participate in them. But counterbalancing this are medical, psychological, and religious discourses that would eliminate homosexuals as eligible dialogical partners. Attempts at locating genetic causes for homosexuality are largely framed in popular discourse as part of the process of addressing an illness. Homosexuals are damaged and as such may be objects of care or even of duty, but they do not have status as moral agents. From the psychological perspective, the reparative therapy movement claims that homosexuality is a psychological illness that can be cured. Sexual orientation can be changed. Again, a basis is given for not considering homosexuals as eligible dialogue partners. As mentally ill, they fall into the category of those whose objections are not worth considering, along with children, animals, and trees.[75]

Finally, from a religious perspective, the argument is made that homosexuals are perverted, their natures corrupt. They therefore are not capable of rational discourse regarding homosexuality.

A Habermasean might try to counter these attempts at barring the homosexual from dialogue by arguing that the reasons given are ideologically tainted. But this is not sufficient. What criteria are going to be used in deciding who is eligible to participate in the conversation about who will and will not be a member of the dialogical community? In addition, who is to decide, and how is one to decide, regarding the language to be used in deciding whether to adopt a norm? As will be discussed at length in chapter 4, it is quite possible that the language used in a dialogue regarding norms, as well as the discussion about the language to be used, can themselves act to silence and marginalize in a way that remains undetectable to participants in the discussion. As Marie Fleming suggests, Habermas's view is open to the Foucauldean charge:

> . . . that the theory of communicative action is only partial in that it cannot inquire about the function of the will that gains expression in discourses. Since no one is likely to argue that there is no will in discourse, we should be able to investigate which will it is that gets expressed. Such knowledge is not possible from the perspective of communicative actors who "always have to suppose that only the unforced force of the better argument comes into play under the unavoidable communication presuppositions of argumentative discourse." Thus, Habermas's theory, which begins from that perspective, must, as a matter of methodology, exclude from its object domain the type of data that goes into genealogical researches and that aims at an exposition of the will expressed in discourses through various types of exclusionary mechanisms—prohibitions on what can be said and how, rules about who has the right to speak, class and race specifications, gender specifications, and so on.[76]

Thus, Habermas must attempt to show that there is at least one discourse that can free itself from the power relations that drive it, but this is a dubious project always subject to the suspicion that, as Flemming puts it, "all discourses are in fact derived from power."[77]

What I want to suggest in this chapter is that avoiding these pitfalls begins by recognizing that the primary impetus for engaging in dialogue with the other should not be the goal of establishing universally valid norms, but of hearing the one who speaks. If morality is born out of a sense of responsibility to the other, one cannot predetermine who that other is, who deserves response, or what response it is that they deserve. One must be caught up in listening. Being so caught up may not require a self-reflective, explicit recognition of one's own finitude. There may be modes of listening and responding that do not require such self-consciousness. But listening does require a recognition of what is implicit in the situatedness of human beings, namely, a recognition of the possibility that the other has something to reveal and a legitimate claim to be heard, a recognition that is prior to any determination of which others count or which languages count as legitimate. Concern for equity, justice, and fairness is not enough. It can seduce one into a decision regarding to whom justice and fairness are due, a decision easily lending itself to unjust exclusions. I suspect that this is the insight that Emmanuel Levinas has when he roots ethics in a face-to-face relation preceding discourse, a relation that precedes any attempt to define the other. These are claims that must be fleshed out in greater detail, which will in part be the project of the concluding two chapters.

At the moment, it is possible to approach this entire discussion from a slightly different angle. The modern age is one in which individuals come into their own as persons distinct from their social relations. As Benhabib notes, in the modern era, the spheres of legal right, individual morality, and ethical life were distinguished, leaving individuals to develop integrated lives responding to the distinct demands that the various spheres made upon them. Contributing to this was the breakdown of classical cosmological visions in which accounts of the cosmos and nature were understood to imply certain forms of social life, including values, responsibilities, and norms. With the development of mechanistic visions of the cosmos, such implications could no longer be drawn; knowledge of nature and justification of norms became distinct. These developments required individuals to consider reflectively the moral norms and concepts of the good they would adopt.[78]

With the development of this world-view, it is clear that discourse ethics offers certain advantages over what Benhabib calls conventional moral systems. In conventional moral systems, a distinction cannot be drawn between social acceptance and the hypothetical validity of norms, but a preference can be given to norms because they are the products of a way of life, a vision of things that is simply accepted as being better than others. Discourse ethics is a postconventional ethics in the sense that it does not presume that any particular vision of life is preferable to another and can confer validity upon normative practices. Further, discourse ethics can defend itself against the charge that it too is a conventionalist ethic by pointing to the fact that the conversation that it advocates neither excludes the views and objections of other points of view nor does it exclude itself from critical scrutiny. Those arguing from a conventionalist ethics typically stop the conversation at the point where certain premises, such as articles of faith, which are fundamental to their world-view, are challenged. Benhabib makes the point that moral conventionalism and reflection are not compatible. Once the person operating out of conventionalism recognizes the possibility that practices that are contrary to their own morality may be valid, they are no longer moral conventionalists.[79] Benhabib offers the following important conclusion:

> Moral reflexivity and moral conventionalism then are not compatible; but in a disenchanted universe, to limit reflexivity is an indication of a rationality deficit. That is to say, only a moral point of view can radically question all procedures of justification including its own, can create the conditions for a moral conversation which is open and rational enough to include other points of view, including those which will withdraw from the conversation at some point. In this sense, communicative ethics "trumps" other less reflexive "moral points of view." It can coexist with them and recognize their cognitive limits; communicative ethics is aware not only of other moral systems as representing a "moral point of view" (albeit one which may no longer be defensible on rational grounds), but it is also aware of the historical conditions which made its own point of view possible.[80]

There are three points worth noting here. Despite the fact that discourse ethics can claim to bypass the objection that it is a conventionalist ethics because of its reflexivity, the *preference* for a postconventional ethics is rooted in the perspective of a "disenchanted universe," Max Weber's characterization of the modern world-view. Might it be the case that those operating from conventionalist perspectives would remain unconvinced by such an argument for the advantage of a postconventional ethic? Although there may have been certain sociological forces at play that have placed individuals in contemporary society in the position of having to adopt a reflective stance, at least one option would be to deny the "disenchanted" view of the world that gave rise to the predicament of individuals who must integrate for themselves the demands of right, personal morality, and ethical life. Secondly, would someone arguing from a conventional moral system necessarily care that their position was defensible on rational grounds? Finally, is it necessarily the case that those maintaining a conventionalist ethic would consider a moral point of view advantageous because it creates a context for a moral conversation that could include other points of view?

My point in raising these questions is to suggest that the ground for conversation between individuals living in a pluralist society requires more than establishing the conditions for maintaining a community in which diversity is tolerated or even prized. It requires more than sketching the necessary conditions for the sort of discourse that would allow one to claim that moral norms are valid in a community. It requires a recognition of others, including the insights out of which they act, a recognition that the recognition of one's own situatedness and finitude promotes. Benhabib makes the point that moral conventionalism and reflexivity are incompatible. But one might well choose conventionalism. One might dogmatically choose to prioritize a given vision of life with all that it implies. Of course, others may not be compelled to follow, at least intellectually, but the point that I would like to make is that no amount of argumentation can sway the dogmatist. What is called for, ironically, is the sort of conversion to which I referred in the discussion of Habermas. That this is the case seems particularly evident in light of Benhabib's claim that discourse giving rise to valid moral norms cannot abstract from the embeddedness of human beings in concrete forms of life and cannot preclude questions of the good life. Benhabib may be right when she says of communicative ethics, "Precisely because such a framework can challenge all its presuppositions, and precisely because it is ready to submit its fundamental

principles to debate, it can provide the bases for the public philosophy of a pluralist, tolerant, democratic-liberal polity."[81] But taking
seriously the point of view of someone operating from a conventional
moral system might well mean not taking such an argument to be
morally compelling. Even if Habermas is right that claims to moral
validity require that certain conditions for argumentation be met,
the person operating from a conventional perspective may have no
difficulty in limiting membership to the discourse community. They
may opt out of the game of communicative discourse when the community in question is a pluralist one. Only by a conversion from
one's conventional standpoint to a standpoint that recognizes the
finitude of all standpoints and their potential power for stimulating
insight, can the impetus for engaging in something resembling the
sort of conversation that Benhabib has in mind materialize.[82] It
seems to me that the sort of mutual recognition that discourse
ethics supposes requires such a conversion, but it also precludes
reading all world-views through the lens of modern secular culture.

In closing, it seems to me that many advocates of communicative ethics such as Benhabib are interested in establishing a theoretical stance that, if adopted by society, would support pluralism
and tolerance, a stance that would protect members of society from
the forces of oppression. The position that I advocate provides no
such guarantee if this is understood in terms of the "logic of the argument." However, adopting the reflective stance of this essay, recognizing the finitude of one's existence calls for one to curb one's
own coercive tendencies while at the same time providing ground
for attending to the reservations that one would have in the face of
others' dogmatic claims. The position that I am advocating would
not require that one simply be tolerant of any practice or vision of
life from which it stems, for tolerance is a close cousin to apathy. For
instance, I would agree with Evans that the kind of patriarchal
stance that leads to the degradation of gays and lesbians and, more
generally, the abuse of women, is intolerable. If someone wishes to
convince me of the wisdom of supporting a given social policy that I
perceive as operating out of such a stance, it belongs to the other to
show me that I am mistaken either in regard to my appraisal or in
regard to the world-view out of which I am operating. Willingness to
listen genuinely and to communicate does not preclude militancy,
especially when listening and communication incorporate a critical

moment. But what I am suggesting does suppose that a militant position must be adopted in fear and trembling, with the awareness that its resolution into dogmatism results in a terrible loss. At times, people will simply stand in disagreement and will act according to their best lights. At such times, a powerful guard against tyranny is recognition of one's own finitude.

The value of such recognition, working in tandem with a willingness to critically engage the other, becomes apparent in the following chapter, which looks at what it means to own a sexual identity. In what has preceded, I have argued for attending to the discourses and narratives of others as testimony regarding possibilities for being in the world and for the power of myths and symbols to serve as the bearers of possible worlds. At the same time, I have stressed the dangers of absolutist accounts of reality and of neglecting the situatedness of all discourses and narratives. The discussion has been driven by the question of the possibility of forming individual and social identities that can sustain meaningful life and action while not succumbing to the attendant dangers of dogmatism, totalitarianism, and authoritarianism. In the following chapter, I will begin considering what is involved in concretely attempting to follow such a course and what is at stake in doing so as regards those claiming gay and lesbian identity, and implicitly, as regards anyone articulating who they are through a marginalized identity. How is the claim to be gay or lesbian to be taken? How should one respond to the claim of the other regarding her or his sexual identity? Is tolerance enough? It is accepted among some in queer circles that the adoption of gay and lesbian identity plays into a heterosexist logic and promotes essentialist thinking that ultimately serves to constrain the very people who adopt such identities. On the other hand, are those who have been silenced and marginalized to be discounted when they speak the identities through which they have been constituted / through which they have constituted themselves? More broadly, what responsibilities does one bear regarding the other's voice, whoever the other might be? These are the questions that will occupy us not only in the following chapter, but in the remainder of the text.

CLAIMING ONE'S IDENTITY
A Constructivist/Narrativist Approach

Somehow it seems highly suspicious that it is at the precise moment when so many groups have been engaged in "nationalisms" which involve redefinitions of the marginalized Others that suspicions emerge about the nature of the "subject," about the possibilities for a general theory which can describe the world, about historical "progress." Why is it just at the moment when so many of us who have been silenced begin to demand the right to name ourselves, to act as subjects rather than objects of history, that just then the concept of subjecthood becomes problematic?

—Nancy Hartsock, "Foucault on Power"

⟶

The first person whom I told I was gay was the person with whom I had been involved for almost four years. Through those four years, we had continually had "accidents" with one another. After telling him I was gay, the accidents ended. I left the seminary. He became a priest. Prior to applying the label to myself, I felt all of its power to constrain me, to objectify me, to make me into a determinate entity whose identity and fate would be irremediably fixed. But I also felt the lie that my life had become, a lie taking the form of frustration at the constraints imposed by the identifications through which I was then living. After applying gay identity to myself, its power to constrain was felt, but so too was its power to liberate. At the time, I was not so sophisticated as to be concerned about the legitimacy of the label itself. Nor was I concerned about whether "being gay" was by nature or nurture. I just felt that it said something true about me that had to be said if I was to get on with my life. In retrospect, I recognize that adopting this label was not a choice, not in the sense that I just arbitrarily decided to apply it to myself to take up the project of "being gay," nor in the sense that I constructed the label for myself. In retrospect, I wonder at the power of this identification to operate in configuring reality. In retrospect, I wonder at the power of this identification still to speak to and about me. In retrospect, I wonder if there is a choice here, and if so, how we should understand the nature of that choice.

The question of whether sexual orientation is a choice has taken multiple forms and has been endlessly debated in modern popular culture. At its most facile level, the issue has been considered important because on it is supposed to hinge the question of how people espousing a same-sex orientation should be treated. The old saw goes that if sexual orientation is not chosen, then those who claim to be homosexual should not be blamed for their condition; it is not "their fault." But ironically, those attempting to use such an approach in order to support gay and lesbian rights now face the serious consequences of their strategy. If sexual orientation is somehow culturally determined, then the project could become changing the environment. Conversely, if it is biologically determined, then the project could become biological manipulation. Realizing these dangers has served as an occasion for gender theorists to recognize that the whole discussion serves merely to reinscribe the privileging of heterosexuality, ultimately to the detriment of any liberatory praxis.[1] Whether nature or nurture is "to blame," the goal is inevitably to cure, and the "homosexual" who is to be cured must wonder whether elimination by cure is preferable to those more severe, though in a certain ironic sense, more honest forms employed in the past, such as genocide or lobotomy. All of these end in destroying the person that one is.

A promising path to deprivileging heterosexuality is by thematizing the constructed character of sexuality and the artificiality of making sexual identity and orientation the pivotal axis for determining personal identity. But taking this path poses a number of challenges, which is not to say, however, that following it is not worthwhile. My strategy will be to introduce what appears initially as a superficial challenge, but one whose dimensions will prove to be significant, in order to show how following this path can actually lead in a certain way to the kind of affirmation of identity that can sustain liberatory praxis. What I propose is neither to challenge the wisdom of dropping the question of choice, nor to deny the legitimacy of surrendering essentialism. Instead, I want to explore a particular sense in which it is right to claim that, while sexual orientation and identity are constructed, they are nonetheless real, and that recognizing this particular sense carries with it important implications for approaching life in community.

The challenge that I should like to pose comes from the direction of those who, like myself, perhaps after struggle, have come to explicitly identify themselves as lesbian, gay, queer, bisexual, heterosexual, etc. At least on the surface, one might suppose that people attesting to their sexual identity, especially those claiming that their sexual identity is integral to who they are, must resist claims that sexuality and sexual identity are constructed. It is worth noting the precise sense in which this is so. Take the person who tells the story of how she came to realize that she is a lesbian. Clearly, the story she tells could have gone another way. One might hold with thinkers like John D'Emilio and Michel Foucault that gays and lesbians did not always exist, but are made possible in modern Western culture, and that had this person been born at another time, she simply would have assumed an identity along a different set of matrices.[2] But this is not what is essential to many people who have undergone such an experience. What they want to say is that their identification of themselves as lesbian or gay constitutes a response to something about themselves that they had to integrate into their identity if they were to be true to themselves.[3] The question is whether the claim that sexuality and sexual identity are constructed provides a space for honoring such an attestation on its own terms, or better yet, provides a context for deepening rather than just dismissing it. Unless an affirmative answer can be given, one has to wonder whether those who own such identities as bisexual, gay, and lesbian would be willing to explore this avenue for moving beyond the nature/nurture debate, and whether any opening could be found for engaging American society generally. I should like to signal the possibility of such an answer by considering the work of two thinkers operating in two very different milieus, Paul Ricoeur and Judith Butler.

The Constructed Character of Gender Identity: Ricoeur and Butler

Ricoeur's initial contribution to this discussion will be to offer a description of cultural language that supports the view that articulations of sexuality and sexual identity, while culturally informed, can nonetheless have disclosive power, though as we shall see, the sense in which this is so must be carefully nuanced to avoid essentialist claims or the privileging of any sexual identity formations. Butler's work will be used to lend support to Ricoeur's position because it arrives at a similar conclusion by a different route, but deepens the discussion by explicitly looking at sexual identity formation, and by addressing the peculiar dangers attaching to all articulations of sexual identity. Engaging Butler's discussion of the latter will make clear that dismissing professions of sexual identity as misguided or mistaken because such identities are "mere constructions" constitutes a form of violence against those who claim them, while refusing to problematize those very identities leads to still other forms of violence. It is in this context that Ricoeur will make a second contribution to the discussion. Ricoeur's account of personal identity as a narrative formation will afford a way of thinking about claims to sexual identity which honors Butler's concerns by making it possible to think about attestations of sexual identity as at once legitimate and subject to the sort of contestation essential to liberatory praxis. In so doing, he will enable us to move the discussion of sexual identity beyond the nature/nurture debate to a richer understanding of the possible meanings of claims to sexual identity and what is at stake in them.

In *Ideology and Utopia,* Ricoeur makes the following case:

> The very flexibility of our biological existence makes necessary another kind of informational system, the cultural sys-

tem. Because we have no genetic system of information for human behavior, we need a cultural system. No culture exists without such a system. The hypothesis, therefore, is that where human beings exist, a nonsymbolic mode of existence, and even less, a nonsymbolic kind of action, can no longer obtain. Action is immediately ruled by cultural patterns which provide templates or blueprints for the organization of social and psychological processes, perhaps just as genetic codes—I am not certain—provide such templates for the organization of organic processes. In the same way that our experience of the natural world requires a mapping, a mapping is also necessary for our experience of social reality.[4]

Ricoeur goes on to argue that such mappings can perform integrative, legitimizing, and distorting functions. Importantly, he suggests that they have disclosive power. To understand these claims, it is helpful to think of them in the context of Marx's discussion of ideology. According to Ricoeur, symbol and myth, which are understood in Marxist terms as "ideological," function first to integrate the community by giving it a common vision of life, a common language, a common set of practices. It is on the basis of this integrative function that symbol and myth can be used to legitimate a given set of power relations. Here, the distortive potential of ideology, which is one of the central insights of Marxism, comes into play. In Ricoeur's view, this potential for distortion arises because the claims to authority that the rulers in a community make require a level of belief on the part of the ruled that can never be rationally warranted.[5] Ideology can serve to fill the gap between claim and belief, and it is precisely here that ideology becomes distortive. It is important, however, to recognize the specific character of this distortion as Ricoeur interprets it, for here, he is very far from Marx. A typical Marxist would argue that ideologies are distortive when they provide accounts of reality, in particular, accounts of social relations; these accounts are untrue to what is really the case and perpetuate the social relations, which in fact obtain. Ricoeur would have reservations about such claims insofar as they suggest that there could be real social relations, or accounts of real social relations, which were not symbolically and mythologically mediated. More pointedly, Ricoeur would deny the claim that there is some bedrock "reality" with

which symbols and myths more or less agree. Rather, he understands ideology to function distortively when it is used to justify the
claim that there is one and only one legitimate form of social relations and corresponding vision of life.

But according to Ricoeur, the possibility of ideological distortion
presumes a more primary capacity of myths and symbols to reveal or
to disclose.[6] This disclosive power does not lie in their ability to reveal a preestablished, given reality, any more than they distort such
a reality. How, then, are we to understand myths and symbols as disclosive? A first step is to dissociate the notion of disclosure from the
correspondence theory of truth, one holding that truth is the agreement of a proposition to a state of affairs. As Martin Heidegger would
say, such an account relies upon a more primordial experience of
truth as aletheia, as the disclosure of a possible way of being in the
world that carries with it the foreclosure of other possibilities.[7] Ricoeur sees symbols and myths as operating on the borders between
disclosure and foreclosure. They disclose not what is, but what is possible. At the same time, their disclosure operates as a founding, a realizing of the possibilities to which they refer, insofar as they inform
the life of a community. It is important to note that Ricoeur sees in
symbols and myths both referential and creative dimensions. They
act to establish what they articulate, but that articulation is not an
arbitrary construction. It is born of insight into possibilities for being.
Correlatively, it is important to recognize that such insight is realized at the price of other possibilities that remain closed, and hence
that the adoption or rejection of a mythic vision cannot operate on
the same plane as the sort of correspondence theory of truth popu-
larly assumed by those captivated by a modern scientific ideology.

If we adopt Ricoeur's account of the various possibilities of
myths and symbols for disclosure, integration, legitimation, and distortion, it becomes possible to conceive of gender identity as constructed and as making claims to truth, and perhaps even . . . to legitimacy? As we shall see, Ricoeur's turn to narrative identity
formation in his more recent works affords a way of thinking identity, including gender identity and sexual orientation, as constructed and as speaking the truth of the subject, even as it makes
room for the limits and dangers of any such articulation. But, as
previously noted, the contribution that Ricoeur can make to the discussion benefits through an encounter with Judith Butler's work.
Butler provides a nuanced account of the constructed character of

gender identity. This account fleshes out the tension between the necessity of rejecting the very possibility of certain identities if others are to be realized, and the violences that just such rejections can incur, violences resulting in particular from the refusal to recognize the contingency of particular identity formations and their accompanying foreclosures.

In *Bodies That Matter,* Butler adopts the position that sex is not a biological given on which gender is built, but rather is itself a regulatory ideal materialized in the body through normatively governed reiterative practices. Further, she maintains that it is only by virtue of assuming a sex that one becomes a subject. Her distinctive development of this position weaves together an articulation and defense of the following claims:

1. The materialization of sex in the body is never fully realized, and it is therefore possible to contest regulatory ideals of sex that underlie gender identity;[8]

2. Nonetheless, to claim that the sexed body is a construct does not allow for the conclusion that we can do without a construction, for it may well be that constructions are necessary conditions for thinking, living, and making sense;[9]

3. Simultaneous with the construction of possible sexual identities is the foreclosure of other identities, and this dialectic of the permissible and the abject determines who counts as subjects and what bodies matter;

4. Finally, while Butler does not claim to offer a program for feminist/bisexual/queer/lesbian/gay practice or theory, she is clearly interested in exploring the possibilities for disturbing the boundaries of the thinkable and the unthinkable, livable and abject identities, and believes that this ought to be done.

The first claim attributed to Butler attests to the constructed character of sex and gender identity and is consistent with her earlier work.[10] But the second marks a shift in emphasis that occurs in *Bodies That Matter*. As early as the introduction, Butler seeks to distance herself from a constructivist position that would illegitimately have to suppose a subject "doing" the construction, or a position that

would have to see the constituted subject as the product of a deter-
ministic process. Instead, she suggests that recognizing that there
are conditions for the emergence of a subject neither requires a
"subject" before the constitution of a subject, nor the foreclosure of
agency by making the subject the product and puppet of sociocultural processes.[11] This is important because Butler hereby distances
herself from positions that would discount the constructed subject
as either an artificial construct "hiding" the "real" subject lying underneath, or those that would discount the constructed subject as a
genuine agent. Butler marks the reality of the subject, but the subject as made possible through certain processes and continuously
constituted through citationality.

    This leads us to the third claim cited above. Butler follows
Lacan in recognizing that for a subject to emerge requires a delim-
iting of what might metaphorically be called an unlimited, indeterminate flow that constitutes the domain of the unsayable, which
Lacan nonetheless speaks through his designation of it as the
"Real." At the stage of the imaginary, this delimitation begins
through the constitution of a unified ego, but this occurs at the
price of imposing an image which, in Richard Boothby's words, "fulfills its function of unity only by imposing an intrinsic limitation—
only, in effect, by leaving something out. A quantity of energy is
pressed into the service of the drive, but there is always an excluded and un-imaged remainder."[12] In other words, in the imaginary, a single, unified ego is formed through an image with which
one identifies. But this at the same time entails an alienation of desire. Through the interference of the linguistic community, this
identification with the image is broken, and one is introduced into
the realm of the symbolic. By taking up the language of the community, it becomes possible to question imaginary identifications,
and to raise the question, "Who am I?" However, this does not involve an unmediated return or rehabilitation of the Real, as if the
Real were to be understood as some determinate thing essential to
the self to be reincorporated into one's identity.[13] Rather, by entry
into the symbolic, it becomes possible to name one's desire as that
which is unnamable, and to come to terms with oneself as an incomplete being desiring a completeness, a self-realization that one
can never have. This requires, however, assuming a place in language. It is in the symbolic realm that the sexed subject emerges
through the injunction to be a given sex and thereby to assume an

identity through which the lack of that which would bring completeness can be expressed. That is, in linguistic communities, sexed positions emerge which take on meaning by announcing what identities are possible, and importantly, thereby establishing a realm of the unsayable, unlivable, and unnarratable. Sexed positions constitute the terms in which a subject can be realized through the performance of the sexed identity. What is important about Lacan's account, especially as taken up by Butler, is that it suggests how it is possible to assert that the claim that sexuality is constructed implies neither that such construction is somehow the "free" construction of a preexistent subject, and hence arbitrary, nor that it is determined and immutably fixed. Rather, normative constraints determine the very possibility for the process of performativity that enables the subject to emerge.[14] At the same time, it is vitally important to recognize that precisely because the subject is constituted through the injunction to assume a sex, the subject cannot purely and simply be identified with the sexed identity. There is an instability at the heart of gender identity that refuses to surrender the possibility of contestation. This last point is one that Butler emphasizes in marked contrast to Lacan.[15]

In the story of sexual development that Lacan offers, the child experiences an initial identification with its mother which is disturbed during the oedipal phase when the child realizes that union with the mother is impossible because of the presence of the father. Sexually, it is the father that is the privileged object of the mother's desire. This recognition takes the form of a prohibition of access to the mother, which in Lacanian terms is designated as the law of the father, and which is constituted as fear of castration. The phallus comes to represent the authority and privilege of the father. It thereby becomes the mark of access to the lost wholeness or completeness that the child seeks to regain. The phallus, then, signifies that which one must have in order to be complete. The fear of castration is an expression of the anxiety that one feels when the imaginary identification with the mother breaks down, and libidinal drives which cannot be accommodated surface. This threat of castration points to the fact that the seemingly original wholeness that has been disrupted was, in fact, illusory. The phallus promises a retrieval of desire that cannot be realized. Given this account, assuming a sexual identity in a linguistic community through obedience to the law of the father, to the fear of castration, can occur as an attempt to surmount the loss of wholeness signified by the phallus. Sexual identities as such can operate as political signifiers, that is, as identities constituted in the linguistic community which actually produce what they signify, those who do and who do not count as whole subjects capable of political action. But because the phallus cannot deliver on its promises, and because sexual identity is only realized through continual performance of that identity, disidentifications with sexual identities become possible.[16] In Butler's view, this opens a space for disturbing reified sexual identities and for debate regarding such issues as heterosexual privilege.[17]

Further, given the failure of the phallus as a signifier to fulfill its promises, Butler questions the supposition that political action requires the sorts of identifications which political signifiers attempt to realize. That is, she questions whether such identifications as "gay," which can function to unify a group, must operate in this way. Why, Butler asks, might disidentification not also be a "ground" for political praxis?[18] In other words, might we at once identify and disidentify with such identity formations as "lesbian," and might this interplay itself be individually and socially transforming? The challenge that Butler poses is formidable and intriguing. On the one hand, she is careful to note that "the demand to overcome radically the constitutive constraints by which cultural viability is achieved would be its own form of violence."[19] It would literally deny the reality of the subject simply because that reality is constructed, and therefore contingent. It would deny the force of the recognition of oneself as gay. On the other hand, the refusal to problematize those constraints promotes two other sorts of violence, violence against the subject by refusing a fundamental condition of subjectivity, potential for transformation, and violence against society by refusing its potential for transformation by turning a blind eye to the partiality of identity categories that claim to be all-inclusive.[20]

The Narrative Character of Gender Identity: Ricoeur and Butler

I should like to turn now to consider what contribution Ricoeur's narrative approach to identity formation can make for navigating between these various threats of violence. A rich contribution should address three questions:

1. How to respect the claims of subjects regarding their gender identity?

2. How at the same time to challenge those very claims when they fail to recognize their own contingency and status as conditioned possibilities?

3. How to exploit the contingency of gender identity formation for liberatory praxis?

To appreciate Ricoeur's account of human identity as narratively configured, it is necessary to turn to his treatment of the narrative structure of human time in *Time and Narrative*. His thesis is that "time becomes human to the extent that it is articulated through a narrative mode, and narrative attains its full meaning when it becomes a condition of temporal existence."[21] Borrowing from Aristotle's account of plot as the mimesis of action, Ricoeur distinguishes three moments of mimesis in order to describe the way in which temporal experience becomes meaningful.[22] By mimesis 1, Ricoeur denotes a preunderstanding of the world and of life and action. By mimesis 2, he distinguishes the construction of a narrative plot. Drawing upon mimesis 1, creative imagination selects from experience and arranges it into a coherent whole with beginning, middle, and end. By mimesis 3, Ricoeur understands the reception of the text by a reader. This reception can become the occasion for at once reinterpreting and actually refiguring the world of one's life and action.[23] To appreciate Ricoeur's narrative account of time, it is necessary to approach it in the context of the aporia between the scientific conception of time as a sequence of moments in which one moment follows another and every moment is identical to any other, and the human experience of time as a relationship between past, present, and future that constitutes a coherent whole. While we are familiar with the scientific account of time as clock time, every second being equal to every other, to consider imaginatively what it would be like to live as if each moment were the same brings with it a sense of incoherence, and ultimately, meaninglessness. What provides a context for meaningful human action and constitutes the fabric of a coherent life is the interrelation of past, present, and future such that one's characterization of the present conditions one's intending of the future, and these taken together mark the significance that one assigns to the past. Ricoeur's account of a threefold process of mimesis is meant to capture two insights:

1.   that meaningful human life is structured narratively;

2.   that the construction of a meaningful narrative underpinning human life and action is a creative process that cannot be reduced to a simple recounting of life as lived.[24]

If we turn for a moment to consider life as lived, we note that there are thinkers like Hayden White who argue that life simply is not lived narratively. The narrative structure, he and others argue, is "added on" through reflection.[25] Ricoeur, in his discussion of mimesis 1, on the other hand, provides ground for thinking that narrative coherence guides the living of a human life. He grants that there is good reason for claiming that life as lived does not have the well-rounded, coherent unity of a single, all-encompassing narrative. As lived, there is an open-endedness to life; there are a plethora of events and experiences that resist unification into one coherent narrative; there is the real possibility of being engaged in a number of distinct narratives running concurrently which refuse integration into one another. On the other hand, Ricoeur insists that it would be a mistake to think of anything that could be called human life taking on the purely homogeneous character of clock time.[26] The barriers to a well-rounded narrative are not sufficient to undermine the claim that the domain of human action contains within itself at least an "inchoate narrativity."[27] As Alasdair MacIntyre notes in his exploration of the intentional character of human action, what distinguishes an action from an occurrence is precisely that an action is intentionally undertaken. For this to happen requires that one recognize oneself as operating within a certain set of circumstances in which a given action is appropriate. But this is just to locate oneself in a narrative whole with a beginning, middle, and end.[28] Ricoeur's account of the movement from mimesis 1 to mimesis 3 traces a movement from an engagement in life and action informed by the sense of a narrative, or narratives, to a reflective engagement of life conditioned by the intention to comprehend one's life as a unified narrative whole. One suspects that, at its outer limits, such an intention might lead one to take up the construction of social and cosmic narratives as well.

At the end of Volume III of *Time and Narrative,* and in *Oneself as Another,* Ricoeur shifts his attention from exploring the potential of the narrative construction of human time for bridging the aporia between scientific and phenomenological conceptions of time to treating the aporias pertaining to human identity. Specifically, he is interested in showing how an account of narrative identity can avoid both an essentialist account of personal identity that entails holding the subject to be self-identical even when passing through different states, and a view of the subject as "nothing more than a substantialist illusion, whose elimination merely brings to light a pure manifold of cognitions, emotions, and volitions."[29] Such an account would go a long way towards meeting the concerns of this book. It would preclude employing categories such as gay, lesbian, and straight as if they were unproblematic, or at worst, incomplete, articulations of the identities of subjects that are irremediably "fixed." Conversely, it would preclude reading all professions of personal identity as arbitrary and misguided constructs.

According to Ricoeur, much of the difficulty that we have with the notion of personal identity results from a conflation of identity with sameness. When we look back at ourselves as children, we typically want to claim that we are the same person. Yet, at the same time, there is clearly a sense in which we are not the same. The tendency to favor one or the other of these valences results in a rigid identification of the self as the same, or in the denial of identity itself based on the fact that we are not the same. To counter this, Ricoeur argues for a replacement of the conception of identity as being the same (idem) with a conception of oneself as self-same (ipse).[30] This latter conception arises by applying the narrative account of human time to personal identity:

> The thesis supported here will be that the identity of the character is comprehensible through the transfer to the character of the operation of emplotment, first applied to the action recounted: characters, we will say, are themselves plots.[31]

The process of emplotment constitutive of a narrative consists in drawing together the heterogeneous elements of a story into a unified whole. In the configuration of a narrative, differences are not simply abolished. In particular, there is a dispersal of episodes that are nonetheless interrelated with one another to form a unified whole.[32] With respect to characters in a narrative, their identities are secured through the coherence of the narrative. But what Ricoeur is suggesting is that we can apply the notion of narrative configuration to an understanding of personal identity itself. Personal identity is realized by drawing together into a unified temporal whole the life of the person.[33] Following Hannah Arendt, Ricoeur maintains, in short, that to tell who someone is means to tell the story of that person's life.[34] In this telling, the individual events and occurrences making up the life of the person, including transformations in modes of thinking and self-conception, at once contribute to the constitution of the self, and pose a challenge to the realization of unified coherence.

With this account of the narrative construction of identity in hand, we can now turn to an admittedly incomplete, but perhaps suggestive, consideration of the three questions with which we began this discussion of Ricoeur. Firstly, how respect the claims of the subject regarding her or his own gender identity? It is possible to approach this question from two different directions. In *Oneself as Another*, Ricoeur notes that the tendency to equate identity with sameness finds support in the recognition of character understood as those distinctive marks of individuals that enable one to identify them as the same through time. Ricoeur maintains that it is in fact character that comes closest to marking a person's identity as the same. However, even character carries with it a temporal dimension, for character is realized through acquired dispositions. Firstly, there are habits. Habits are acquired, but become so determinative of the self that their acquisition is covered over. This gives to the self a permanence in time tantamount to identity as sameness. The second sorts of dispositions constituting character are the norms, values, and models, etc., that are inculcated into the person through socialization. This is the entrance of the other into the self actually contributing to the constitution of the self, but again, in a way that covers over or annuls its own contribution.[35] In light of such an account of character formation, it becomes possible to recognize the legitimacy of a claim to a given gender identity without bowing to essentialism or dismissing the person's testimony as misguided. This is indeed who the person has become.

But this first approach, while key to contributing to a nonessentialist account of identity as nonetheless real, only takes us so far, for it ultimately operates as the sort of causal explanation that cannot sufficiently account for agency or for personal determination. Through his claim that characters are themselves plots, Ricoeur affords a way of supplementing this approach. He accommodates agency by opening a second avenue for respecting claims of gender identity without bowing to essentialism. When one *attests* to being gay, this does not amount merely to acknowledging a sedimented character formation. Rather, it entails taking up a vision of reality understood at the very least as the articulation of a possible way of being-in-the-world, and adopting it as the framework for writing a personal narrative, and by extension, a social and cosmic narrative. The issue of authorship in narrative theory is a complex one. Ricoeur would not claim that we author ourselves. He would agree that it is only in and through the other that becoming a person is possible. We always already find ourselves enmeshed in relations with an identity, and as identified. As Butler notes, as early as infancy, we are assigned an identity as male or female through which we become socially recognized as human.[36] An identity is assigned that we do not determine, but with which we cannot fail to be concerned. On the other hand, Ricoeur recognizes, with Heidegger, that who we are is an issue for us. We are not handed the book of our lives as a completed, well-rounded, definitive story. Still, it might be appropriate to say that we are given what could metaphorically be called a gift. Though it would be unwarranted to posit some independent subject as gift-giver, residing in the idea of gift can be the idea of otherness as a source of possible meanings and significance outside the control of the one on whom the gift is bestowed, the idea that one is beholden to that which is other than oneself for one's possibilities for being-in-the-world in such a way that calls for response and at times exerts authority. Heidegger gives us an inkling of this in *The Origin of the Work of Art* through his description of the origin of the work of art as Art. The origin of art is not the self, not even the artist. Rather, according to Heidegger, art works are born of the struggle between earth and world. They set up a world and set forth the earth, thereby revealing even as they conceal, possibilities for being-in-the-world which call forth and constitute those who enter into them as preservers.[37] In short, human beings do not give themselves their possibilities for being-in-the-world, but stand in need of a disclosure of those possibilities, a gift.

Gifts, of course, can be equivocal in a variety of ways: they can disclose and mask; they can liberate and enslave; they can enliven and oppress. It is precisely because of this ambiguity that we can figure our past as a gift given to which our account of ourselves is a response opening us to the future as affording determinate possibilities and projects. Because we are uniquely positioned with respect to our own lives, uniquely situated with respect to our own-most possibilities, it is possible to understand our respective accounts of our personal identities as operating on the plane of what Ricoeur calls attestation. Our account of ourselves is a response to the past that we have been given projected into the future. When I testify as to who I am, I am at the same time testifying as to what I believe in based upon the person that I have become and the possibilities that I can imagine. This by no means implies a simple acceptance of the identities afforded by the community in which one finds oneself.

Though employing a very different vocabulary, Butler in *Excitable Speech* provides insight into the ambiguity of what I have called "gift," and the multiple possibilities for response. Drawing upon the idea that one comes to "exist," to be recognized and recognizable, to be a subject, through the address of the Other,[38] Butler raises a series of provocative and disturbing questions:

> Could language injure us if we were not, in some sense, linguistic beings, beings who require language in order to be? Is our vulnerability to language a consequence of our being constituted within its terms? If we are formed in language, then that formative power precedes and conditions any decision we might make about it, insulting us from the start, as it were, by its prior power.[39]

Our relation to our own past, to our language, to our communities, to the names that we have been given, is deeply ambiguous. We do not choose our identities, but neither is the choice made for us. We respond to what we have been given, thereby testifying to and transforming who we are. "We're here, we're queer, get used to it." This slogan, reiterated at virtually every gay pride parade, invites an embrace of an identity traditionally marked as abject, the impossible identity of a nonsubject. This identity is not chosen, nor is it essential; it is the mark placed on one through which one constitutes one's identity as a response. One testifies to this identity, and in so doing, calls others to a possibility for being-in-the-world.

Such testimony does not operate at the level of episteme understood as self-founding knowledge. But this does not mean that it does not command a hearing. The power of testimony lies in the belief that one has in the one who testifies. Such belief may be only in the sincerity of the one testifying. But this need not be the case. It might also be that the compelling character of the testimony of someone testifying to her or his identity lies in the very narrative that he or she constructs. If we turn again to the question of respect for the claims of the subject regarding gender identity, we might conclude that there is reason for seriously entertaining such claims if we regard the fragility of our own claims about who we are and the world in which we live, claims themselves which are rooted in no more than what the gift of being-here affords.

But perhaps it is at this point that we should take up our second question, the question of how to challenge those very claims to gender identity when they fail to recognize their own contingency, their status as conditioned possibilities. Ricoeur makes the following interesting suggestions about the sort of challenge appropriate to attestation:

> The fragmentation that follows from the polysemy of the question "who?" . . . gives to attestation its own special fragility, to which is added the vulnerability of a discourse aware of its own lack of foundation. This vulnerability will be expressed in the permanent threat of suspicion, if we allow that suspicion is the specific contrary of attestation. The kinship between attestation and testimony is verified here: there is no "true" testimony without "false" testimony. But there is no recourse against false testimony than another that is more credible; and there is no recourse against suspicion but a more reliable attestation.[40]

We have spoken of the reality of a constructed gender identity. We might go so far as to signal such a reality as a necessary contingency. In other words, while one's history may be contingent, in constituting oneself, one must of necessity come to terms with who one has become by virtue of it. But there are at least two dangers that arise here. Firstly, one might mistakenly suppose that there is only one possible story that can be told out of one's past projecting one into the future. Secondly, one might suppose that what it takes to count as a subject is necessary and fixed. However, when confronting the claims of others to be telling the whole truth, the only possible truth, about themselves and by extension about everyone else, can we not turn once again to the fragility of our own claims to find testimony to mount a significant challenge? Can there be any more solid ground for impinging such testimony offered by the Other? For people who have struggled with the question of whether to assume a lesbian or gay identity, the decision to adopt such an articulation is almost always accompanied by feelings of ambivalence. The experience of owning such identities is liberatory to the extent that it frees one from the determination by others of what counts as a good and meaningful life, preempts those who would use the derogatory power of such labels to police the actions of others, and provides a language for articulating who one has become. At the same time, because these identity terms carry with them layers of meaning, and in particular insist upon the conflation of sexual identity with identity, their adoption can be experienced as constraining and inhibiting, as illustrated at the beginning of this chapter. It is the experience of wrestling with just such difficulties that makes it possible to challenge those who would presume the unproblematic privileging of the heterosexual matrix in determining identity.

This leads us to our third question: How exploit the contingency of gender identity formation for liberatory praxis? As we ask who we are and who we are to become, we recognize in the question itself that no one answer is necessary. If it were, there would be no question; decision is born of the recognition that things could be otherwise. On the other hand, there would be no decision if there were nothing about which to decide. Decision is based on something, presumably on the orientation afforded us in the world which I have called gift, keeping in mind that this gift has an ambiguous status, for we must not forget that whatever gifts we have were given us through the constitutive exclusions to which Butler has called our attention. Further, our decisions are not made in isolation, but in social contexts which constitute the conditions of their possibility. Recognition of the contingency, not only of gender identity, but of individual and social identity in general, provides a context and impetus for dialogue aimed at taking seriously the various testimonies that we have to offer regarding the possibilities for living well with and for one another.[41] What this implies is that liberatory praxis cannot operate within the limits of promoting some normative ideal, or even of evaluating possible candidates for social action, such as the realization of social justice. Rather, it must expand its parameters to engage critically the stories informing people's lives, stories that likewise inform the social ideals pursued. For such critical engagement to occur, it must promote strategies that encourage vulnerability to the stories of others, for one cannot engage critically what one does not take seriously. Finally, it must engage in enabling those who have no voice and who have no language that can do justice to the stories that they might tell to gain voice and to appropriate language, which in turn means enabling the speakers in society to hear the silence required for listening and to develop an attunement to the disruptive power of poetry at work in transformative stories. The dimensions and advisability of this project are the concern of the following chapter, while the final chapter turns to the question of its viability.

SPEAKING WHAT HAS YET TO BE SAID
The Call for Giving Voice to Responsive Narratives
and to Hearing beyond Them

What I am after, it seems, is a noncontrolling art of writing that will leave the writer more receptive to love than before. That will not be guilty of writing's usual ruthlessness toward life. For the fashionable idea that writing is a form of creative play, and that everything is, after all, writing, seems to me to ignore the plain fact that much of human life is not playful at all, or even creative. And writing's relation to that nonplayful side of life is deeply ambiguous. Writing records it, to be sure. But even as it does so it goes to work fixing, simplifying, shaping. So it seems difficult for it not to be the enemy and denier of mystery and of love. Overwhelmed by the beauty of some landscape, the power of some emotion, I run for my pad of paper; and if I can put it into words, set it down, I breath a sigh of relief. A kind of humble passivity has been banished. Writing, then, seems not to be everything, but to be opposed to something—say, waiting. Beckett tries to find a way to use language to undo, unravel the simplifications and refusals of language, undermining stories with a story, words with words. If I were not so determined to survive, I'd try to write like that.

These are thoughts she might have had. They don't entirely
suit me. She probably reads Heidegger too, heaven help her.

—Martha Nussbaum, "The Fragility of Goodness"

—~~~—

Science fiction is remarkable for its capacity to guide science.
What scientists claim to be impossible, science fiction writers
take for granted, and in thirty, or sixty, or a hundred years, the
scientists' impossibility is a reality. Computers are a case in point.
For at least half a century, science fiction writers have been rou-
tinely exploring the conundrums accompanying the existence of ro-
bots. Today, science is beginning to make those conundrums real by
creating machines capable of teaching themselves, capable of adapt-
ing to the environment and making decisions not by being pro-
grammed, but by actually learning through adaptation much in the
way that children grow and develop. Recently, I heard a young scientist say that he took on the project of developing a "thinking"
robot after having seen *2001: A Space Odyssey* as a teenager.

My interest in this phenomenon is not to unravel the genius of
science fiction writers, but to point to the significance of narrative
as a medium and form through which human beings figure the possible so that they might make it real, or irreal, in their lives. More
narrowly, my concern is with the implications of this for those of us
who are interested in addressing not only the inequities that gays
and lesbians face in contemporary Western societies, but also the
danger to their very existence that opens up if one adopts what
might be a paranoiac, but nonetheless possible, narrative perspective. In Richard Rubenstein's *The Cunning of History,* Rubenstein
argues that the Holocaust was not an aberration from Western culture, but rather a manifestation of some of its most basic currents,
in specific, the disenchantment of nature, secularization, and ra-
tionalization. Through these processes, human beings have been reduced to parts in the machine of society, expendable parts whose
value is measured in terms of utility. Human beings have no rights
except those given by the state, revocable rights which, when ter-
minated, permit the termination of those no longer under their protection. Rubenstein's picture finds support in the work of numerous

thinkers and a multitude of texts. For instance, Carolyn Merchant's *The Death of Nature* traces the evolution (or devolution, or transformation?) from organic to mechanistic metaphors for construing nature, society, and the person in the West. It suggests that among the implications of this transition is the reconceptualization of human beings from parts in an organism whose relation to the whole is one of reciprocity to cogs in a machine that, when worn out, are to be replaced. In the organic metaphor, the well-being of the parts is realized through the well-being of the whole and vice versa. More pointedly, what well-being means requires consideration of both parts and whole. It would make no sense to think of the social and the individual as separable with respect to their well-being. On the other hand, from the perspective of the mechanistic metaphor, while the individual may make a calculated judgment that her or his well-being would be served through the promotion of some social goal, and while the state might make an analogous calculation with respect to the individual, the two entities stand as quite distinct and do not find their essence, one in the other. This means that, on either side, a calculation of expediency is sufficient for elimination. Again, when Heidegger asserts in *Being and Time* that those of us who are the heirs of Western culture have lost sight of the question, what does it mean to be? he lays the groundwork for exploring the implications of turning human beings into objects subject to manipulation. Among these implications is the possibility of treating human beings as what Heidegger, in *The Question Concerning Technology,* calls a standing reserve, a resource to be used and used up in the realization of whatever goals are arbitrarily assumed. We reduce ourselves and the world to nothing more (or less) than a monochromatic field of stored energy to be called upon at will. A final example, one closer to Rubenstein, is Hannah Arendt's discussion of the apatrieds after World War I. Through denaturalization, unwanted populations could be stripped not only of all rights guaranteed by the state, but also of any claim to consideration as human beings. As a first step to creating communities of total domination leading ultimately not to quixotic attacks upon the Jews and other "undesirables," but to their systematic elimination, denaturalization was essential, according to Rubenstein.

What makes Rubenstein's account so compelling in comparison to more academic or theoretical discussions of the ideological currents in motion in the West is his engagement of the sheer reality of the Holocaust. The fact that an advanced industrialized nation in the West could systematically eliminate part of its population combined with the claim that this was no accident but was tied to the culture itself is a powerful brew that can prove intoxicating. Indeed, the Holocaust has loomed large in the public imagination generally and, I believe, in the gay and lesbian population in particular. One part of the story which Rubenstein glosses over, however, but that should provide no comfort to those who identify themselves as gay, lesbian, bisexual, queer . . . , is that, while the ideological ground may be in place for reducing any and all human beings to their resource value, the reality is that an additional step is needed. It is not simply the case, as Rubenstein claims, that "a hitherto unbreachable moral and political barrier in the history of Western civilization was successfully overcome by the Nazis in World War II and that henceforth the systematic, bureaucratically administered extermination of millions of citizens or subject peoples will forever be one of the capacities and temptations of government."[1] As Rubenstein himself notes, before such elimination could occur, the Jews had to be given the identity of a *Tiermensch,* a subhuman.[2] In the final analysis, one is not willing to eliminate oneself; the other must become an other whose being as other justifies elimination. Rubenstein's general narrative capitalizes upon the predominance of utilitarian, calculative thinking at work in much contemporary decision making. He thereby makes understandable not only why the Jews, Palestinians, . . . and Irish, etc. share a mutual anxiety regarding the establishment of a homeland through which to secure rights, but also why gays and lesbians as such are anxious to secure legal status so that their actions and very persons might not become the pretext for the elimination of rights guaranteed by the state. The addition that I made to Rubenstein's story, or more accurately, the tension inherent to the story occasioned by the necessary inclusion of the fact that the population to be eliminated must be given a paranthropoid identity, makes understandable the anxiety of many gays and lesbians to be considered "just like everyone else," members of the community who share the same concerns, goals, and aspirations as everyone in the community, and who simply want, in the words of Bruce Bawer, "a place at the table."[3] It also makes understandable the desire on the part of many gays and lesbians to discover ways of disturbing the narrative, or the predominant narrative at work in contemporary Western culture, often joining ranks with those feminists who believe that the oppression of women can truly be addressed only if the patriarchal suppositions at work in the culture are supplanted.

For my purposes, it is not important at this stage to engage in polemics about:

1. the veracity of the two predominant narratives invoked, that of Rubenstein and the narrative that he attributes to Western culture;

2. the veracity of the readings assigned to these two narratives;

3. the strategy or strategies that lesbians and gays should adopt to constitute meaningful lives, engage in liberatory praxis, or defend themselves from annihilation.

The exigencies of the moment do require not only that such polemics be underway, but also that those who in some sense identify as gay, lesbian, or bisexual develop strategies for meaningful political action. Yet, it is equally as vital to recognize that our current understandings, including the most idiosyncratic and least invoked understandings, are narratively configured. It is important for at least three reasons:

1. Seeing that our understandings of who we are and how we stand in relation to the world and to others is narratively configured sets the conditions for meaningful discourse.

2. Understanding how the process of narrative configuration can contribute to the production of the abject, and attending to the fact that such understanding itself does not occur from some transcendent vantage point, but within a narrative context, is essential if gays, lesbians, and others who are figured as the "no" that constitutes the permissible are to create a space for listening/discovering not only new stories, but new kinds of stories by attending to what remains undisclosed but present as undisclosed in the narratives through which they have become who they are.

3. Attending to the kind of story that one tells about narrative understanding can provide gays, lesbians, bisexuals, and others with clues for engaging in meaningful political praxis and constituting full and satisfying lives.

To anticipate, it is quite possible to be a dogmatist and at the same time recognize that human beings' understandings of their lives are narratively configured; one need only maintain that there is a single, true story to be told, and that one knows it. However, as I have discussed in the preceding chapter and shall here again briefly indicate, there are reasons for believing that recognizing that one's understanding is narratively configured militates against such dogmatism, provides impetus for not being at home in one's own narrative universe, and thereby opens a space for meaningful dialogue, understood as dialogue that engages the other in his or her otherness. At the same time, such recognition creates a space for considering how the narrative structure of human understanding poses obstacles to dialogue that engages the other as other. If one were to maintain that people operating out of different narrative visions can and should form communities, not only of discourse, but in which there is genuine discourse, one is faced with at least two obstacles. Firstly, this claim should not be taken to mean that fully formed persons who have somehow constituted themselves and created their own narrative visions can and should come together as dialogue partners standing on some mythical even playing field that is itself the construction of a modernist liberal dream. Rather, if discourse is about hearing the other and making oneself heard by the other, the realities of the real historical and geographical contexts in which discourse, whether genuine or not, occurs cannot be ignored. Concretely, this gives rise to a number of concerns: Is it possible to conceive of a discourse between people operating out of different narrative visions that would be something more than a power play? Might people be effectively silenced by the narratives available to them? Might the narratives that people articulate about themselves in fact be narratives into which they have been violently initiated? Secondly, and more stubbornly, if the narrative language that we have been taught, regardless of the specific narratives that we construct, conspires with a heterosexist logic, then the very course of all narrative possibilities will be irremediably confined such that the place at the table for gays and lesbians cannot be that of dialogical partner. The stories that gays and lesbians could tell would have to be hopeless ones, or ones that would allow solace to be taken in the fact that they fought the good fight to mimic the heterosexual in a homosexual key, even if they could not possibly succeed. In brief, I believe that it is neither possible nor desirable to abandon narrative understanding. Therefore, in order to survive, those of us who have, by virtue of the narratives available to us, come to understand ourselves as lesbian, gay, or bisexual, must discover some way of negotiating those contexts in which narrative logic and heterosexist logic form an alliance that affords only oppressive and oppressing life-stories. If this is to occur, it will be necessary to disimbricate heterosexist and narrative logic, and more fundamentally, to weave a tale of narrative that encourages the telling of tales.

The Story: Narrative Constructions

What does it mean to say that human beings come to terms with themselves and their world narratively? Most fundamentally, narratives traditionally contain three moments, a beginning, middle, and end. Even when the three moments do not line up in a neat temporal sequence, or when some attempt is made at short-circuiting, transforming, multiplying, or dismissing these moments, they return as the necessary conditions for mounting any challenge. Additionally, their relation is not merely sequential. The significance of the past is determined by the goals of the future. What one values in the present depends upon one's goals for the future. The goals and purposes available for consciousness and pursuit are a function of one's past and present circumstances. It is unnecessary, and I believe impossible, to assign a causal priority to any of these three moments in terms of the other two; what is important to note, rather, is that each entails the other as its necessary condition. In a narrative, each moment is not like every other.

To say that human beings come to terms with themselves and their world narratively is to say that they engage in the process of integrating the past, present, and future into a coherent whole in both thought and action. It further requires, to speak metaphorically, that nothing in the world or out of it be left out. Properly speaking, while I wholeheartedly agree with Heidegger and others that one cannot take the world as an object for investigation, the point here is not that a narrative must provide an account of the world, but that it must take the world into account. This does not mean that one must believe that the story that one tells about one's life, or about the world, is the only story that can be told, the best story, or the right story. Stories have at once referential and performative power. They set up possible ways of being in the world, invite one to the realization of those possibilities, but they do so by drawing together what has already been, is now, and can be. This opens a space for multiple, at times conflicting, and at times incommensurable stories. To say this is to recognize that human beings are never simply at home in their stories. Even seemingly trivial narratives, how I spent my summer vacation, carry embedded in them narratives articulating how things have been, are now, and can be in the future, narratives that may demand assent, but that cannot preclude another reading, or the writing of another story.

To put this in a somewhat different key, using the language of Jean-Francois Lyotard, I would argue that beneath the surface of even the most casual, limited stories that we tell, such as the various ways in which my cat annoys the hell out of me while I write this chapter (which could explain a lot), there lurks, if not an overarching narrative sufficiently rich (read cosmic in dimensions) to make sense of one's life, at least the impetus toward one. This impetus militates against articulating multiple possible stories, leading to the claim that there is one and only one possible and/or appropriate narrative. This forces a reading of the world that is not necessary, but that fails to acknowledge this, and by privileging a single story, it silences others, thereby silencing other possible voices.[4] It is for just these reasons that Lyotard eschews grand narratives for their totalizing, exclusionary tendencies, and for the violences to which they give rise.[5]

More pointedly, through his account of *un differend,* by which he signifies the inability of one of two parties in a conflict to articulate the wrong that has been inflicted upon him or her because the conflict is articulated in the idiom of the opposing party,[6] Lyotard makes the point that, between two narratives, as well as between two genres of discourse which claim to be hegemonic, there can be no deciding, if by deciding we adopt the model of a putatively "objective" legal decision. This is so because any proposed criterion for judgment would itself require legitimation, and this could not be done because one would have to step out of all language games in order to accomplish it. In fact, Lyotard makes the point that the quest for a criterion of judgment that could be used in the project of legitimation is itself part of the language game of modern science, and is not found in traditional narratives.[7] In *The Differend,* Lyotard employs a discussion of Faurisson's denial of the Holocaust to illustrate his point. Analogously, it is easy to see that, once the homosexual, like the Jew, is turned into a *Tiermensch,* there is no longer any recourse in the narrative universe outlined by Rubenstein for the homosexual to protest the wrong done to him or her. Finally, human beings do not operate out of one and only one language game or one and only one narrative. What one finds satisfactory in a scientific discourse is different from what one finds satisfactory in a religious one, and presumably, one does not always feel the need to reconcile the two. Analogously, human beings do not always feel the need to weave into one narrative the various stories that they tell or entertain about themselves, or do they? True, it may not be possible to legitimate a grand narrative, understood as a narrative that claims universal hegemony. True, there may not even be a felt need for such legitimation. But what is demanded for the subject by the subject is, to repeat my formulation above, a narrative that takes the world into account, not one that necessarily provides an account of the world.

Obviously, this creates a space for the generation of many narratives, many articulations of possibilities for being in the world, that have little bearing on one another. But just as obviously, there is plenty of room for conflict, most perniciously, for conflicts not even perceived as such by those who have opted, or who have been constituted/co-opted by a given narrative. For instance, in contemporary American society, the only possibility for homosexual relationships to gain recognition as legitimate, significant, meaningful relationships is through marriage, which is the very reason that many Americans are so anxious to bar the possibility of gay marriage.[8] But the point here is that it is inconceivable to most Americans that they could commit a wrong, a violation, with respect to gay relationships if these relationships do not mirror marriage. To recognize this would require hearing a different story, one which, even if heard, might not be able to be accepted, or allowed, if the first were to be pursued. Certainly, for individuals and for communities, not all stories can be pursued. Choices are necessary. But recognizing this at the same time opens a space for recognizing the contingency of one's story, a space which, if not available, might be made—and filled—by those not content with the story.

Recognition of one's own fragility and of the possible contingency of one's narrative can, and I believe should, provide impetus for listening to the other and allowing transformation both of oneself and one's stories. But the difficulties that the narrativity of narrative poses, particularly for someone interested in those who are marginalized, made invisible, or whose exclusion is constitutive for given narratives, cannot be forgotten. That human beings make sense of their lives narratively, but are unable logically to eliminate conflicting narrative possibilities even when they refuse them, means that when one reflects critically upon the narrative universe informing one's existence, and on conflicting narratives, one cannot decide between them in some objective way. Nor can one establish criteria for social discourse and praxis that could forestall all objections to any claims to legitimacy that these conflicting narratives might make. Recognizing this carries with it the advantage of making one sensitive to the inevitable coloring that one's deliberations takes on given the language employed. But this advantage contains a danger: to use the language of Gadamer, one cannot escape all prejudices (pre-judgments). It is a prejudice to think that such escape would even be desirable, for it would amount to foreclosing all possibilities. But it does mean continually putting at risk the other, reading the other to the other's disadvantage. It therefore poses serious challenges for those seeking to live meaningful, satisfying lives in a pluralist society. These challenges dovetail with those raised at the end of the preceding section relating to the fact that people who enter into discourse with one another, or who fail or refuse to do so, do so as narratively informed in social contexts that are narratively informed. This danger is exacerbated by the second concern that was also mentioned at the conclusion of the preceding section: What if the very structure of narrative itself carries within it the tendency to exclude and to marginalize? Might there be something about the logic of narrative structure that contributes not only to conflicts between people, but also to the exclusion and silencing of those who cannot be accommodated within the narrative? The remainder of this chapter will take up the first danger, while the final chapter will engage the second one.

Can We Talk?

On initial reading, the first difficulty might seem to carry within it the following presumptions:

1. that one should listen to the other;

2. that one should listen to the other to reach some sort of consensus regarding not only public policy or law, but regarding the narrative framework informing society, or at least, the modes of life that are to be permitted therein;

3. that following some due process of listening to the other and making a decision lends some legitimacy to the decision that follows.[9]

I do not, in fact, want to operate with any of these presumptions. Each is problematic, each would at the least need qualification. The last is simply false: If a sadist, a Jewish masochist, and an Arab nationalist, who thinks that all Jews should die, have a conversation that concludes with the Jew should be killed, it does not follow that the decision is legitimate or justified. However, as I suggested above and in the previous two chapters, recognition of the fragility and contingency of one's own story, and recognition of one's own finitude, together with recognition that the other may have something worth hearing, opens a space for listening to the other in a way that is significant if a pluralist society is to survive and if the people in it are to materially and spiritually flourish as people operating out of different convictions. The point that I should like to focus on here is that listening to the other finds itself at a disadvantage if the model adopted is agonistic.

It is no secret that in the past few decades there have been sustained critiques of those totalizing structures of language and knowledge that preclude and silence various minorities while presenting themselves as neutral, objective, and thus just. These critiques have been developed and inspired by such thinkers as Jacques Derrida and Luce Irigaray. They have extended to a profound suspicion, on the part of Foucault and others, of all discourses as both instituting and circulating in power relations that act violently to silence and marginalize, and have promoted a view of discourses as standing in conflict with one another. This suspicion of discourse has fueled much of the productive work done by feminists, gays, and lesbians, such as Butler's account, discussed in the preceding chapter, of the development of gender categories that function to marginalize, exclude, silence, and render certain identities impossible. To question the agonistic metaphor in terms of which the relations between discourses have been read might therefore appear as dangerous and retrograde, for it might be interpreted as an attempt to reinstitute a single, hegemonic discourse, one that might lead to reinstating women and queers as marginalized. On the other hand, it seems deeply ironic for those who find themselves marginalized in Western society to adopt a metaphor for language that is decidedly colored by traditional Western patriarchal values. Doing so risks the development of strategies for engaging society that will perpetuate the very same sorts of marginalization and silencing that are at issue. What I hope to show is that it is possible to challenge the agonistic metaphor without supporting the search for a hegemonic discourse.

The Agonistic Metaphor: Lyotard

To get a better sense of the agonistic metaphor, the rationale for adopting it, and the reasons for questioning it, I want to turn to its articulation by Lyotard when he claims, in *The Postmodern Condition,* that "to speak is to fight."[10] I want to suggest that adopting this militaristic metaphor is disadvantageous because it sets up as primary, when considering the character of dialogue, the framework of arbitration, judgment, and the demand for criteria (expectations which, it should be noted, Lyotard seeks to forestall, saying that between genres, phrase regimens, etc., there exists *un differend,* not a litigation). While it is true that there are good reasons for adopting this metaphor, while it is true that narratives can conflict, that de-

cisions do have to be made, that challenge is important, these activities cannot occur if one has not first listened. It is on listening
that the marginalized and forgotten must ultimately pin their
hopes. I want to suggest that, while to speak may be to fight, it need
not be so. If one's interest is in the marginalized and the forgotten,
it will be well to recognize the fertile power of Lyotard's metaphor,
and at the same time to attune one's ear to other possibilities, such
as that opened up when Emmanuel Levinas proclaims, "The face
speaks."[11] Such a claim does not preclude the possibilities opened
up by Lyotard's metaphor, but it does invite one to hear something
quite different.

Why is to speak to fight? To address this, it is necessary to look
at Lyotard's approach to language. There are two aspects of it that
are striking. Firstly, he seeks to develop a notion of language that
enables the recognition that there are distinct and incommensurable universes of discourse. He does this to great effect *in The
Postmodern Condition* by borrowing Wittgenstein's notion of language game to note that there are different modes of discourse,
such as prescriptive, performative, and pragmatic, each of which
has its own rules for acceptable moves, etc.[12] Secondly, he wants to
capture the idea that reality is always already mediated by language such that there is no reality, and no subject, outside of it. In
The Differend, he replaces the term *language game,* which suggests
that language is a tool independent of the user, with the term
phrase regimen, to signal the pervasiveness of language while re-
taining the idea that there are a variety of language games that
are ultimately incommensurable.[13] In the words of Geoffrey Bennington, according to Lyotard, "Reality is never given, but always
situated by particular narratives as referents: just as story-teller
and addressee do not precede the story told but are positioned by
it."[14]

The one indubitable, the only given, according to Lyotard, is not
reality, but rather what he comes to call in *Le Postmoderne explique
aux enfants,* "phrases,"[15] which can be understood roughly as the
units of discourse, whether they be literal phrases, sentences, or
even physical gestures, that are linked together according to the
rules provided by language games, or phrase regimens.[16] Shifting
our typical way of thinking about things, Lyotard argues that there
is not first an addressor and addressee and then a phrase which

passes between them. Rather, addressor and addressee "are instances, either marked or unmarked, presented by a phrase," just as are reference and sense.[17] Hence, what is in a phrase, according to Lyotard, is a universe setting forth in relation addressor, addressee, sense, and referent:

> It should be said by way of simplification that a phrase presents what it is about, the case, ta pragmata, which is its referent; what is signified about the case, the sense, der Sinn; that to which or addressed to which this is signified about the case, the addressee; that "through" which or in the name of which this is signified about the case, the addressor. The disposition of a phrase universe consists in the situating of these instances in relation to each other. A phrase may entail several referents, several senses, several addressees, several addressors. Each of these four instances may be marked in the phrase or not. (Fabbri and Sbisa, 1980)[18]

Lyotard insists upon the indubitability that *there is* a phrase (not, it must be noted, on the indubitability of the universe presented by it),[19] for even to call into question a phrase requires a phrase. He insists that reality is never given except as the referent of a phrase. He insists that a phrase presents a universe. But phrases do not stand alone. A first phrase calls for a second to present it: "A presentation can be presented as an instance in the universe of a phrase . . . But the phrase that presents the presentation itself entails a presentation, which it does not present."[20] As Tim Jordan puts it, "A phrase is just the "there is"; it is just the fact that a universe exists, which means the phrase does not itself tell us that its universe exists. It is necessary for at least one other phrase to link to a phrase for the first phrase to be presented, otherwise it would not be known that the first phrase existed."[21] It is in this way that Lyotard moves from the phrase to phrase regimens, which provide rules for linking phrases, and ultimately to genres, which employ phrase regimens, such as prescriptives, performatives, constatives, to various ends.[22] Thus, following much structuralist and poststructuralist thought, Lyotard conceives of language as a differential system in which phrases are linked together according to various competing and incommensurable phrase regimens and genres, or language games.

Different phrase regimens offer different, heterogeneous rules for linking onto phrases, much in the way that the rules of different games are heterogeneous; this is the source of conflict underpinning the agonistic metaphor.[23] It is necessary "to link onto a phrase that happens," but how to link onto it is contingent.[24] "Incommensurability, in the sense of the heterogeneity of phrase regimens and of the impossibility of subjecting them to a single law (except by neutralizing them), also marks the relation between either cognitives or presecriptives and interrogatives, performatives, exclamatives . . . For each of these regimens, there corresponds a mode of presenting a universe, and one mode is not translatable into another."[25]

One might try to resolve the conflict between phrase regimens by appealing to a genre to determine the appropriateness of a given linkage, but then one is left with the difficulty of privileging one genre over another, and attempts at validating such privileging itself leads to the privileging of a certain genre, for, according to Lyotard, "Validation is a genre of discourse . . ."[26] Stated differently, genres are able to employ various phrase regimens, fixing rules of linkage according to the ends pursued, thereby eliminating conflict by providing criteria for appropriate linking, but this merely shifts conflict "from the level of regimens to that of ends."[27] Again:

> The idea that a supreme genre encompassing everything that's at stake could supply a supreme answer to the key-questions of the various genres founders upon Russell's aporia. Either this genre is part of the set of genres, and what is at stake in it is but one among others, and therefore its answer is not supreme. Or else, it is not part of the set of genres, and it does not therefore encompass all that is at stake, since it excepts what is at stake in itself. The speculative genre had this pretension (Result Section; Hegel Notice). The principle of an absolute victory of one genre over the others has no sense.[28]

Only one linking is possible at a time, for the stakes of different genres differ. The success of one genre is not that of another, and the "victory" of one genre, the linkage it realizes, entails that other possible linkages "remain neglected, forgotten, or repressed possibilities."[29]

Thus are we led to the agonistic claim that to speak is to fight,[30] the force of which surfaces when we consider that the social is indissoluble from phrase regimens and genres, for it is in and through the latter that social bonds are effected.[31] In the political realm, it is possible that a number of genres will be in play, but it is inevitable that they will conflict. Consider for a moment the phrase, "the Jewish plague." The presentation of this phrase by the Nazi myth of Aryan supremacy must suppress the linkage made by queer culture theory, where the uses made by the Nazis of the language of "plague" might be compared to the use by contemporary Americans of the word "plague" in relation to gays and lesbians. Importantly, one cannot forget that the reverse is also the case. To the extent that one genre, and I would say more pointedly, one narrative, becomes hegemonic, violence is necessarily done to other genres. Certain things can no longer be said, and we are left with the disturbing prospect, outlined in the preceding section of this chapter when discussing *le differend,* that at least one of the parties to a conflict will be unable to articulate the wrong done to him or her because the idiom available does not allow it.

But given that no logically compelling criterion of judgment for deciding between heterogeneous phrase regimens, genres of discourse, and narratives is available, it does not seem that Lyotard could convincingly argue that a given narrative should not become hegemonic. Ironically, he in fact unsuccessfully attempts to do just this in *Just Gaming* by simultaneously and thus inconsistently privileging a prescriptive language game, and arguing that "just gaming" requires that no language game *should be* privileged over another.[32] All that can consistently be said is that there is no criterion for adopting a language game that somehow stands above all others, and that while the "fight" might come to a halt in a given community, it necessarily comes at the price of silencing other narratives and other genres, and of wronging those who are silenced thereby, where "wrong" is given the specific sense that Lyotard assigns to it, a damage that cannot be proved because the framework available for speaking it does not allow the evidence.[33] From a somewhat different perspective, it leaves open the recognition that, while one may be forced to submit to some grand narrative, there is always a gap, a leap to adherence that need never be made.

Yet this is not the end of the story. At least one thing has been left out that is relevant to our concerns: the importance that Lyotard assigns to "the event." It is impossible to do justice to this here. Understood historically, an event is unique, unrepeatable, that after which nothing will ever be the same.[34] Assimilating it, incorporating it into a general history as a moment, results in the loss of its singularity as an event.[35] It should be noted that writing a history, constructing a cultural narrative, and telling a tale are all events which, as such, are incapable of taking account of themselves. There is always an excess, something more to them than what is said in them, their occurrences as events, which may be taken up by other discourses, narratives, tales. According to Bill Readings, Lyotard's discussion of "the phrase" in *The Differend* is actually his "most fully developed account of the 'event' as pure happening."[36] The phrase happens; it takes place, presenting a phrase universe that affords various linkings. From all that has been said, it should be clear by now that, according to Lyotard, there is no grand narrative in terms of which one can determine which linking is true. But this is not an invitation either to indifference or to relativism. The linking effected makes a difference: It silences some; it betrays the silence of others; it leaves open the possibility that the obscene can become hegemonic without any legitimate way of declaring the obscenity as such. From the fact that there is no criterion for judging between incommensurable genres, or between those parties in conflict who seek litigation by appeal to incommensurable narratives, it does not follow that all judgments are equally valid. Distinct from the question of truth, we can raise the question of justice. Because various linkings are possible, but only one can be accomplished at a time, it is inevitable that an injustice is done to the other possible linkings, to those that are suppressed, and to the phrase event itself as event. It is on this basis that we can speak of *un differend* such that the inability of one of the parties to a dispute to state his or her case in the language in which the dispute is to find its resolution constitutes an injustice. A judgment must be made between conflicting parties, but it must be an indeterminate judgment, a judgment without criteria, and justice demands that it be a judgment that testifies to the incommensurability of the conflicting claims.[37]

From a different perspective, Lyotard introduces his own idiosyncratic reading of Kant's sublime to suggest the requirement of justice that the unrepresentable be somehow presented. "One's responsibility before thought consists . . . in detecting differends and in finding the (impossible) idiom for phrasing them. This is what philosophy does."[38] The sublime is the feeling that one wants to place the totality in phrases, together with the feeling of the impossibility of doing this. The sense of the sublime consists in recognizing both thought's capacity to make new phrases, and its limitations before the unrepresentable event. More pointedly, to feel the sublime is to feel the call to present the unpresentable.[39] I would suggest that it is precisely this call that is the source of the responsibility to detect differends and to find the idiom for phrasing them. Without the feeling of the sublime, one could not feel the injustice of a hegemonic discourse, or be drawn to the multiplication of phrasings. Without it, it would make no sense for Lyotard to speak of the despair at "never being able to present something within reality on the scale of the Idea," and "the joy of being nonetheless called upon to do so,"[40] or to make the following demand upon politicians:

> But, supposing that a change took place, it is impossible that the judgments of the new tribunal would not create new wrongs, since they would regulate (or think they were regulating) differends as though they were litigations. This is why politicians cannot have the good at stake, but they ought to have the lesser evil. Or, if you prefer, the lesser evil ought to be the political good. By evil, I understand, and one can only understand, the incessant interdiction of possible phrases, a defiance of the occurrence, the contempt for Being.[41]

But if this is so, then there is in fact a double movement here that requires more than the multiplication of discourses, idioms, narratives, and the proliferation of conflicts whose resolutions rely upon indeterminate judgment. While it is true that any presentation of the event, and any linking of the phrase, must constitute a betrayal which is sensed in the feeling of the sublime, at the same time, if one is to attend to the testimony of the other in another idiom, or to the silence borne of refusal or incapacity to testify in a discourse that has achieved de facto hegemony, then one must cede to these worthiness to be heard. This means attending to *what* they are saying. That is, the proliferation of phrases and the uncovering of *differends* is not enough if this becomes the only concern, for then the multiple phrases, phrase regimens, genres, multiple discourses, and narratives themselves are in an important sense silenced, their substance ignored. There is a failure in speaking and remaining silent, there is a failure in listening, if the truth claims and the claims to justice that are made in a particular genre or discourse are not taken seriously.

To show what is at stake here, bringing *differends* to language, defending the right to phrase, can only be accomplished if it is able to take into account the cry of the Holocaust survivor that justice demands the silencing, the banishment, of the Nazi narrative. One must be able to make two moves at once. One must recognize the failure of any narrative's claim to hegemony, the failure of any narrative to achieve a totalizing vision, if for no other reason than that it cannot take into account itself as an event. At the same time, one must recognize in the midst of this failure, that at least some narratives may constitute gifts, presentations of what cannot be presented, springing from nowhere, bestowing the grace of meaning and the possibility of justice. One must attend to the possibility that what is said, and the silences that are there when one attends to them, are gifts that make demands upon us. Above or below the inevitable conflicts between narratives, discourses, genres, phrase regimens, and phrases, one is called to listen because of their failures and because of the possibility that they speak in their various ways what demands to be, and what must be, heard. And yet, this means being placed in the impossible position not only of listening, but of being called upon by some narratives to discard others because they bear false testimony. One cannot escape the decision, for to do so is already to decide. In the end, Lyotard's emphasis upon the incommensurability of genres of discourse and upon the injustices to the other that can spring therefrom moves one beyond the various conflicts to the demands to be heard which stand at their origin, demands that at times incorporate demands for condemnations of those discourses that fail, mislead, and commit injustice.

But how is one to decide? The only thing that seems incontestable from what Lyotard has given us is that no criterion employed would be incontestable. But if one recognizes that there is a demand to listen, a demand to be heard, made by no one from nowhere, beyond and below all possibilities for speaking, or by someone from somewhere who can never be turned into just anyone, a demand that requires recognition that cannot be achieved through argumentation, might this itself provide clues for listening and for responding responsibly? To approach this question, I should like to turn to Emmanuel Levinas's consideration of responsibility as arising from what he describes as recognition of the face of the other in *Totality and Infinity,* and as proximity to the other in *Otherwise than Being.*

Words That Don't Fight: Levinas

Levinas's work pushes beyond being, not to nothing, but to the other,[42] and because of this, there is a spirit of superabundance to it that is unique and requires special attention. To begin, it is helpful to recall Hegel's description of irony in his *Introductory Lectures on Aesthetics,* where he discusses Friedriche von Schlegel. Hegel maintains that Schlegel follows Fichte in taking the abstract, formal "I" as the absolute principle of knowledge, of cognition and reason. Because the "I" is a purely formal, empty unity and the absolute principle of all cognition, it follows that the "I" does not discover meaning and significance for itself in the other, but rather is the sole determinant of value, the origin of meaning and significance.[43] But this means that nothing has value in itself, and according to Hegel, "it follows that the I is able to remain lord and master of everything, and in no sphere of morality or legality, of things human or divine, profane or sacred, is there anything that would not have to begin by being given position by the I, and that might not, therefore, just as well be in turn annihilated thereby."[44] Hegel draws the conclusion that all that is independent of the "I" would have to be viewed as mere semblance, or appearance, arbitrarily ordered and valued according to the caprice of the "I." If we turn to art for a moment, this implies that the work of art as an expression of the self seeking realization would have no other content than the free creation of semblances; there could be no earnestness in art, for earnestness implies a regard for something of intrinsic value. For the artist to be earnest would require that he or she consider the content of the work to have an essential value that is independent of the artist's determination.[45] Irony consists in deflating the values hitherto held as independent of human appraisal and replacing them with the principle of absolute subjectivity.[46] Interestingly, Hegel says that the ironist can have no sense of obligation, of meaningful ties or commitments, of the independent value of particular actions, and that she or he is left to the "bliss of self-enjoyment."[47] Eventually, Hegel notes, the ironist may come to feel the emptiness of being left with nothing but himself, an empty, hollow self, and may therefore seek an absolute, objective reality that constitutes a sphere of transcendent value, though he or she may ultimately be unwilling to undertake the pursuit, not wanting to forsake its absolute unity and "inward harmony."[48] The alternatives with which we seem to be left from this account are either to follow Fichte's and Schlegel's accounts of the "I" as absolute, or to maintain that beyond semblance there is an Absolute that is the origin of meaning, significance, value, an Absolute that is the proper goal of cognition.

As should be clear from the preceding chapters, both of these alternatives are unpalatable for those finding themselves marginalized in contemporary Western culture. The former typically leads either to relativism or to totalitarianism, opening itself at once to the war of all against all and to indifference. To make the self the locus of meaning is to reduce the other to one's own vision, or to admit a multiplicity of arbitrary visions. While this may create a space for those who find themselves marginalized to contest the claims to legitimacy of the status quo, it leaves them with little recourse but the arbitrary and violent assertion of their own will.

But appeal to an Absolute that is the proper goal of cognition carries its own dangers. At least one way of characterizing the Enlightenment project is as the attempt to discover the reign of reason in reality. If we look to Hegel, we will see that the strategy for accomplishing this is to privilege sameness, singularity, and unity over diversity. A metanarrative is constructed employing a conceptual apparatus that enables the understanding and identification of differences as moments in the constitution of a single, unified whole. On the one hand, this strategy promotes the tolerance of difference. By understanding differences in terms of their contribution to the whole, they are brought into an economy of the same and are thereby given place. But this toleration comes at the price of sacrificing the difference of difference. As A. T. Nuyen puts it, "Encouraged by the Hegelian account of difference in terms of the same, modernity teaches us to see sameness in difference, unity in diversity, universality in the multitude of things. We are urged to think that those who differ from us racially, sexually, culturally, are 'really the same as us.' We should tolerate because there is really no difference to fear."[49] We hear this logic when we gays and lesbians profess that we are the same as you; we are your sons and daughters, your neighbors and fellow workers. Our differences do not make us different, do not make us other than you. Or, our differences ultimately contribute to the cultural tapestry that makes us strong, creative, and vibrant, a people, so long as we are included, made one of you.

This assimilation of difference into sameness constitutes a certain violence, a refusal to take difference on its own terms, and a refusal and silencing of difference which cannot be assimilated. A Kantian approach to ethics aptly illustrates this. Kant's ethics is built on the demand to respect the other as an autonomous moral agent like oneself. This respect can incorporate a tolerance for the other as different from oneself regarding temperament, aptitude, life choices, etc. But because this tolerance is built on a recognition of sameness, it is revocable. The other who is not like oneself does not qualify. Perhaps more importantly, because the qualifying mark becomes determinative, no one can be respected in her or his uniqueness. This failure manifests itself in Hegel through his dismissal of whatever is simply unique—whatever cannot be fitted into the conceptual net woven by reason to account for everything—as unimportant, transitory, "lazy Existenz."[50] But as Wendy Farley notes, this is precisely to denude the individual of those features that are essential to concrete existence, and to frustrate "philosophy's own eros for the truth" by perpetrating a distortion in the name of understanding.[51]

Stated otherwise, a totalizing account of reality provides a conceptual grid which enables us to identify only those differences that count in terms of the whole picture, and that require us to read them in terms of the whole. It further requires a conceptualization of the self that reduces the self to the same, either the same as everyone else in all relevant respects, or the same as all others whose difference operates in the economy of the whole, a conceptualization that determines moral status. Leaving aside for the moment Senator Trent Lott's characterization of the homosexual as sinner, a characterization presuming moral agency and an underlying sameness between the homosexual and everybody else that would ground duties towards the homosexual, Lott's pseudomedical characterization of the homosexual as someone subject to a compulsive disorder aptly serves to suggest how genuine difference is occluded or made to serve an economy of sameness when appeal is made to an absolute, overarching structure to reality. In Lott's universe, the homosexual becomes either a freakish aberration deserving of pity or the other of the same that must be negated if moral agency is to be achieved and if one is to attain the status of a being deserving of respect.

The spirit of superabundance characterizing Levinas's work comes into play at this juncture, for Levinas offers a third alternative, one that moves beyond an absolutization of the knowing self, and beyond being conceived as a totality subject in some sense to cognition. Indeed it is with the latter alternative that Levinas is most concerned, for as Merold Westphal notes, Levinas is alive to the dangers it poses when he sees in Western philosophy's "attempts to totalize the world and our experience in it, to make everything fit within its conceptual schemes, . . . a series of attempts to make the world safe for a Self unimpeded by any Other which is not its own other, that is, the necessary condition for its own possibility, something to be used, possessed, enjoyed."[52] Turning to infinity as "origin" of value and meaning, Levinas points to this third way through his characterization of eschatology in *Totality and Infinity*:

> Eschatology institutes a relation with being *beyond the totality* or beyond history, and not with being beyond the past and the present. Not with the void that would surround the totality and where one could, arbitrarily, think what one likes, and thus promote the claims of a subjectivity free as the wind. It is a relationship with *a surplus always exterior to the totality,* as though the objective totality did not fill out the true measure of being, as though another concept, the concept of *infinity,* were needed to express this transcendence with regard to totality, non-encompassable within a totality and as primordial as totality.[53]

To anticipate, this suggests that, otherwise than thinking of discourses as potentially incommensurable but nonetheless agonistically related because of their various totalizing pretensions, it might be possible to recognize them as springing from an origin beyond being such that any totalizing pretensions are short-circuited. This would not preclude agonistic relationships between discourses. But it would create the possibility that a plurality of discourses might have something to say worth hearing, that they might not be either mere semblances or totalizing discourses, that they might in addition open a legitimate demand that one attend to silences as well as to the word.

It is possible to approach this third alternative with the fairly abstract observation that Levinas's project consists in placing ethics before ontology.[54] We saw above in the discussion of the Enlightenment appeal to reason that it is possible to think of traditional ontology as attempting to provide a rational, justifiable account of the fundamental structure of reality that would in turn be available to ethical discourse for determining the nature, and depending upon one's stance, in some instances, the criteria, for moral action. Crudely stated, one can find in the Western philosophical tradition a long series of attempts to explicate and justify the following three theses:

1. There is a meaningful, rational structure to reality.

2. Human beings are capable of comprehending this structure, of employing this understanding to determine the meaning of specific human situations, and of deciding what actions are appropriate and morally justifiable in these particular situations given the structure of reality.

3. Human beings are free and therefore responsible for their actions and capable of following their own reason, which means that they are autonomous moral agents.

Given these theses, the project of philosophical ethics is to discover rationally justifiable, universal criteria for moral decision making, criteria to which any rational moral agent could be held accountable. I would add that this project, broadly construed, could include approaches to ethical decision making that do not incorporate the construction of formal laws, such as Aristotle's virtue ethics, though it would take us far afield to explore how this is so. The purpose of this sketch is simply to situate Levinas's claim that ethics precedes ontology. The claim is significant because it affords an approach to listening and responding responsibly to multiple and conflicting narrative discourses (and to the silences that they impose) that foregoes the alternative posed in Hegel's treatment of irony. Levinas offers an alternative between treating all discourses as mere semblances (ultimately, semblances that cannot even be properly so called as they neither dissemble nor resemble), and eliminating or subsuming these discourses into one totalizing discourse providing an absolute account of the Absolute.

So, what has Levinas in mind when he claims priority for ethics? In *Totality and Infinity,* Levinas, much like Heidegger in *Being and Time,* focuses on the fact that to be Dasein is to be a being-in-the-world. But, in contrast to Heidegger, Levinas's attention centers on the fact that finding oneself existing in the world means finding oneself among others who are indeed *other* than oneself.[55] The importance of this shift cannot be underestimated, and while I cannot do justice to it here, dwelling on it at some length is essential both to coming to terms with the alternative that Levinas offers and to appreciating its viability.

In *Being and Time,* Heidegger claims that those of us standing in twentieth-century Western culture have lost sight of the question of what it means to Be and have instead concerned ourselves with beings. He proposes that we raise once again the question of Being by turning to the place where Being discloses itself, to Dasein. That is, according to Heidegger, it belongs to human beings as beings-in-the-world to raise the question of Being, and it is by attending to their own Being as beings for whom Being is an issue that the meaning of Being is revealed.[56] What is important to note here is Levinas's view that Heidegger sees the relation between Dasein and Being as primarily one of comprehension.[57] What this implies for Levinas is an inability to account for an encounter with the Other as Other. Thus, in what many would consider to be a contentious reading of Heidegger, Levinas returns him to the history of Western philosophical ontology. Heidegger attempts a comprehension of what it means to Be privileging Being over beings in such a way that the alterity of the Other is occluded.

It is possible to gain a better understanding of this if we consider Dasein as being-in-the-world and as being-unto-death. One of the most extraordinary moves that Heidegger makes in *Being and Time* is to dissolve the problem, most trenchantly posed by Descartes, of how the subject is to move outside of the self to discover the truth about the external world. Heidegger does this by disclosing that the subject/object dichotomy is itself an abstraction that presumes a more primordial experience of being-in-the-world. To be Dasein is to be-in-the-world and to be the place where the possibilities for Being are disclosed through Dasein's being questioningly. As such, it makes no sense to talk about absolute alterity. The other is always an other for Dasein and is thereby subjected, in Levinas's view, to the economy of the same. Again, Heidegger does not see Being as an agent or as an entity; but rather Being is the granting of possibilities for being, and in this granting, Being is also the foreclosing of other possibilities. Hence, it makes no sense to talk about what lies outside of, or beyond, Being. Even those possibilities for being that remain concealed or foreclosed for Dasein have their being for Dasein as concealed or foreclosed.

According to Heidegger, Dasein's mode of being-in-the-world is care. It is by virtue of the things that one cares about, one's projects, goals, etc., that beings in the world take on meaning for one. It is by virtue of one's projects that the possibilities for beings in the world are disclosed. At its outermost limit, this care is for the being of Dasein itself. Through Dasein's recognition of itself as a being-unto-death, the possibilities for being become an issue, and it is in terms of these possibilities for being that the being of others becomes an issue. Others are not encountered in their own right, but in relation to Dasein's care. It is because of this that Levinas breaks with Heidegger. Levinas insists that we retain the Otherness of the other in the disclosure of the possibilities for Being that Heidegger calls the happening of truth, aletheia:

> In the modern terminology, we disclose only with respect to a project. In labor we approach the Real with a view to a goal conceived by us. This modification that knowledge brings to bear on the One, which in cognition loses its unity, is evoked by Plato in the *Parmenides*. Knowledge in the absolute sense of the term, the pure experience of the other being, would have to maintain the other being *Kath auto.*[58]

It is interesting to note in this regard that in his discussion of Heidegger and Levinas, Alphonso Lingis makes the case that Heidegger takes account of our being "beset with the fact of being."[59] Through his existential analytic of Dasein as a being always already in a world, as a being thrown into the world, Heidegger, according to Lingis, recognizes that our own being "is exposed from the start to the being of the most alien and remote things, exposed to the dimensions of remoteness in which beings can be exterior; the weight of the being of the world presses down on us."[60] But the difficulty is that Heidegger recognizes this only in the context of our confrontation with death, with the possibility that we may cease to be, the possibility of nothingness that makes of our being an issue. As such, those things that confront us do so not in their own right, "but as means, as supporting gear, or obstacles and snares, in the way of our movements into the world."[61]

Levinas, on the other hand, takes his cue from our experience of the weight of being. Because the encounter with beings in Heidegger, at least the Heidegger of *Being and Time,* is from the very start conditioned by utility, Heidegger is unable to take account of the sensuous, the experience that one has in material contact with the other. In the sensuous encounter with the other, prior to any attempt to explore the instrumental potentialities of that which one encounters, one is affected by the sheer presence of tone, color, solidity, by the material presence of the other, the sensual experience of which is marked by enjoyment.[62] Shifting for the moment to an encounter with another person, the first time that I caressed a man's body, that I touched his shimmering, smooth, brown flesh, I felt an inexpressible intimacy and pleasure that had nothing to do with conceptualization, definition, or utility, a pleasure that, true, encompassed a sense of union, of communion, but that stemmed most deeply from having crossed a divide, a divide that most crucially did not disappear with the touch, but that remained stamped as mystery and awe. As Levinas has it, "In voluptuosity the other is me and separated from me. The separation of the Other in the midst of this community of feeling constitutes the acuity of voluptuosity. The voluptuous in voluptuosity is not the freedom of the other tamed, objectified, but his freedom untamed, which I nowise desire objectified."[63] Central to the touch, to the caress, though the caress cannot be reduced to it, is the sense of no longer being alone, but a sense curiously shadowed by delight at not being able to absorb the other, for to do so would be precisely to be alone again . . . the other would no longer differ from oneself.

From a different angle, in his works prior to *Totality and Infinity*, "De l'evasion," *Existence and Existents*, and *Time and the Other*, Levinas focuses on the feelings of vulnerability and pain that one experiences when one finds that one cannot escape Being, that Being in general and one's own Being enchain one to oneself. Because one cannot escape one's being in the present moment, one is irremissibly bound by the Other as such. In *Existence and Existents*, Levinas chooses the phrase, *il y a*, there is, to denote the being that is prior to human comprehension, the other with which one is confronted, the other that one knows *is* without knowing *what* it is. That there is *(il y a)* prior to consciousness, or other than consciousness, implies that consciousness, as well as subjectivity and identity, must be understood as what Levinas calls an hypostasis, the emergence out of anonymity of a separate existence.[64] This emergence is effected through the Other, through the demands that the Other places on one. In *Time and the Other*, Levinas picks up on Heidegger's notion of *Geworfenheit*, of being thrown into the world, to argue that, logically, such a being thrown entails an existence independent of the existent that is "thrown," and that the existent, therefore, subjected to being, is unable to become master absolutely. Escape from the weight of being comes not through mastery, but as Levinas develops later, through transcendence of self by going out to the other in love. This transcendence of self through the love relationship has its completion in fecundity, the birth of an other who is oneself and who yet is other, escaping the moment into the future.[65] We shall return to this later. For the moment, what is important is feeling the strength and comprehending the nature of Levinas's prioritization of alterity, the fact that one's relation to the other is one that stands outside the bounds of comprehension because it overflows any attempts to dissolve the otherness of the other, to reduce the other to the same.

In *Totality and Infinity*, Levinas is quick to point out that the awareness of otherness is not one's first concern. Initially, there is an egocentric bias; one attempts to control one's environment, to fulfill one's needs, and thereby to enjoy one's existence (note in this regard Hegel's reference to enjoyment in the discussion of irony).[66] To this end, one seeks to turn the other into the same, to extend one-

self, understood either as the individual self or the social self, to include the other, making it the same as oneself, or to reduce the other,
making it subject to oneself. Indeed, this focus on self-enjoyment
marks a resistance to turning oneself into an entity that is to take
its place, among others, in the totality, in the order of things; it
marks a move away from participation in Being to ontological au-
tonomy.[67] But while one may attempt to subdue the other or to commit a violence against the other by reducing the other to the same,
one cannot escape the otherness of the other, the experience of the
other that occurs in what Levinas calls in *Totality and Infinity* the
face to face relation and characterizes in *Otherwise than Being* as
the experience of proximity. It is an experience of the other as
unique, strange, and as quite possibly not occupying the same world
as oneself, an experience of the other as making a demand addressed to oneself not as one subject among many, but as this
unique and uniquely responsible subject. In the face to face relation,
one cannot escape the expression of the other, the demand that the
other makes not to be understood as an entity, but as soliciting response.[68] It cannot be too forcefully stated that, for Levinas, this experience of being summoned by the face precedes and directs all attempts at comprehending the Other; it is in view of this summons
that any attempt to come to know the other person occurs. As Levinas puts it, "The relationship with a being infinitely distant, that
is, overflowing its idea, is such that its authority as an existent is already *invoked* in every question we could raise concerning the
meaning of its Being. One does not question oneself concerning him;
one questions him."[69] Ethics precedes ontology. More pointedly, the
attempt to reduce the Other to the Same by prioritizing the cognitive relation to the other, by reducing the other to what can be com-
prehended through one's conceptual framework, is itself an ethical
violation.[70] Finally, one cannot escape what Levinas calls desire, the
longing for that which is other than oneself, that draws oneself beyond oneself, the longing that cannot be quenched as can needs,
which subside once their objects are appropriated.[71] It is through
the sheer experience of the other as other that one becomes responsible for the other and to the other. This is so because the experience
of the otherness of the other contests any attempt at reducing the
other to the same, at conceiving a single, unified, total system that
cannot respect genuine alterity,[72] and that resists placing the

conception of this totality in service to one's own enjoyment. One is called to account.

According to Levinas, to respond to this call means taking up language, for it is through language that one can place one's world before the other in a genuine conversation, a conversation that supposes that one is speaking with someone who is not the same as oneself:

> We shall try to show that the *relation* between the same and the other—upon which we seem to impose such extraordinary conditions—is language. For language accomplishes a relation such that the other, despite the relationship with the same, remains transcendent to the same. The relation between the same and the other, metaphysics, is primordially enacted as conversation, where the same, gathered up in its ipseity as an "I," as a particular existent unique and autochthonous, leaves itself.[73]

Through language, one exposes one's world with all of its suppositions and assumptions to the other and thereby opens oneself to being responsible to the other.[74] It is in this way that one establishes the conditions for communication and the possibility of genuine community. In other words, by responding to the other as other, by being responsible to the other as other, one escapes one's egoism and opens oneself to the possibility of dwelling with the other.

This calling to account by the other, this demand by the other to be responsible to and for the other is a demand made uniquely to oneself, and in fact is that which individuates the self. The experience of the face of the other is an experience of being *the one* who is called to account, and it is this experience that is the ground of ethics. As Tina Chanter says so well, "What is beyond being for Levinas is not an abstract or ideal conception of the good, but the social relation, which first takes place not in terms of Hegelian recognition where the I is contested by the other, but as welcome, as a giving in which I am answerable for the other. The face of the other signifies my obligation to the other, not solely because the other has empirical needs—but because I am put in question by the very existence of the other."[75] In light of this, it should be clear why and in what sense Levinas gives priority to ethics over ontology. If one starts with a totalizing vision of reality that cannot respect alterity because it reduces the other to the same, that refuses to recognize the other as uniquely other, one does violence to the experience of the other and to the responsibility that that experience entails. It is one's obligation to the other that is the appropriate context for placing one's world before the other in language.

There are three issues raised by the preceding discussion that require some response before proceeding to a consideration of the contribution that Levinas's account of responsibility in the face of the other makes to how the narrative discourses and silences of the other are to be engaged. Firstly, it is possible, of course, that one will refuse to recognize the other as other, or will refuse to recognize one's responsibility to and for the other.[76] Indeed, has it not been the case traditionally that ethical obligations are considered to obtain with respect to those who are the same as, or like, oneself? In fact, it is worth recalling that prior to stripping Jews, gypsies, the mentally disabled, homosexuals, etc. . . . . of their rights, the Nazis found it necessary to reduce them to subhumans. Analogously, the rationale commonly given today to support "coming out" is to show that "we" are "just like everyone else," and presumably are therefore subject to "the same" treatment as "they." Concurrently, the attempt on the part of the religious right to characterize gay and lesbian efforts to secure nondiscrimination protections as "special rights," and the response by lesbian and gay activists that what they are advocating is "equal rights" employ the same logic. Secondly, it might be possible that one will remain content not to strive for community and communication. Finally, for an obligation to be an ethical one, it has typically been supposed that it must in some sense obtain universally. How is this to be the case if the demand is made uniquely upon oneself by the other?

Regarding the first issue, it is of course possible that one will seek to refuse such recognition. At a certain level, there seems to be no argument here. Levinas's account hinges upon an experience that he does not believe can be escaped, but only denied. " 'To leave men without food is a fault that no circumstance attenuates; the distinction between the voluntary and the involuntary does not apply here,' says Rabbi Yochanan. Before the hunger of men responsibility is measured only 'objectively'; it is irrecusable. The face opens the primordial discourse whose first word is obligation, which no 'interiority' permits avoiding."[77] Further, it is an experience that shatters the shallowness of the view that one is responsible only to those "like oneself"; the experience itself testifies against the restriction of value to the self that such a stance implies. But is there something more to offer regarding such a pivotal point? At its most extreme, the refusal of the other becomes negation, murder. Levinas takes as the first ethical command, "you shall not commit murder":

> The Other who can sovereignly say *no* to me is exposed to the point of the sword or the revolver's bullet, and the whole unshakeable firmness of his "for itself" with that intransigent *no* he opposes is obliterated because the sword or the bullet has touched the ventricles or auricles of his heart. In the contexture of the world he is a quasi-nothing. But he can oppose to me a struggle, that is, oppose to the force that strikes him not a force of resistance, but the very *unforeseeableness* of his reaction. He thus opposes to me not a greater force, an energy assessable and consequently presenting itself as though it were part of a whole, but the very transcendence of his being by relation to that whole; not some superlative of power, but precisely the infinity of his transcendence. This infinity, stronger than murder, already resists us in his face, is his face, is the primordial *expression,* is the first word: "you shall not commit murder." The infinite paralyses power by its infinite resistance to murder, which, firm and insurmountable, gleams in the face of the Other, in the total nudity of his defenceless eyes, in the nudity of the absolute openness of the Transcendent.[78]

This command comes from the Other; why is it a command from which I cannot free myself through my elimination of the Other? The force of "thou shalt not commit murder" does not rely on my recognition of some legitimate authority that imposes it or on obedience to my own will. I am not free to take a Kantian approach and ask whether or not I would be willing to live in a world where murder, or perhaps more tellingly, the murder of Jews or homosexuals, is permissible. Rather, this command's power lies in the fact that even if I murder, I shall not murder: I shall not eliminate the Other. That I have decided to take a murderous stance towards the Other calls me to the fact that I share this world with the Other, that I have an identity precisely because I distinguish myself from the Other, that the Other's presence puts in question how I have decided to dispose of my power and freedom. Certainly, I can murder another individual, but I cannot free myself from the command because I cannot nullify the Other. The Other places a demand on me that I can violate but cannot escape.

With respect to the second issue, it is possible that one desires neither community nor communication, especially with certain others and under certain circumstances. Still, the experience of the face of the other precludes freedom from responsibility to the other. There is an ineluctable demand that one lay one's world before the other, though this does not entail being appropriated by the other or the other's projects. Levinas breaks from those who would give priority to the freedom of the subject.[79] Because it is the call of the other that individualizes the subject, the subject always already finds himself or herself responsible to the other.[80] It is, in fact, this responsibility to the other that is the condition for freeing one from one's self-concern, for making the choice of a response an issue, for bestowing the freedom to do what no one else can do because of one's unique position with respect to the other.[81] More pointedly, as Alphonso Lingis has noted, "In the face to face, the Other gives my freedom meaning because I am confronted with real choices between responsibility and obligation towards the Other, or hatred and violent repudiation. The Other invests me with genuine freedom, and will be the beneficiary or victim of how I decide to exercise it."[82] From a somewhat different angle, as Levinas suggests in *Time and the Other,* "a free being is already no longer free, because it is responsible for itself."[83]

Finally, with respect to the question of universality, Levinas maintains that the demand upon the self by the other is asymmetrical.[84] The experience of this demand is direct, immediate, and non-contingent. Ethics does not have its origins in the search for universal criteria by which to determine what one can demand of the other or what one owes to the other because the other is like oneself. I do not have a responsibility to the other because the other has a responsibility to me. Rather, I am actually the subject that I am because I am situated towards the other in a way that no one else is, and am therefore uniquely responsible to and for the other.[85] However, the dimension of universality is not simply left behind.

Because the face of the other places a demand upon each and every one of us, a demand that is actually constitutive of our subjectivity, it is in that sense universal. But this demand is addressed to each of us uniquely;[86] in addition, it is important to highlight that the universality of the demand does not presume a reduction of each individual to the same, being like everyone else by being called. Levinas protects against this by shifting from the language of the face of the other in *Totality and Infinity* to that of proximity in *Otherwise than Being,* emphasizing thereby a unique relationship that can only be spoken in the first person, the relation that I have with my neighbor.[87] I am always already implicated in this relation such that I can never distinguish myself from it to become a one like any other. The accent here is on the fact that it is I who am summoned; I am uniquely called in my proximity to the other. Yet, as Fabio Ciaramelli puts it, "Each and every person is called upon to become a 'me' in a relation of responsibility for the other. In this we can recognize the universal dimension necessary for an ethical discourse. . . . The claim made upon me by another, insofar as it is addressed not only to me but to everyone, is the basis of the universality of ethics."[88] More pointedly, in addition to one's relation to the other, Levinas highlights the relation of oneself and the other to the third party. By recognizing a third party, I recognize that the one before whom and to whom I am responsible is likewise responsible to and for another. Moreover, through the eyes of this third party, I come to recognize that I, too, am one for whom and to whom others are responsible. In this way, we are led from our individual, asymmetrical responsibilities to the other to the question of universal justice. But it must be emphasized that we commit a profound injustice if we forget that this question of universal justice is founded on an original experience of alterity. The question of universal justice does not spring from an insistence that like beings be treated the same, but from the recognition of one's responsibilities to a plurality of others.

It is precisely the individuation of the subject beyond ontological conceptualizations which is not only at play in all three of the issues just mentioned, but also at the heart of the contribution that Levinas can make to our consideration of how to engage the narrative discourses and silences of the other. We can begin to approach this by recalling that the face of the other calls one to place one's world before the other in language, to be responsible and responsive to the other, to make oneself vulnerable before the other.

This is at the same time a call to bring one's relation to the other to language.[89] It is important at this juncture to recognize that this move to language need not be viewed as a totalizing gesture. In *Totality and Infinity,* Levinas offers an account of language that resists reducing the function of language to suppressing the other, constituting a totality. His account is worth recording at some length:

> But to make the thinker a moment of thought is to limit the revealing function of language to its coherence, conveying the coherence of concepts. In this coherence the unique I of the thinker volatilizes. The function of language would amount to suppressing "the other," who breaks this coherence and is hence essentially irrational. A curious result: language would consist in suppressing the other, in making the other agree with the same! But in its expressive function language precisely maintains the other—to whom it is addressed, whom it calls upon or invokes. To be sure, language does not consist in invoking him as a being represented and thought. But this is why language institutes a relation irreducible to the subject-object relation: the *revelation* of the other. In this revelation only can language as a system of signs be constituted. The other called upon is not something represented, is not a given, is not a particular, through one side already open to generalization. Language, far from presupposing universality and generality, first makes them possible. Language presupposes interlocutors, a plurality. Their commerce is not a representation of the one to the other, nor a participation in universality, on the common plane of language . . .
>
> The relationship of language implies transcendence, radical separation, the strangeness of the interlocutors, the revelation of the other to me. In other words, language is spoken where community between the terms of the relationship is wanting, where the common plane is wanting or is yet to be constituted. It takes place in this transcendence. Discourse is thus the experience of something absolutely foreign, a *pure* "knowledge" or "experience," a *traumatism of astonishment.*[90]

But there is nonetheless a difficulty here that Levinas explores in *Otherwise than Being* through his distinction between the saying and the said.[91] The call of the other is immediate and individuates one prior to any articulation of one's identity, especially to any ontological account that would place one under a universal category. Language, the said, is the medium in which everything past, present, and future is drawn into a whole, made subject to presentation or representation. As Alphonso Lingis puts it, "it is logos that assembles into a system, that establishes togetherness, that institutes synchrony."[92] Through language, individuals are categorized under universal concepts, are brought into relation to one another, and meanings and values are set into a world that can be shared with another.[93] "Language does not exteriorize a representation preexisting in me: it puts in common a world hitherto mine. Language *effectuates* the entry of things into a new ether in which they receive a name and become concepts."[94] But what escapes the universality of the logos is precisely the saying itself, which is born of the absolutely unique, unrepresentable relation to the other that nonetheless founds the said. That is, the face to face relation in its immediacy and singularity escapes all attempts at articulation. Therefore, the saying, the response demanded by the face of the other, is betrayed in the said insofar as the said erases the saying in its pretensions to totality. It is the response to the call of the other of the sort, "Here I am," that effects one's exposure to the other, that gives voice to it, that testifies to alterity, that enables the Infinite to touch language. But when the move is made to thematize the Infinite, to bring it into language, to represent it, then the otherness of the other is covered over through the institution of a totality in which everything is reduced to the singularity of a system, and the saying is betrayed in the said.[95] As Tina Chanter puts it, "Words can signify intentions, but not without already losing sight of another meaning, not without already substituting the categories of being for the pre-original sensibility which signifies as the-one-for-the-other."[96]

However, the said cannot and should not be dismissed.[97] There are at least two considerations that come into play here. Firstly, it will be remembered that one is responsible to a third party before whom and to whom the other in the face to face relation is likewise responsible. This complex set of relations gives rise to a concern for universal justice that requires language in order to come to terms with the demand for justification. According to Lingis:

Little by little Levinas means to found reckonings, rationality, systemization, labor, the State and technology on the exigency for assembling and synchronization, which in turn is required by the exigency for justice. Even the very assembling of Being effected in all these registers is founded on this ethical exigency. "It is in view of justice that all things show themselves." It is as a text, a context and system, that things are synchronized in justice. And thus the articulated logos, the said, and the beings thus put forth and fixed in identities, and even the very movement of being that verbalizes them and promotes these identities—all this is founded on the exigency for justice, and the pluralism of ethical instances. Levinas gives an essentially human meaning to the exigency for justice. The simultaneity of the other and the third party is the original locus where this exigency for justice emerges. It is as this exigency, this purely ethical bond, that the three are compossible.[98]

Secondly, it seems to me that the demand that one place one's world before the other in language calls for a kind of double attention to the said. One must first attend to what one says, the story that one tells about oneself. This is not immediately apparent in Levinas. Levinas maintains that it is the face to face relation that individuates one, that makes this one the unique one responsible to the other. In the face to face relation, it is not the case that what one is comes to light, but rather that one is marked as an individual prior to every question about who one is: "The face is not a modality of quiddity, an answer to a question, but the correlative of what is prior to every question."[99] But to be responsible to the other is to place one's world before the other, and in doing this, one cannot be disembricated from his or her self-understanding, from what I take to be the implicit story or stories out of which one lives and acts. Paul Ricoeur points to this in *Time and Narrative* when he notes:

1. that in our everyday experiences, we tend to see the episodes of our lives not as mere chronological sequences, but as stories that are as yet untold;

2. that part of the psychoanalytic process is to draw together conflicting bits and pieces of lived stories into

"a narrative that will be both more supportable and
more intelligible," and that "the subject can take up
and hold as constitutive of his personal identity";[100]

3. that Wilhelm Schapp's example of the judge who attempts to understand a person's actions by untan-
gling the plots in which the subject was caught up
rightly captures the sense in which people experience
who they are in terms of the stories in which they find
themselves.[101]

To be responsible is to be responsible to the other as the one telling
a story, to be responsible for the telling, for the story, and for the possibilities for being in the world that the story makes available to the
other. It is in fact through the story, through what is said, that one
gives oneself to the other, makes oneself vulnerable as this very self,
and in the last analysis gives what one has to give. One therefore is
responsible for the story that one tells, or I should say lives, and it
is for this story that one is held to account by the other.

But, again drawing upon Ricoeur, a story functions to integrate
heterogeneous events into an intelligible whole, to configure past,
present, and future to form a single temporal whole, and ultimately,
through emplotment, to integrate all of the elements of a story, including character, situation, goals, interactions, etc., into a unified
whole.[102] It is this pretension to totality that poses the danger of
forgetting the saying in the said, forgetting the origins of the story,
especially as a response to the other, and turning the story into an
absolute, the only story, in which the self and the other are consumed. This pretension fuels agonistic approaches to discourse because it affords little room for thinking about differences except in
terms of eliminating those discourses which either fail or are less
successful in providing a compelling "total picture" than are their
competitors. It is the immediacy of the face to face relation that can
short-circuit this, opening one to the response of the other, a response that can be taken up as a gift making possible the transformation of the story, and thereby the transformation of oneself and
the other.[103] This does not imply a simple abandonment of the story
or a replacement of it by a story offered by the other. It may be apropos here to remember that one is responsible to a third party as
well. It does mean not taking a simple agonistic stance toward the

other's response, story, or silence, recognizing the contingency of one's own story.[104] But perhaps most difficult of all, it means becoming responsible for the other's short-circuiting of one's story. This last point is crucial but elusive. In *Otherwise than Being,* Levinas uses the term substitution to suggest the relation that one bears to the other, not as a subject in general, but as me, as this irreplaceable one who is responsible for the other, and who is therefore responsible for substituting myself for the other.[105] This responsibility extends beyond merely listening to the other or respecting the other, in particular respecting the other as like myself, to taking on responsibility for insuring the other's short-circuiting of my story, so that I may thereby be responsible to the other. Concretely, this means that I must create opportunities for the other to speak, attend to the ways in which discourses silence, and at times allow silence to overwhelm me.

But now it is necessary to turn to the second sense in which it is necessary to attend to the said. Because one is responsible to and for the other, one is responsible to and for the other's story. This should not be understood in terms of reciprocity. I am neither at liberty nor required to disrupt the story of the other or to respond to it because the other is at liberty or required to respond to mine. I am responsible to the other to disrupt and to respond to the other's story, or at times, to give voice to the other, or to respect the other's silence, regardless of whether or not the other takes responsibility for me. One might say that my responsibility extends to being the other for the other. It is in this way that one is truly responsible, for it is in this way that one does not merely attend to the said, but to the saying in the said of the other, even when (and especially?), as in the case of the victims of the Holocaust mentioned by Lyotard, that saying is a silence.

The Story: Narrative Response-ability

It is worth recalling at this juncture that this discussion of how we might approach our own narratives and those of others was undertaken out of a recognition that a certain danger attends narrative understanding. Given that we must come to terms with ourselves and our world narratively and that there are no logically binding criteria for deciding between the plurality of narratives that we might construct or adopt, we risk injustice by adopting a narrative which silences, or commits a violence against, the other by imposing a language that corrupts the testimony of the other. So long as the primary approach to narratives is agonistic, where the options are elimination of one of the competitors, amelioration, or the construction of some sort of field of cohabitation, it is difficult to see how to come to terms with this danger. But recognition that narratives are born out of responsibility to the other shifts the terrain in an important way. It requires that one be attuned to the otherness of the other in listening and speaking. This means that it is not enough to decide between narratives, or to reconcile them in some way, or even to multiply narratives endlessly. One must attend to them in the ways suggested in the preceding paragraph, as being responsible to and for the other, as requiring an attitude of listening to the said, to silences, and for the saying in the said. Again, in *Time and Narrative,* Paul Ricoeur makes the point that human beings require understanding, the grasping together of the whole that occurs in and through narrative, in order to act and function.[106] To the extent that narratives operate to this end, it is easy to see how multiple narratives relate agonistically, and how operating within a narrative context opens the possibility for injustice. But placing narratives in the context of a response to the face of the other works to short-circuit this by introducing into the heart of narrative formation the call for justice, the call to attend somehow to the saying in the said which is the origin of all sayings, but which cannot be said.[107]

Can more be said? Can responsibility to the other, and responsibility to and for one's own and the other's narratives, place demands and restrictions upon the content of the narratives themselves? It is interesting in this regard to note Levinas's claim that in the game of Being, everything possible is permitted, but that the pre-original saying demands a response of the one for the other.[108] All things possible are not permitted. Returning to the question at hand, I would answer it with a hesitant yes, remembering the virtually inevitable betrayal of the saying in the said, and therefore including the caveat that pursuing such a project reintroduces the danger being addressed here if it results in criteria used to silence the other's discourse, and if it itself issues forth in a monologue that ignores its own origins.

Rather than concentrate on generating such criteria, I should prefer to make some provisional suggestions about what it might mean, as someone who finds himself identified as gay in the discourses at play in mainstream American society, to assume responsibility with respect to the other. It is important to be careful here. Levinas locates individuation as deriving from the face to face relation, and emphasizes that the inquiry ". . . concerned with the *otherwise than being* catches sight, in the very hypostasis of a subject, its subjectification, of an ex-ception; a null-site on the other side of the negativity which is always speculatively recuperable, an *outside* of the absolute which can no longer be stated in terms of being."[109] It is therefore misguided to reduce consideration of responsibility in the face of the other to the responsibility that one has as gay, lesbian, a bus driver, etc. At the same time, with Paul Ricoeur, I maintain that one understands oneself, has an identity, through the quasi-narrative in which one finds oneself, and out of which one lives and acts.[110] Language, according to Ricoeur, is born out of an attempt to orient oneself to the situations in which one finds oneself as a being in the world, an attempt to orient oneself to the world. In language which is obviously reminiscent of Levinas, but which seems to veer significantly from him by not taking up the formulation "otherwise than being," Ricoeur says that language belongs to the order of the Same, while the world is its Other, and that language "knows itself as being *in* being in order to bear *on* being."[111] Importantly, according to Ricoeur, it is because of this orientation to the world which takes place in language that one has something to say, something to share with others.[112] In short, while responsibility to the other finds its origin in the "otherwise than being," meeting that responsibility means placing before the other a narrative bearing on what it means to be in the world born of one's experience. What I would like to consider is what it means to be responsible for this narrative. Before doing this, I want to emphasize that the attempt to chart a course between reading narratives as candidates for absolute accounts of reality or as mere semblances concocted by individuals, cultures, or civilizations—a course that finds in narratives the potential for opening up possibilities for being in the world that constitute invitations from one to the other, and that are born of one's responsibility to the other—is precisely what makes possible the shift in focus from judging between narratives to being concerned for one's own narrative. At the same time, lest there be any misunderstanding on this score, this concern does extend to the

other's narrative, a narrative for which one is responsible in a way
that is particularly acute when one considers that one stands before
a third party as well. Concretely, this means that even if one identifies oneself as an adult, gay male, one must take on responsibility
for the narratives out of which people act who place teenage gays
and lesbians at risk by creating hostile environments at schools
across the nation. Indeed, to say that "even" such a one must take
on such responsibility misses the point that such a one bears a responsibility that no one else can bear, even another such one.

So what is to be said about taking up this responsibility? Firstly,
it must be said that what needs to be said in response to this question simply cannot be said. It is a question addressed to a unique individual who holds a position that no one else can, and who therefore has a responsibility that can belong to no one else. Concretely,
I am not a poet, a politician, a policeman, an African-American, a
woman . . . I am not even the author of my story, but I have a story
to tell, and I must tell it in the way that I can tell it, not in the way
that either a storyteller or an illustrator, or someone who tells stories without narrating them would tell it. So, I am responsible for
telling my story in the way that I can tell it, and I am responsible
for the story that I tell. But as this chapter has suggested, this poses
a greater challenge than may at first appear. As Paul Ricoeur notes,
narratives involve an interplay of tradition and innovation. In an
account that draws heavily upon an analogy between emplotment
and Kant's notion of the productive imagination, Ricoeur maintains
that paradigms pertaining to formal features, genres, and types, i.e.,
individual works serving as models, have evolved through time.[113]
These paradigms act as rules for determining what counts as an acceptable narrative, as an acceptable way of configuring the world for
those finding themselves in a given tradition who must draw upon
this tradition to articulate the narratives informing their lives.
However, such paradigms constitute only one pole of tradition. The
other is innovation. "There is always a place for innovation inas-
much as what is produced, in the *poiesis* of the poem, is always, in
the last analysis, a singular work, this work."[114] The singularity of
each work does not permit simply abandoning all rules: "Innovation
remains a form of behavior governed by rules. The labor of imagination is not born from nothing. It is bound in one way or another
to the tradition's paradigms."[115] Yet, the possibilities for response to

the paradigms are vast and can engage all three levels of paradigm: form, genre, and type. "Rule-governed deformation constitutes the axis around which the various changes of paradigm through application are arranged. It is this variety of applications that confers a history on the productive imagination and that, in counterpoint to sedimentation, makes a narrative tradition possible."[116] To be responsible to the other with respect to the narrative out of which one speaks, acts, and lives means honoring the interplay of sedimented paradigms and innovation.

To adhere blindly to the paradigms is to collude in instituting the violences to which Lyotard called attention in his discussion of the *differend,* and in the betrayal of the saying in the said marked by Levinas. In this regard, for a person whose attraction is to someone of the same sex to embrace blindly the paradigm of young heterosexual love triumphing over adversity to achieve marriage as the privileged narrative, as the only truly worthy story to adopt for the living of one's life, is to fail in one's responsibilities. By simply perpetuating this narrative, one does not make available to the Other, other possibilities for being in the world born of one's experience. One fails in one's responsibilities to those others who embrace this narrative, to those excluded and marginalized by it, and to those in search of a new narrative because they cannot find in the old one a way to give voice to their experiences. Of course, one may have nothing more to give. But even here, one may have failed one's responsibilities, for *at least* to the extent to which a narrative fails one's experiences, one is responsible for going in search of a narrative. It is worth considering here Ricoeur's claim that events require the expectations established through narratives in order to be intelligible as events.[117] What counts as a turning point, a reversal, a decisive moment, is so determined in the context of the narrative, and part of the function of the narrative is, in turn, to make events intelligible. For someone designated as gay or lesbian, to be responsible to the other is to attend to the way in which sexual orientation is marked as an event in the narrative of the other and to attend to one's experience of this event for testimony with respect to the way in which it is inscribed.

Conversely, it will not do to attempt a narrative from nowhere, even if this were possible. To ignore the sediment of tradition, to refuse a voice to the other by not taking into account in one's own narrative the narrative paradigms informing the lives of others, or to do so in a way that reduces the other to an excluded or marginalized other, is to fail in one's responsibility to the other. It is to fail to recognize the other as one who has a story to tell, a story for which one is responsible in the telling and in what is told. In not taking the sediment of tradition into account, one becomes incomprehensible to the other, and must therefore either impose one's narrative or render oneself superfluous.

What it might mean to engage the narrative of the other in a responsible way will, of course, vary tremendously from situation to situation; there are no rules. In the face of a tirade or a monologue, perhaps what one must offer is a conscious silence, a refusal to engage, which calls the narrative to account. Several years ago, I delivered a paper at an NEH Summer Seminar after which one of the participants, an evangelical Christian theologian, engaged me in conversation and made the comment that, of course, living life as a gay person could never be satisfying because gays are unable to sustain long-term commitments. Given the limitations of time, circumstance, the history and commitments of my interlocutor, would it have been responsible to question the link made between a satisfying life and long-term commitments, or to have simply testified to my eleven-year monogamous relationship? I am not interested at the moment in answering this, but in suggesting that being responsible to the other means demanding of oneself the consideration of such a question. Further, it is important to recognize that this question should not be raised in order to determine the best strategy for co-opting the other, for winning an argument, or for paternalistically caring for the unenlightened. It should be raised from a recognition that I am responsible to the other, that this responsibility extends to listening to what the other is asking of me, and to responding as best I can given who I am, the experiences I have had, my capacity to be touched, to be vulnerable, to be transformed. In addition, it should be raised from the recognition of my responsibility to others whose lives might be touched by my response, such as the students of that evangelical theologian.

As I suggested earlier, this discussion of responsibility can in nowise be complete, nor does it even pretend to be a partial sketch. It is less than that. But I should like to interrupt it to observe that, while my professed interest is in the responsibilities of gays and lesbians, their consideration has really been only incidental to the overarching discussion. I make no apologies for this. There is no reason that this discussion should be relevant only to gays and lesbians, even if its impetus lies in a specific concern about them. However, there is an opportunity here to shift the discussion to more particular challenges faced by lesbians and gays given what has been said. A central motif in the writings of many working in queer theory has been that queers have traditionally constituted the other, the excluded, necessary for realizing the heterosexual narrative. It will be recalled that a central reason for undertaking the discussion of this entire section was to find an alternative to agonistic conceptualizations of narratives, conceptualizations that continually threaten marginalization and silence. What has resulted, admittedly, is a narrative that depends upon something other than logical necessity for adherence. But consideration of this must be left for another time. For the moment, it is more important to attend to the fact that what has emerged is an account of narratives that calls upon those who entertain them to be responsible for their narratives and for the narratives and silences of others, including the very ones who are marginalized, excluded, and silenced by them. To gays and lesbians who are marginalized and silenced by the predominant narratives at play in our culture, this may seem very agreeable. But as someone who identifies as gay, I feel a responsibility to call myself to something more, to a refusal simply to construct a competing narrative, or to ignore tradition, or to seal myself off from the demands of the other for an account, including others who identify as gay and lesbian, and I feel a responsibility to make these reflections available to gays and lesbians in case they desire to take them up.

But a peculiar difficulty arises at this juncture. Among the responsibilities that one has to the other that I have not mentioned is the responsibility not to strip them of the art of storytelling. Without this art, one can no longer engage the world to think and to act. Further, one is not only thereby freed from the constraints of one's narrative, but one is also rendered forcibly silent, unable to testify or to have anything about which to testify. According to Ricoeur, "We tell stories because in the last analysis human lives need and merit being narrated. This remark takes on its full force when we refer to the necessity to save the history of the defeated and the lost. The whole history of suffering cries out for vengeance and calls for narrative."[118] Why is there a peculiar challenge that lesbians and gays face at this juncture if they are to be responsible to the other? A difficulty indeed arises if there is something about narrative logic which itself conspires to silence or to marginalize gays and lesbians. If this is so, then gays and lesbians are placed in a peculiar situation. Incapable of but responsible for narrating their stories, they must preserve the capacity of the other to pursue the art of storytelling and at the same time find some way of addressing whatever peculiar difficulties narrative poses so that they might fulfill their responsibility to lay their world before the other. It is this rather bizarre difficulty that will be the focus of the final chapter.

Levinas: Epilogue/Supplement (?)

Before turning to that discussion, it seems fitting to attempt to exceed the boundaries of this text, which has so relied on Levinas, someone who finds in the said a betrayal of the saying. Appending an epilogue or supplement seems an appropriate way of marking the violence that occurs when one tries to make everything fit in. But does allowing what exceeds the body of the text, to overflow into an epilogue, result de facto in a marginalization, or banishment, or reinstatement of a hierarchical organizational structure? In any event, this text may itself mark a betrayal if it fails to consider whether Levinas's own philosophical work conspires in marginalizing and silencing the Other. In approaching this, I should like to examine the responses of people working in women's studies, most notably, Luce Irigaray, to Levinas's work, and to some of the concerns that surface in Derrida's landmark essay on Levinas, *Violence and Metaphysics*. In what follows, I want to suggest that Levinas's work does require a supplement, one that I marked out above when I said that the other must not be stripped of the art of storytelling, or more to the point, that the expression of the other calls me to my responsibility for enabling the other to speak in the first place.

The Feminine as the "Other": Irigaray

An initial brush with Levinas's discussion of the feminine can be off-putting to feminists because he casts the feminine in the position of "the Other," thereby, presumably, placing the male in the subject position. As noted in the preceding chapter, what it means to be a subject is realized in part through exclusion, through determination of what a subject is not and cannot be, the other. Traditionally in the West, to be a subject has been at least to be an adult male. To be a woman is to be the other, the non-subject, the other necessary to the constitution of the subject. To be a woman and a subject requires no longer being a woman "as such." It is to say the least, then, interesting that Levinas emphasizes an identification of the Other as feminine. What is at stake here is perhaps best expressed by Luce Irigaray:

> Is there otherness outside of sexual difference? The feminine, as it is characterized by Levinas, is not other than himself. Defined by "modesty," "a mode of being which consists in shunning the light" (see *Time and the Other*), the feminine appears as the underside or reverse side of man's aspiration toward the light, as its negative. The feminine is apprehended not in relation to itself, but from the point of view of man, and through a purely erotic strategy, a strategy moreover which is dictated by masculine pleasure *(juissance)*, even if man does not recognize to what limited degree his own erotic intentions and gestures are ethical.[119]

The discomfort that this might cause is not alleviated by Levinas's uncritical use of the word "feminine" to denote certain physical and emotional characteristics traditionally associated with women, such as receptivity, passivity, tenderness, thereby reinforcing an ideal of femininity that has not been determined by women and that is insensitive to the diversity among women. Finally, Levinas develops an account of maternity that relies heavily upon and supports a traditional, idealized version of motherhood in terms of responsibility and sacrifice.[120]

Perhaps the latter two concerns are mitigated somewhat by the fact that Levinas distances himself from any sort of crude biological determinism: "Perhaps, on the other hand, all these allusions to the ontological difference between the masculine and the feminine would appear less archaic if, instead of dividing humanity into two species (or into two genders), they would signify that the participation in the masculine and the feminine were the attribute of every human being."[121] However that might be, I intend to focus on the first area of concern, as it is most pressing to the current discussion.

If Levinas's account of the feminine simply turns the feminine into the other of the masculine, and more tellingly, into the other of the subject, then Levinas returns the feminine to an economy of the Same, thereby instituting a totalizing vision that does violence to the other as other. Does Levinas indeed do this? If the feminine is identified with the other, and if Levinas reinstitutes an economy of the same through his treatment of the feminine, does he undermine his entire project? A lot is at stake here.

Levinas's most sustained treatment of the feminine is in his discussion of the love relationship in Section IV of *Totality and Infinity*, "Beyond the Face." It is possible to approach this relationship by recalling Levinas's discussion of being enchained to one's being. In the life of enjoyment, one lives from the world, taking the other as something to be consumed, taking the other as for oneself. "Nourishment, as a means of invigoration, is the transmutation of the other into the same, which is in the essence of enjoyment: an energy that is other, recognized as other, recognized, we will see, as sustaining the very act that is directed upon it, becomes, in enjoyment, my own energy, my strength, me."[122] But inherent in enjoyment is the threat of insecurity. There is a continual reliance on food, shelter, and clothing, needs that might not be met. Through domestic life, through human sociality, this instability decreases, for in society it is possible to gain a distance between oneself and that which one needs to live. But it is precisely this that is necessary if one is to enter into the face to face relation, for as Tina Chanter notes, according to Levinas, "until the I has learnt to identify itself as an I and as distinct from that which it enjoys, there can be no bread to give the Other."[123] It is in the erotic relationship that there is a relation to the Other not as one who expresses needs or makes demands, but as one who is vulnerable, and whose vulnerability calls one beyond oneself. It is a relation beyond the face to face relation that makes an identification of the self in distinction from the Other possible, that makes the face to face relation, a relation that issues in discourse, possible.[124] At the same time, through the erotic relation, through the caress of the other, one comes to experience the weight of one's being, of one's life as the ongoing fulfillment of needs, by experiencing the desire to transcend oneself by going to the Other.

As already noted, Levinas characterizes the love relationship in *Totality and Infinity* as an encounter with the feminine other. What is the character of this encounter? Key to Levinas's description of the love relationship is his discussion of the movement of eros as one that occurs as both voluptuosity and as fecundity. I had occasion to discuss voluptuosity above. It will be recalled that the movement of love towards the other is not a movement towards an object to be grasped, nor is it a response occurring in the face to face relation. It is an experience of desire, understood not in terms of need, but in terms of transcendence, the desire to flee one's existence through one's love of the other, to abandon one's enjoyment through surrender to the tenderness and fragility of the other. In my first touch of a man's naked body, there is an intimacy beyond words, but an intimacy that escapes all attempts at reducing the other to myself, all attempts at canceling alterity, and certainly, all attempts at categorization or speech. Levinas describes this in terms of the caress, which "consists in seizing upon nothing, in soliciting what ceaselessly escapes its form toward a future never future enough, in soliciting what slips away as though it *were not yet*."[125] Again, Levinas describes the caress in terms of a movement aimed at the tender, understood "as a *way*, the way of remaining in the *no man's land* between being and not-yet-being. A way that does not even signal itself as a signification, that in no way shines forth, that is extinguished and swoons, essential frailty of the Beloved produced as vulnerable and as mortal."[126] Finally, in his description of voluptuosity, Levinas describes a relation to the other that is a discovery of the other as hidden.[127]

But Levinas insists that inherent in this movement as voluptuosity is a return to the self. As voluptuosity, love does not take the other as individual for its object, but rather takes delight in, enjoys, the voluptuosity of the other. In voluptuosity, love is "love of the love of the other."[128] Given that this relationship aspires to transcendence, to following a desire that leads one beyond oneself, but returns one to oneself in the pleasure deriving from the love of the love of the other, Levinas marks it as an equivocal relationship standing between desire and need.[129] More pointedly, because Levinas identifies the beloved with femininity, the feminine occupies the site of the equivocal. Levinas's description of the love relationship is a description of an encounter not between two subjects, but between a lover and a beloved, where the beloved is marked as feminine and as equivocal, leading the lover out of himself through desire and returning the lover to himself by becoming that which satisfies a need.

In Levinas's view, it is not through voluptuosity that one achieves transcendence, that one escapes the weight of being, but rather through fecundity. The relationship between lovers gives birth to a child, and thereby gives birth to a movement towards the infinite. Tellingly, Levinas describes the parental relationship in terms of the paternal relationship between father and son. In the son, the father transcends himself into the future. The father both discovers himself in the child, and discovers himself in the child as other, as a stranger. The erotic relation enables a movement towards transcendence, towards infinity by engendering a child who is at once the same as oneself and different from oneself, freed from one's being and consigned to a future of his own.[130]

If we examine this account of femininity in the love relationship, there are several things that can be said on Levinas's behalf regarding the issues raised by Irigaray and others.[131] Levinas's account of the feminine does not comprehend the feminine as a complement to the male subject, thereby reinstating an economy of the same in which a duality is produced that privileges the male. His insistence on the genuine alterity of the feminine is meant in part to preclude reading the male and female in terms of a binary constituting a larger whole, especially where the feminine is defined in relation to the male as one who is lacking. In "Judaism and the Feminine Element," Levinas comments, "If woman completes man, she does not complete him as a part completes another into a whole but rather, if one may put it thus, as two totalities complete one another."[132] More positively, as Tina Chanter notes, "For Levinas, the fact that woman is different from—other than—man does not imply her inferiority. Difference does not have to mean deference."[133] Hence, Levinas's insistence on the irreducibility of difference works against the erasure of the feminine and against the subjugation of women that is at play when women are at once identified with the feminine but told that they can be "just like men." Again, Chanter's remarks in this regard are to the point:

Once we understand Levinas's statement that alterity accomplishes itself as the feminine in the context of the priority Levinas gives to alterity, otherness and exteriority over the same, the one, totality, we cannot say Levinas is simply keeping the woman at home, in her traditional place. Rather, he has taken femininity seriously and not merely defused the feminine either by putting it down as "weak" or by dressing it up to make it acceptable but only on male terms. It is the world of male values, the universal rule of reason, the law of totality that Levinas is reacting against when he says "the virile judgement of history . . . of 'pure reason' is cruel" . . .[134]

Nevertheless, there is much that remains troubling here: Levinas's presumption of a heterosexual matrix, even granting that his uses of masculine and feminine are not to be reduced to designations of biological sex; his insistence on understanding fecundity in terms of the birth of the child; and his reduction of the parent/child relation to the father/son relation. But what is most troubling given the concerns of this chapter is that when it comes to the other as feminine, the disclosure of this other is the disclosure of the other as remaining hidden and therefore as silent, unable to speak. Can this work to reinforce the marginalization and silencing of those who occupy the site of the feminine? It is useful at this point to return to Irigaray. Though Irigaray does seem in the passage quoted above to see Levinas as returning the feminine to a patriarchal economy of sexual difference, she is in fact inspired in her own work by Levinas's attempt to depict a relationship between two persons in which they remain distinct.[135] The difficulty that she poses for Levinas is actually more complex. Levinas's identification of the lover with the masculine and of the feminine with the beloved does not allow for a feminine lover. In "The Fecundity of the Caress," Irigaray introduces the term, female lover (amante), to suggest that the love relationship is a relationship between two desiring beings, and further suggests that it is a relationship in which each bestows on the other life, prior to any procreation.[136] Through these moves, she reintroduces the notion of reciprocity in the love relationship, and she refuses a consignment of the feminine to what she calls the abyss, while the masculine lover achieves transcendence through his relation to the son. Irigaray is in accord with Levinas in his attempt to maintain the integrity and difference of the feminine. But she recognizes that even if Levinas seeks to articulate the feminine outside of the economy of patriarchal sexual difference, he may in fact be entrapped in it if he cannot make room for a distinctly feminine subject capable herself or himself of desire and transcendence. More concretely, it seems to me that one occupying the site of the feminine, whether it be a lesbian, a straight woman, a gay or heterosexual male, must have a voice not independently of occupying that site, but precisely as occupying that site.

This is very difficult terrain. There seems to be something true to the experience of the intimacy of the love relationship in Levinas's description of it as lying beyond speech and beyond the face of the other. But my point is that his use of the masculine/feminine dichotomy to articulate this relationship carries with it a recognition that certain people are culturally assigned to these positions. As such, they may be deprived of speech, marginalized, or allowed to speak only in so far as they are successful in distinguishing themselves from their identification as feminine. Indeed, in "At This Very Moment in This Work Here I Am," Jacques Derrida notes that Levinas in fact makes sexual difference secondary to the difference between human beings in essays such as "Et Dieu crea la femme," distinguishing between woman as woman and man as man on the one hand, and woman and man as human beings on the other.[137] It is by doing this that Levinas loses a key insight, that the face to face relation cannot abstract from the concrete other as one who is identified. Doing so leads to a silencing of the other. In this case, it threatens to reinstall male privilege, for as Derrida notes: "Once sexual difference is subordinated, it is always the case that the wholly other, who is *not yet marked,* is *already* found to be marked by masculinity . . ."[138] In order to respond to the other, one must be able to respond to the other who is socially identified as feminine, and more importantly, to the other actually occupying the site of the feminine as Levinas interprets it. But for this to occur the other must be permitted expression, and this is what Levinas's account does not so easily accomplish. So, while Levinas may seek not to reduce the feminine to the other as male, he nonetheless leaves the feminine and those occupying her place (has she a place?) without language, except for a receptive language of self-effacing welcome, a language which forces the other as feminine into hiding or makes him or her vulnerable to objectification, the object of need. Unless Levinas can create a space for men and women to be feminine subjects, he runs the risk of reinstalling a category, a designation that serves to exclude those assigned to it the ability to express themselves and to thereby solicit the other. Irigaray's attempts at giving voice to a female subject who is distinct from the male subject is promising in this regard, though one suspects that the use of "male/female," however metaphorical, deserves trouble. Does a third person necessarily break the intimacy of the erotic? In any event, Levinas's language of love, his use of masculine and feminine, does violence to lovers, for it forces them to speak their love in dichotomous terms that fail to do justice to the polyvalent positions that lovers occupy—their experiences of giving and receiving, and of receiving in giving—that constitute their lovemaking, and perhaps more to the point, their experiences of collapsing boundaries between self and other that occur in erotic ecstasy. Finally, it fails to give lovers a language to testify to the fecundity of their relations prior to any child, which Irigaray signals when she speaks of another energy, "neither that of the one nor that of the other, but an energy produced together and as a result of the irreducible difference of sex."[139]

In sum, it certainly seems that Levinas's work benefits through the supplement (or revolution?) suggested by Irigaray. But there is a challenge harbored by this entire discussion that is not so much a challenge to Levinas, as one that issues forth if one is convinced by him. In "Violence and Metaphysics," Derrida asks if the Other can make an appeal if the Other is not only recognized as other, but also as alter ego, and hence, in a certain way, the same as I.[140] Is this the difficulty into which Levinas falls in his discussion of the feminine, namely, that to the extent that he discusses it at all, he betrays it by reinstalling a discourse that threatens to turn the feminine into the male other, or abandons it by allowing it to sink into the abyss? It seems to me that if Levinas is truly to insist on the primacy of the ethical relation understood as the expression of the other calling for response, he must recognize that the response must be not only to the other as other, but also to the other as a full-blooded, particular other who is constituted in part through relation to a variety of identities. Otherwise, he does violence to the other by turning the other into an abstraction.

Language as Violence: Derrida

Derrida introduces a fundamental difficulty when he notes the inevitable tension between Levinas's claim that philosophical discourse, through its attempt to grasp the other by imposing conceptual frameworks, reduces the other to the same, and Levinas's
dependence on philosophical discourse.[141] Through reliance on
philosophical discourse, Levinas seems to be put in the position of
reducing the Other to the Same, thereby betraying his own intentions. This is not a critique of Levinas, but rather the statement of
an impasse inherent in his thinking. It is indeed a difficulty that
spurs Levinas's distinction between the Saying and the Said and his
reflections on the betrayal of the former in the latter in *Otherwise
than Being or Beyond Essence,* a work published after Derrida's
"The Violence of Metaphysics," which some consider to be a response
to Derrida.[142] Derrida, for his part, recognizes in Levinas's discussion of language a distinction between the intention of speech aimed
at responding to the Other (peace) and its historical emergence in
language that perpetrates violence on the Other by reducing the
Other to the Same. But while Levinas maintains the primacy of
peace at the origin of language,[143] Derrida maintains the primacy
of violence:

> How to think the other, if the other can be spoken only as ex-
> teriority and through exteriority, that is, nonalterity? And if
> the speech which must inaugurate and maintain absolute
> separation is by its essence rooted in space, which cannot
> conceive separation and absolute alterity? If, as Levinas
> says, only discourse (and not intuitive contact) is righteous,
> and if, moreover, all discourse essentially retains within it
> space and the Same—does this not mean that discourse is
> originally violent? And that the philosophical logos, the only
> one in which peace may be declared, is inhabited by war?[144]

Given Levinas's view that thought consists in speaking and is
thereby tied to language, that language is the medium of comprehension and conceptualization and is thereby reductive of alterity,
then Levinas is confronted with the problem, in Peter Atterton's
words, of "how to think and not think the Other, how to have any re-

lation to someone (peace) which is not mediated by reflection on her or him and *ex hypothesi* language (violence)."[145] Derrida claims that the only counterbalance to the violence of speech is another speech. He further claims that this violence extends even to silence, for only speech as violence can act to liberate one from the violence of oppressive silence.

The question that I should like to raise is why the prominence assigned the metaphor of violence. It is a metaphor that perhaps works in light of the totalizing pretensions of philosophical discourse, though perhaps not in terms of other pretensions of such discourse. By insisting on the primacy of peace in the origin of discourse, Levinas is complicit in privileging the metaphor of violence by prioritizing its complementary term. But by emphasizing speech not as an absolute origin, but as already a *response,* a dual response to the face of the other, a response to a command issued from that face always and never spoken before speech, the command, "Thou shalt not kill," and a response to the welcome of the Other, Levinas creates a space for thinking outside of the dynamics of peace and violence. He points to a double origin precluding the determination of origin. While it is true that the Said may betray the Saying, perpetrating violence, it is at least as possible that the Said may fail the Saying, falling short of the Saying. But this falling short only perpetrates violence when it claims not to be falling short, when it takes on the pretensions of a philosophical discourse that has succumbed to pride(?) This leaves open the possibility of a language that is dynamic, at play to allow what needs to be said to be continually on the way to being said, the language of symbol, myth, and most significantly for us at present, narrative. Atterton suggests in response to Derrida that he reads Levinas's assertion that "thought consists in speaking" too narrowly, quoting Levinas in *Totality and Infinity:* "Language thus conditions the functioning of *rational* thought: it gives a commencement in being."[146] Atterton draws from Levinas the suggestion "of a thought which isn't simply reducible to reason (or understanding), a language not simply reducible to language."[147] What I want to highlight here is the reference to a language that is not simply reducible to language. Atterton goes on to distinguish Levinas's characterization of language as an attitude of the Same towards the Other, in Levinas's words, "irreducible to an intention of thought, irreducible to consciousness of . . . language as an *attitude of mind.*"[148] This returns emphasis to the relation of language to speech as response to the Other. Inevitably, language will fail speaking, but this failure need not constitute a violence so long as it retains its responsiveness, and so long as those speaking are called, and call themselves, to responsibility, a theme that becomes increasingly prevalent in Derrida's own later work. In taking up this alternative to reading language as violence, it becomes possible to resist another violence, the violence that occurs when one dismisses the other by dismissing what the other has to say simply because this saying accomplishes itself as language. By appealing to the violence of language, one ironically violates the speaker by refusing to hear him or her, and by refusing, thereby to respond to her or his expression. In taking up this alternative to reading language as violence, one protects against a violence that Derrida takes very seriously: the violence involved in silencing the other.

In light of this discussion, I want to return in the final chapter to a consideration of narrative discourse, its potential for avoiding the totalizing tendencies of philosophical discourse, and its capacity, thereby, for offering a language that accommodates responsibility to and for the other. I have suggested that narrative, through its play between tradition and innovation, might constitute a form of discourse that can respond responsibly to the Other. But here we return to the basic problem: What if there is something inherently heterosexist regarding the very structure of narrative itself that thereby makes it complicit in a totalizing gesture?

CONFLICTING STORIES/CONTROLLING NARRATIVES

A solitude ten thousand fathoms deep
Sustains the bed on which we lie, my dear:
Although I love you, you will have to leap;
Our dream of safety has to disappear.

—W. H. Auden, "Leap Before You Look"

Stories That Marginalize Gays and Lesbians

Ellen *and* The Fifth Element

In the spring of 1997, I, along with thirty-four million other Americans, watched the "coming-out" episode of the television show, *Ellen*. Also, with many fewer Americans, I went to see the movie, *The Fifth Element*. The primary function of the plot in the latter was to create an excuse for some very interesting visual effects, but it is to the plot that I should like to attend for a moment.

The movie begins by establishing that there have been special stones stored on earth for centuries by a superior intelligence. When these stones, each representing one of the four elements, are brought into combination with a fifth element, they produce a force capable of overcoming the sheer evil that threatens to destroy the world at some point in the future. The movie shifts to that future date. The "fifth element" turns out to be a "perfect woman," who appears in this futuristic world as an alien who must enlist Bruce Willis, a "guy's guy" in search of such a perfect woman, to recover the stones and save the world from destruction. After many, many chase scenes, the stones are recovered and activated in the nick of time. All that remains is for the fifth element to take effect. But as the audience realizes before it even occurs, what this means is that Bruce Willis must "activate" the woman: he must tell her that he loves her and "take her." He does just that, and a beam of light shoots up from the couple into the heavens, destroying the evil globe and saving the world.

In *The Poetics,* Aristotle says, "A likely impossibility is always preferable to an unconvincing possibility."[1] This story certainly seems impossible, but it just as certainly seems likely. As already suggested, the plot is not provocative; it serves as a hanger on which to place special effects. The audience expects the result, and finds it satisfying, pleasing. Though the particular tale seems impossible, there is a story here that is told over and over again, the story of the heterosexual couple surmounting obstacles in order to join together, become whole, and produce offspring, thereby realizing a sort of immortality. In the case of the film, the couple's coupling destroys evil, saving the world for future generations. The movie is satisfying to the extent that we recognize in it a story that informs our culture, though it may not be satisfying from the standpoint of innovation, nor give much solace to those who are marginalized by it. (It is diverting to consider whether or not the story would have been satisfying had the couple been gay. I can only speculate that it would have been appreciated as a joke or a farce, while as preposterous as the actual ending was, it nonetheless somehow functioned as a believable, if ultimately too predictable, consummation.)

Turning now to *Ellen,* given the moral objections that many Americans voice regarding homosexuality and the proclivity of many to view it still as a "lifestyle choice," one would expect that the story of Ellen—"discovering" in her mid-thirties that she is "really" a lesbian, and that this has been at the heart of her inability to form meaningful romantic relationships—would be unsatisfying. Yet, even for those who disagree with the construal of homosexuality as "natural" for some people, and with the message that homosexuals are just as "good" as everybody else, the *story* can still work as a story. It makes sense. People can follow it. The story develops a set of causal relationships that signal the significant events of Ellen's life, and integrates them into a meaningful whole. In brief, Ellen's inability to realize her "true nature" has left her incapable of really connecting with others and leading a meaningful, fulfilling life. Through the intervention of someone like herself who has this self-knowledge, and who has reconciled her "true nature" to her public persona, Ellen is given the opportunity to come to terms with herself. In so doing, she brings the story to a close, giving the events of her life coherence and unity. The search for self—for the true self that can provide a core being in terms of which to situate the various and at times conflicting roles which people occupy in modern society, and the discovery of which is supposed necessary to personal fulfillment and social productivity—is a central plot line organizing many people's lives. *Ellen* draws on this to construct a story that is probable, recognizable, and hence satisfying, even if many consider it to be impossible.

But if we consider *The Fifth Element* and *Ellen* together for a moment, something rather disturbing emerges. We may suspect that, when Bruce takes home his "perfect woman" at the end of the day, their mundane lives may fall far short of the promises held by their coupling. But what does it really matter? They have produced the right ending: they have saved the world. In *Come As You Are*, Judith Roof offers the following quote from W. Somerset Maugham's *The Razor's Edge:*

> Death ends all things and so is the comprehensive conclusion of a story, but marriage finishes it very properly too and the sophisticated are ill-advised to sneer at what is by convention termed a happy ending. It is a sound instinct of the common people which persuades them that with this all that needs to be said is said. When male and female, after whatever vicissitudes you like, are at last brought together

they have fulfilled their biological function and interest passes to the generation that is to come. (P. 1)

Things are not so simple with Ellen. An important element in the overarching plot of *Ellen* is Ellen's sense of isolation. While she has friends, she ultimately plays a secondary role in their respective lives, their heterosexual relationships being central to them. She is alienated from her parents because she does not share their aspirations for her; she is not interested in being a wife and mother. She has no love interest. By coming out, a certain gap between herself and others is lessened, but hardly closed. She still plays a secondary role in the lives of her friends; she still fails to satisfy her parents' expectations; she still has no love interest. Of course, as we saw in the notably final second season, it is possible for her to form a love relationship and a network of relations operating as a substitute family. Still, it is difficult to see in any of these developments anything more, and perhaps something significantly less, than the creation of a simulacrum of the heterosexual couple and the American family.

At first blush, this might not seem so bad from the perspective of gays and lesbians. It enables them to develop coherent narratives that give their lives meaning and significance. In addition, keeping in mind the previous chapter, it facilitates a certain respect for the life-stories of others, for the narratives that inform their identities and express what they have found to be meaningful and significant in their lives. Finally, it shows promise for promoting social justice. However, three difficulties soon emerge. Firstly, in the pervasive heterosexual narrative, the homosexual has traditionally operated in the middle of the story as a choice that must be excluded or surmounted in order to consummate the heterosexual union. Queers may find it quaint when heterosexuals raise the objection that if homosexuality were permitted, there would be no more human race. Who would have the babies? That such logic is so prevalent leads one to wonder if Freud was right when he said that everyone has made an unconscious homosexual object choice.[2] Still, it eloquently articulates the formulation of homosexual identity as an excluded option on the way to heterosexual coupling. Within the confines of the story, the homosexual can at best imitate the heterosexual role, and in so doing, must reinforce the exclusion of homosexuality as an appropriate option if any other is available. Hence, while homosexuals' lives may be accorded meaning and significance, this comes at the price of supporting a narrative that renders their lives of secondary importance and marginal.[3] Meaning is realized in the sense of overarching coherence; significance is assumed in the context of the larger story; but the homosexual's story leads nowhere. Secondly, this placement of the homosexual left unchecked and unquestioned tempts heterosexuals to assume positions of privilege and to pursue egocentric courses that make them deaf to the call of the other. It fails heterosexuals by tempting them to an impoverished existence. This is not to suggest that one would be doing heterosexuals a service by dismissing or denigrating the stories or narrative types informing their lives, but that one does not fulfill one's responsibilities to them without somehow going further than simply reiterating their tales. Finally, by reinforcing not only the marginalization, but the potential threat of the homosexual, it threatens the pursuit of justice for those who are so positioned now and in the future.

If one is to fulfill one's responsibilities for engaging the heterosexual narrative, given the pervasiveness of the narrative itself and its capacity to absorb subplots such as Ellen's "coming out," might drastic measures be required? Might it be necessary to somehow explode not just the story, but to disrupt the very process of spinning narratives? Is such a thing even possible? As importantly, recalling the end of the preceding chapter, might this strategy likewise result in a failure to meet one's obligation to those identifying themselves as heterosexuals by silencing them, and by failing to attend to their stories as anything other than tactics that give privilege to what are socially constructed relations and identities by making the tactics appear natural, universal, and necessary?[4] To make some gestures towards addressing these two sets of issues, I should like to turn to Judith Roof's *Come As You Are: Sexuality and Narrative* to consider why so drastic a measure as disrupting the very process of spinning narratives might be thought necessary, and whether or not it is indeed so.

Narrative Structure and Heterosexist Logic: Roof

In *Come As You Are,* Roof makes the brilliant observation that what counts as a narrative, and I would add, as a satisfactory narrative, depends upon the story that one tells about what narratives are.

The question of the book is, "How do twentieth-century Western cultural understandings of narrative inflect, mold, determine, and/or reproduce understandings of sexuality and how do understandings of sexuality influence, define, configure, and/or reproduce narrative?"[5] Her thesis, in brief, is that contemporary Western ideas regarding narrative and sexuality are mutually imbricated, or form a marriage the offspring of which is a heterosexual, capitalist ideology.[6] Roof begins with the claim that we cannot do without narrative since it is the register in which we understand, define, reason, analyze, criticize, and recognize others. In addition, she cites approvingly Roland Barthes' claim that narrative is transculturally and transhistorically omnipresent.[7] Through narrative, we draw together into a unified, coherent whole the various elements composing our world and the temporal arch of our lives. If narrative understanding is central to human life, then an understanding of narrative that marries narrative to the modern Western heterosexual narrative as characterized in the discussion of *The Fifth Element* and *Ellen* would seem to make the marginalization of gays and lesbians virtually necessary. Or, as Roof would have it, "Something in the way we understand what a story is in the first place or something in the way narrative itself operates produces narrative's 'heterosexually friendly' shape. If this is the case, then simply changing people's minds through good public relations would not change the story all that much."[8] It would seem that the only hope for gays and lesbians would be a short-circuiting of the process of narrativization itself. But even if such short-circuiting were possible, sustaining it would seem unlikely, undesirable, and, if the general argument made thus far is in any sense appealing or compelling, irresponsible. But before facing this challenge, it is necessary to explore further Roof's claims regarding the mutual imbrication of contemporary Western ideas of narrative and sexuality.

Roof recognizes that the inability to leave narrative behind or to somehow step outside of narrative to come to terms with narrative and its ideology poses an insurmountable problem. In face of this obstacle, she proposes as a strategy examining the place where the suppositions of narrative presumably are most likely to surface, in narratives about narratives, particularly narratives that pose as theories of narrative, such as those of Levi-Strauss, Greimas, and Barthes.[9] It is not possible to follow her through her close readings of these figures to demonstrate how their accounts of narrative structure employ a heterosexual logic. I will rest content with a very general description of the narrative expectation under which we operate that will suggest its compatibility and usefulness to a heterosexual logic. In brief, we expect a narrative to move from a state of equilibrium to disequilibrium to the reestablishment of equilibrium. In addition, this movement involves the joinder of disparate elements into a coherent whole that is effected through causal relationships. There is a movement from beginning, through the middle, to the end that involves some sort of risk or conflict and that can be understood by an appeal to motives. Finally, a satisfying ending must in some sense be productive, productive of knowledge, or mastery, or victory.

Turning now to sexuality, Roof makes the interesting observation that Freud rejected the popular view that the development of sexuality follows a smooth course, being absent in childhood, becoming present in puberty, and reaching maturity in an irresistible attraction to the opposite sex, because it made for a bad story, "going from nothing to something without threat, risk, conflict, impediment, or motive."[10] Freud replaced this story with one that involved risk, the surmounting of conflict, driven by the reproductive imperative, a story that naturalized heterosexuality and produced homosexuality as perversion, as that which threatened to short-circuit the story, making it come to a premature end in the middle. Indeed, homosexuality operates in the middle of the story as the threat to be surmounted, as that which threatens either too much sameness or too much difference, thereby circumventing the joinder of those whose differences are complementary and can be brought into union to produce a satisfying ending.[11] The story that results is one that moves from equilibrium, undifferentiated union with the mother, through disequilibrium and the process of bypassing inappropriate joinders, to heterosexual union and reproduction. While we read this Freudian rendition of the (hetero)sexual narrative of sexual development as a response to narrative expectations, we could just as easily invert this and find in the heterosexual narrative a paradigm narrative shaping narrative expectations. A certain synergy is thereby created whereby the organizing structure of narrative finds its legitimation by appeal to a paradigmatic story, the timeless tale of heterosexual development and reproduction, while this timeless tale is rendered satisfying and natural through narrativization, leaving gays and lesbians out in the cold, or I should say, in the middle.

In the second half of her book, Roof looks at the extraordinary difficulty attaching to breaking this synergy, and examines and assesses various strategies employed by lesbian writers to accomplish this. She is particularly interested in exploring how our understandings of narrative might actually be shifted or transformed so that narrative and sexuality might be disimbricated, thereby creating the potential for developing alternatives to the heterosexual narrative whose logic requires the marginalization of gays and lesbians. But even as Roof explores the promise of the strategies employed by writers such as Wittig, Brossard, and Barnes for loosening what she calls the "hegemony of heteronarrative,"[12] she recognizes the following formidable difficulty:

> Wittig's and Brossard's narrative maneuvers may in some ways avoid the oppositional economy by which lesbian and even its concept are culturally located. Made more viable by a postmodern aegis, their writings offer disturbing narrative alternatives. But even if their strategies have dissimilar purposes and finally work differently than other postmodern projects, their surface similarity to the postmodern threatens to relegate lesbian narrative experiments to the same intellectualized and generally popularly rejected group of narratives as the literary postmodern. The potential association between a lesbian narrative praxis and one perceived as effete jeopardizes the possibilities for cultural change any lesbian practice might introduce. For this reason as well as for the many reasons that already inscribe a particular cultural pleasure in narrative structurally understood, Wittig's and Brossard's understanding of the power of narrative itself unfortunately promises little but very slow change.[13]

Immediately, one might reply that "slow" and "fast" are relative terms when it comes to cultural change, that what effects such change and how is not so easily read, and in any event, that the significance of these works need not be measured in terms of global or historical impact. These replies aside, what interests me is the extent to which Roof's reservations corroborate Ricoeur's insistence, discussed in the preceding chapter, that understanding a story requires understanding "both the language of 'doing something' and the cultural tradition from which proceeds the typology of plots."[14] While it would be false to see Brossard, Wittig, and Barnes as simply disengaged with the narrative tradition of the West, might their work transgress the interplay of sedimentation and innovation that Ricoeur finds necessary to a narrative which is followable? This should not be read as a critique; I am not interested in posing either/or alternatives. But it does create an occasion for wondering if there might be some way of engaging this narrative tradition in a way that could allow the possibility that there is more to be found there than just a tool in the service of heterosexual privilege. To make the reduction of conceiving narrative as nothing more than such a tool seems too precipitate. It commits a violence against the various narratives that have informed people's lives, and fails to recognize the potential of these narratives to say something worth hearing.

I agree with Roof that there is a hegemonic heterosexual narrative at work in Western culture today, and that "our understandings of narrative are both gendered and heterosexually inflected,"[15] such that our conception of narrative and the heterosexual narrative create a synergy that is hard to resist and that is oppressive to gays and lesbians. But I nonetheless wonder if it might not be possible to find a way to work within the interplay of sedimentation and innovation that Ricoeur characterizes as constituting a living tradition in order to fulfill our responsibilities to ourselves and to others to challenge and be challenged by the stories that we tell. This is not a very sexy course to follow. In light of the frustration caused by prevailing conditions, a more dramatic course might seem more pleasing. Yet it is possible that the less sexy approach might operate both to allow the stories of those whose experience has been shaped by the prevailing culture to be heard and to create a loosening, a receptivity to innovation, that could admit works, articulations whose ties to tradition are more tangential, and perhaps subversive. In addition, it might offer the advantage of more effectively generating the cultural change that Roof rightly seeks because it offers a route that is more accessible to most people living in the culture. But perhaps more to the point here is that both choosing strategies, operating in one venue, and not choosing strategies, not operating in one venue, carry risks to justice and to being able to be more than just. In light of this, perhaps what I should say is that what I have to offer, as the person I am given my history and experience, is a foray into the less sexy strategy, while realizing—thinking of Heidegger's account of guilt—that I am inevitably guilty for not having more to offer.

Reclaiming the Story: The Interplay of Sedimentation and Innovation

I would suggest as a first step on this course that we recognize in certain stories from our cultural past narratives that measure up to our sense of what counts as a satisfying story, but that work against privileging heterosexual relationships as those which are truly meaningful and productive. These are stories which roughly follow the narrative arch described above but which form patterns with respect to theme and content that are repeated in multiple individual tales, and which, with an important qualification that I shall have to make explicit below, do not work either to privilege heterosexuality or to marginalize gays and lesbians. Precisely because they draw upon our narrative expectations, these stories are followable, carry with them a sense of probability, cannot be simply dismissed as they engage the values and concerns at play in the hegemonic narrative, and open alternative possibilities for being in the world, even if they are initially thought to be impossible. The three stories that I should like to consider are, roughly speaking, the Christian story of salvation, the Platonic love story, and the story of modernity. To explore their potential, I want to look at the Christian story through the eyes of John Boswell's *Same-Sex Unions*, at the Platonic love story through Martha Nussbaum's *Love and the Individual*, and at the story of modernity through Henning Bech's *when men meet*.

The Christian Story of Salvation

Through a close reading of texts spanning from the Greco-Roman world through the medieval Christian one, Boswell shows that conceptions of love and marriage in the premodern world differed from those that are prevalent today. While Boswell makes it clear that it would be a mistake to paint a unified picture of Greco-Roman views regarding various sexual relationships and their cultural significance, he develops a number of interesting observations regarding these views and how they informed medieval Christian conceptions of the sorts of relationships that should obtain between members of the opposite sex and of the same sex. He notes that there were essentially four sorts of heterosexual couplings operative between 400 B.C.E. and 400 C.E. that were considered acceptable and that were paralleled by four sorts of homosexual couplings: use, concubinage, marriage, and romance.[16] Reading Boswell's account suggests that there were three recognized ends that were pursued in coupling, that these ends sometimes coincided, but sometimes were pursued, and pursued legitimately, in distinction from one another: sexual gratification, affectional gratification, and dynastic/economic gratification. That these could be pursued legitimately independently is nicely illustrated by Boswell's reference to Plautus's *Menaechmi* (1.2), in which "a husband asserts sharply to his wife that his love life is none of her business . . ."[17] Boswell presents much evidence to suggest that same-sex relationships between men in particular were in many cases highly valued, even more so than those between men and women. Of particular interest are his discussions of how such relationships were prized for promoting democracy and military valor[18] and for fulfilling a need for friendship that was not commonly considered possible in relationships between men and women given the generally inferior status assigned to women at the time.[19] In addition, it is interesting to note that dynastic/economic gratification was not realized solely through heterosexual marriage. Among the forms of same-sex union that were practiced was "collatoral adoption," in which a man adopted another as his brother, thereby securing for him a share in his property and wealth.[20] What is important to recognize from this is that the soil out of which Christianity grew provided ground for acknowledging relationships other than heterosexual marriage ending in procreation as valuable, worthy of pursuit.

What is interesting in shifting to early Christianity is the extent to which heterosexual relationships were actually devalued and seen as constituting a possible impediment to realizing the goals of the true Christian. Early Christians understood themselves as preparing for the end of this world and the coming of salvation. In this Christian story, the things of this world, including matters of the flesh, property, and wealth, were seen as possible distractions.

Celibacy, rather than heterosexual coupling, represented the ideal for the Christian enthusiast. Thus we find a narrative in which heterosexual union occupies the middle space as an option ideally to be avoided. "Although a thousand years after its inception Christianity would begin to emphasize the biological family as the central unit of Christian society (including, by a somewhat strained analogy, the Holy Family), for half of its existence it was most notable for its insistence on the preferability of lifestyles other than family units—priestly celibacy, voluntary virginity (even for the married), monastic community life."[21] Boswell references in this regard Paul's first letter to the Corinthians:

> But this I say, brethren, the time is short: it remaineth, that both they that have wives be as though they had none; and they that weep, as though they wept not; and they that rejoice, as though they rejoiced not; and they that buy, as though they possessed not; and they that use this world, as not abusing it; for the fashion of this world passeth away.[22]

Obviously, the same logic would militate against same-sex unions pursued for sexual gratification or for economic advantage. However, in early Christian practice, same-sex unions, and heterosexual ones, too, for that matter, did persist.

But what is most significant for our purposes is the use in early Christianity of certain same-sex relationships as models of lasting love, at times contrasting them with accounts of heterosexual passion as transitory.[23] In light of the fact that a variety of unions were recognized in the Greco-Roman world, it makes sense that early Christians would have seen the possibility for putting unions based upon mutual love and care, such as those forms of same-sex union that did not depend upon power differentials, to work in promoting spiritual growth and fidelity. Boswell cites as examples a number of same-sex couples who were paired as saints and held as models for the Christian community, including the earliest paired saints, Perpetua and Felicitas, who supported one another in their martyrdom,[24] and Serge and Bachus, two highly placed Roman soldiers who converted to Christianity and died for their faith. Boswell relates the following account of Serge's reaction to the death of Bachus, illustrating both the texture of Bachus's and Serge's relationship and how a same-sex relationship could be viewed within a Christian context as valuable and worthy of pursuit:

> Meanwhile the blessed Serge, deeply depressed and heart-sick over the loss of Bacchus, wept and cried out, "No longer, brother and fellow soldier, will we chant together, 'Behold, how good and how pleasant it is for brothers to abide in one-ness!' You have been unyoked from me . . . and gone up to heaven, leaving me alone on earth, now single . . . , without comfort."
>
> (2) After he uttered these things, the same night the blessed Bacchus suddenly appeared to him with a face as ra-diant as an angel's, wearing an officer's uniform, and spoke to him. "Why do you grieve and mourn, brother? If I have been taken from you in body, I am still with you in the bond of union, chanting and reciting, 'I will run the way of thy commandments, when thou shalt enlarge my heart.'
>
> Hurry then, yourself, brother, through beautiful and perfect confession to pursue and obtain me, when you have finished the course. For the crown of justice for me is to be with you."[25]

It should be clear that the narrative *structure* at work in the early Christian narrative is that which was the subject of Roof's critique. However, it would seem highly artificial to say that *this narrative* privileges heterosexuality and marginalizes gays and les-bians. More tellingly, it would probably be appropriate to say that it renders inconsequential the categories heterosexual, homosexual, gay, and lesbian. Key in this narrative is considering what sorts of relationships promote spiritual growth and fidelity. This shift is of central concern, and is one that will be repeated, though not in quite the same way, in the other two narratives to be considered. In brief, it might well be that the heterosexual/homosexual (gay and lesbian) distinction operates in a particular narrative such that being homo-sexual (gay/lesbian) is by definition being marginalized. The Chris-tian narrative may provide a place for same-sex couples whom we recognize as "homosexual," but who would not conceive of them-selves in those terms. Because it is a narrative which is followable and operates in the tradition that informs our lives, but at the same time dislocates our usual conceptual grid, it represents an opportunity for promoting new dialogues and occasions for listening, though I feel immediately compelled to register my recognition that as a narrative it affords numerous opportunities for marginalizing and silencing others and for promoting injustice by promoting a totalizing vision of reality that can encourage blind dogmatism. There are other concerns as well that are more relevant to the chapter as a whole that I shall take up in conjunction with a consideration of the two remaining narratives to be considered.

The Platonic Love Story

Turning now to what I called the "Platonic love story," it is necessary first to acknowledge that there is no such love story. In the *Symposium*, Plato allows a number of different stories to be told, to interact, and it is not so clear that one unified, coherent tale emerges. In addition, Martha Nussbaum makes a compelling case in *The Fragility of Goodness* for seeing love in the Platonic corpus as a complex affair. It is a passion that can lead one to attachment for the individual, making one vulnerable to loss. It can lead to neglect of the life of the mind and of one's obligations to the community. At the same time, it belongs in some sense to the divine.[26] If it is permissible to speak of a Platonic love story, it is through seeing that Plato's dealings with love occur in the context of the Platonic tale that privileges the life of the mind as leading one from the transitory things of this world to insight into the "really, real"—the eternal and true articulated through the theory of forms, a life taking the form of a journey leading beyond the forms, or ideas—to contemplation of that which lies beyond being: the good, the beautiful, the true. In *The Fragility of Goodness*, Nussbaum characterizes Diotima's speech as an attempt to reconcile love to the life of the mind, but at the price of refusing to recognize qualitative differences between individuals with respect to love. That is, Diotima's speech depends upon seeing beauty/goodness, the object of love, as qualitatively the same in all individuals who are loved. It is the goodness/beauty in individuals that is loved, and therefore, what is merely individual in them can be negated. In fact, love should lead precisely to such negation so that one can attain pure contemplation of the good, the beautiful, the true. Through a close reading of the argument, Nussbaum shows that it assumes, rather than demonstrates, that all beauty—spiritual, physical, etc.—is the same, and in fact that the argument can be read as an attempt not to show the homogeneity of beauty, but as an attempt to show the advantages for preferring that which is universal over that which is particular:

> Diotima connects the love of particulars with tension, excess, and servitude; the love of a qualitatively uniform "sea" with health, freedom, and creativity. The claim for the change of perception and belief involved in the ascent is not just that the new beliefs are *true*. In fact, questions of truth seem muted; the gap between "family-related" and "one and the same" indicates that the ascent may be playing fast and loose with the truth, at least as human beings experience it. (Whatever my brother *(adelphos)* is, he is certainly not one and the same with me.)[27]

But as Nussbaum notes, the *Symposium* does not end with Diotima's story. Alcibiades comes on the scene to tell the story of an individual love, his love for Socrates. In this story, Alcibiades claims to tell a truth that is not admitted in Diotima's account, the truth about love that one can only learn through an individual relationship, the truth of the value of love of the individual. To follow the path laid out by Diotima requires leaving the individual behind, but this is to sacrifice the beauty and goodness to be found in that which is unrepeatable. There is no one else like Socrates, and there never will be. In addition, there is a certain wisdom, a certain knowledge attaching to the individual relationship which is lost in the negation of the individual: "Certain truths about human experience can best be learned by living them in their particularity."[28] The *Symposium,* in Nussbaum's view, leaves us in a sort of double-bind:

> You have to refuse to see something, apparently, if you are going to act. I can choose to follow Socrates, ascending to the vision of the beautiful. But I cannot take the first step on that ladder as long as I *see* Alcibiades. I can follow Socrates only if, like Socrates, I am *persuaded* of the truth of Diotima's account; and Alcibiades robs me of this conviction. He

makes me feel that in embarking on the ascent I am sacrificing a beauty; so I can no longer view the ascent as embracing the whole of beauty. The minute I think "sacrifice"
and "denial," the ascent is no longer what it seemed, nor am
I, in it, self-sufficient. I can, on the other hand, follow Alcibiades, making my soul a body. I can live in *eros,* devoted to
its violence and its sudden light. But once I have listened to
Diotima, I see the loss of light that this course, too, entails—
the loss of rational planning, the loss, we might say, of the
chance to make a world. And then, if I am a rational being,
with a rational being's deep need for order and for understanding, I feel that I *must* be false to *eros,* for the world's
sake.[29]

In an extraordinary essay, "Love and the Individual: Romantic
Rightness and Platonic Aspiration," Nussbaum affords a way of negotiating between these two poles without negating one or the other.
Focusing on the experience of the loss of a beloved, Nussbaum refuses the strategy of negating the individuality of the beloved—
which reduces the loss to nothing, thus denying vulnerability—by
valuing the universal instantiated in the individual. At the same
time, she makes the case that there is something right in Plato's account of love, namely, that what one loves in the beloved is not just
the beloved's unique idiosyncrasies, or even the relationship, the
unique history, that one has forged with the beloved and that is unrepeatable. A genuine love must encompass the character and values of the beloved.[30] This is important because it affords a way of
continuing in the face of loss without negating it. Love does not and
need not die with the loss of the beloved; one can continue to live in
fidelity to that love by pursuing the values, concerns, and projects
that constituted much of the fabric of the relationship. It is important to recognize here that the individual relationship is not
negated or rendered superfluous in light of a universal value or
goal. The more appropriate correlate might be found in the *Phae-
drus,* where the beauty of the beloved nourishes the soul of the lover,
enabling the lover to approach the divine through the beloved,
rather than by negating the relationship.

Nussbaum's Platonic love story, like Boswell's Christian story of
salvation, follows the narrative arch that has been our primary con-

cern. Again like Boswell's story, it does not require the marginalization of gays and lesbians. In a sense, in fact, it does not differ from
Diotima's in this respect. Diotima maintains that love must give
rise to reproduction, for it is only through giving birth in beauty that
one can continue to participate in the good given one's mortality.[31]
Yet Diotima places mortal children as the least desirable of progeny,
preferring instead works that are more enduring, such as the poetry
of Homer, the laws of Solon, the noble deeds of great heroes giving
rise to fame.[32] Given such a hierarchy, there would be no reason to
prize heterosexual relationships over homosexual ones. But Nussbaum's story is still more interesting, for while Diotima's tale requires that love relationships between individuals be viewed at best
as stepping-stones to a higher love and at worst as impediments to
transcendence, Nussbaum's affords a way of valuing the intrinsic
worth of such relationships, whether they be between same-sex or
differently sexed partners. Although there are aspects of a relationship that endure, the loss of a beloved remains an irremediable
loss. Relationships cannot be reduced to mere means to ends.
Hence, same-sex and opposite-sex relationships can be viewed in this
frame-work as ones that are worthy of pursuit from both individual
and societal perspectives. We find here a story which is followable,
which engages the tradition, which conspires with the importance
and worth assigned by contemporary society to affective relationships, and, at the same time, which provides a way of visioning
and re-visioning contemporary notions of productivity such that
distinctions between gays/lesbians/bisexuals/straights/homosexu-
als/ heterosexuals/transexuals become irrelevant. In fact, as with
Boswell's Christian story, we find that this different narrative
works to resist the marginalization of gays and lesbians by weaving a tale in which same-sex partners whom we would recognize as
homosexual could have a place, but in which the concepts, gay and
lesbian, would lose any real significance. There is a pattern emerg-
ing here that I will examine after presenting the third story.

The Story of Modernity

It seems bizarre on the face of it to suggest that the story of modernity could be put in service to addressing critically the marginalization of gays and lesbians. The story of modernity that I have in mind

here is the story of man's attempts to master nature, often figured as female, through the use of scientific reason. It is a story that extends to the social environment as well. The chief value at play in the story is efficiency. The ultimate goal pursued is realization of human desires, which are themselves either naturally or socially generated, through ever increasing and efficient productivity. Drawing upon Michel Foucault, Roof argues that it is through the linking of sexuality and productivity in this modern narrative that the heterosexual family and reproductive sexuality are privileged:

> The self-perpetuating motives of bourgeois capitalism rope sexuality into the service of the family, which must restrict sexuality to a non-incestuous heterosexuality. Sexuality's position as licit or illicit depends upon its reproductive use; its intelligibility exists in relation to the reproductive narrative. In the narrative of familial productivity, homosexuality and other "perversions" quickly become the enemies of healthy reproduction; "sexual perverts" descend from afflicted ancestors and in turn produce degeneration. Thus, while healthy heterosexuality produces the proper reproductive narrative—like reproducing like and increasing (similar to well-invested capital)—perversions produce the wrong story: decrease, degenerescence, death. This perception is supported by the narrative logic of production, a logic of combination and increase, and both are susceptible to a deplorable short circuiting through pleasure (bad investment) and the seductive but unprofitable delay of perverse "detours." The bourgeois need for the correct narrative, one effected by proper heterosexual, reproductive sexuality and good timing, positions sexuality as itself causal: perverted sexuality is the cause of the bad narrative, familial disfunction, low production; and good, reproductive sexuality is the cause of profit, continuity, and increase.[33]

It certainly does seem odd to suggest that the modern narrative could be used precisely to undermine this privilege, but Henning Bech's *when men meet: Homosexuality and Modernity* enlists it to do just that with respect in particular to male homosexuality. Bech's treatment of the relationship between homosexuality and modernity is complex; it by no means paints a picture of modernity as purely and simply supporting the acceptability of homosexual relations. In an early chapter entitled "Absent Homosexuality," Bech makes the argument that homosexuality is pervasive in the culture, but pervasive as something that exists "primarily insofar as its existence can be denied."[34] For instance, homosexuality has been used to define what a "real man" is not.[35] In fact, one of the more interesting aspects of the first sections of Bech's book is that he traces a predominating concern by men in the culture regarding what counts as a "real man." This concern manifests itself in a preoccupation with what men can do with one another, with physical appearance, with what constitutes masculinity, a concern which opens the door for erotic interests, for making the move from being interested in being like other men to being with other men, an interest which fuels the peceived need to proscribe homosexual relations even as it secures a preoccupation with them.[36] Later in the book, Bech notes that what it means to be a man and to be a woman in modern societies has become problematic. There are fewer and fewer functions that belong solely to men or to women. At the same time, men and women are required to assume a gender. What becomes decisive, then, for a man to be a man is that he have a penis, and what proves his manhood is having sex with a woman. This—and the images of masculinity and femininity with which men and women are bombarded—is all they have to draw on to meet the imperative of being men and women. Given this, it is clear why homosexuality would be something that is prevalent, but prevalent as a cause for anxiety. Finally, Bech goes so far as to suggest that the homosexual has served modernity as the very incarnation of evil whose only rival has been the Jew. In fact, in Bech's view, the homosexual has surpassed the Jew for this dubious distinction, as is testified by the refusal to acknowledge that homosexuals were victims of the Nazi concentration camps.[37]

However, this is not the whole story. Bech argues that there are reasons for describing modern homosexuals as a species. This is because they share certain common conditions, such as societal disapproval, surveillance by the medical establishment, and the impact of urban life. Bech, of course, does not maintain that all homosexuals share the same experiences with regard to these conditions. Rather, he holds that the conditions are ones that they must address, ones leaving an imprint on their existence and inviting certain answers, and that in the course of history, the answers that have been supplied have in turn set new conditions and raised new questions common to homosexuals.[38] In general, one might say that what homosexuals share in common is that for them, modern existence must be a problem, and one that is uniquely informed by the role assigned them as perverse, deviant.

This has in fact provided homosexuals with a unique vantage from which to become conscious of the conditions informing modern life generally and for developing strategies for dealing with these conditions. For instance, a homosexual male more than any other man must concern himself with his masculinity, with what it means to be a man, since he is defined as "a *man who is not a man*."[39] In other words, the particular conditions that make traditional gender roles problematic are peculiarly problematic for homosexuals. In line with this, homosexuals are particularly sensitive to a certain distinction between depth and surface that is at play in modernity. Modernity affords a wide variety of roles that one can assume and poses the question of how one will relate to these roles. One might presume that the goal would be to assume a role that accords with the depth reality of who one is, but the homosexual feels the difficulty attaching to this more acutely than most because in stripping himself of the role that he was forced to play to assume his "true identity" as a homosexual, he finds that there is no role that will be completely satisfying, with which he can simply identify, since it is necessarily negative: "From the uneasiness of not being able to be himself as a homosexual, he progressed to the uneasiness of having to be himself as a homosexual. There was no self to be."[40] According to Bech, the homosexual experiences acutely what is actually a fundamental condition of modernity, the fact that one can never simply be at one with the role that one plays. While this can serve as a cause for anxiety, what homosexuals have found is that it is likewise an opportunity for freedom, the freedom to experiment, to play various roles, to change, to create.[41]

A final example of how the homosexual is uniquely situated to be conscious of the conditions of modernity and to develop strategies for negotiating them comes through a consideration of the homosexual's problematic relation to the family. For the homosexual, to either establish a traditional family or to attempt some imitation of it is not an automatic choice. Bech cites Edmund White's claim that what is distinctive regarding the homosexual lifestyle is that it separates sexuality, love, and friendship.[42] Paralleling this, modernity has given rise to urbanization, which has made possible a wide variety of relationships outside of the nuclear family. From considerations such as these, one of the conclusions that Bech draws is that homosexuals have had to face certain issues posed by modernity earlier than heterosexuals, but that heterosexuals will likewise have to face them, especially as gender roles become more and more problematic, as the artificiality of roles in general becomes more and more apparent, and most importantly, as the nuclear family dissolves.[43] At one point, Bech actually suggests that homosexuals could someday serve as an avant-garde for heterosexuals, pointing the way to creatively engaging the conditions established by modernity if it realizes its impetus toward, among other things, the dissolution of the traditional family.[44] But more importantly, in his final chapter, Bech argues that, as modernity develops so as to confront heterosexuals with the same challenges facing homosexuals regarding such matters as the negotiation of gender roles, of depth and surfaces, of the variety of affective relationships that modernity makes possible, it will become possible for same-sex relations to be conceived in terms of aesthetic choice. The difference between homosexual and heterosexual relations will become increasingly irrelevant or reduced to a matter of taste. There will be a shift in attitude such that the operative questions regarding same-sex relations will pertain to what one can learn from them, as opposed to how to prevent, eliminate, or protect oneself against them. Bech concludes:

> We haven't yet reached the point where the detachment of surfaces cannot, once again, turn into a longing for what is to be the genuine and authentic: Blut und Boden; Kinder, Kirche, Kuche, *a strong man*. But the more the surfaces are detached and become autonomous, the more the roles are severed from nature, the more accessible they become for staging and pleasure, the more they can be treated *as* surfaces, *as* roles, *as* images. In this way we can free ourselves from the narrow-minded pornography of psychoanalysis, or at any rate place it on a level with other things. We can transcend the "active/passive" phantasm, historically perhaps

the most common blockage of sexual relations between men, when masculinity no longer rises and falls with the cock and where it is placed when it has its orgasm, when the cock's place within masculinity can be determined and varied through the game. We can finally reach the point at which the dangerous in masculinity is maintained all the while it's suspended, the violence, the domination, the power display; it can stop when it isn't fun any more. Emancipation *from* masculinity *to* masculinity. It exists at the junction between culture and nature, where it can come into being and yet can let be.[45]

As with the narratives unfolded by Boswell and Nussbaum, this narrative not only fulfills our traditional narrative expectations, but also works, indeed more self-consciously than theirs, to explore ways in which narratives can be produced that do not insist upon the marginalization of gays and lesbians.

It should be clear that I am not advocating the adoption of any of these narratives. Each is dangerous in its own way. Rather, they are significant because they show that it is possible to enlist our narrative expectations, to operate through the interplay of sedimentation and innovation that is tradition; it is possible for those who have been marginalized to create a voice, a narrative that is followable, and hence that can be heard. In the last analysis, while the face of the other may call one to responsibility, the saying must be said if one is to hear, and one can only hear if what is said is comprehensible, able somehow to enlist the context, the tradition, informing the hearing. It is the responsibility of those who have ears to hear that they do all that is in their power to give voice to the other, without putting words in their mouths, and to attend to the silences when no voice is possible. It is the responsibility of those who speak and who remain silent to care for the ones who should be listening by making their voices and silences as available as possible.

Could this be the end of the story? If narratives threaten a certain violence through their tendency to totalize, to integrate all variables into a coherent whole, perhaps it would be a good idea to leave a loose end (or does the gesture itself really become coherent in the context of this narrative, and the preceding justification given for it? Oh, well . . .). I noted in the discussions of the Christian story of salvation and the Platonic love story, that even as same-sex relations and those who are labeled as gays, lesbians, homosexuals in our society are repositioned, the labels themselves disappear, and in a sense, so too do the identities. Indeed, this is the case with Bech's narrative as well. For according to Bech, if certain economic conditions are met and the modern narrative ends as he would like, it would at the same time result, in his words, in the disappearance of the homosexual, by which he means the homosexual's disappearance as the incarnation of evil, as that which one cannot be if one is to be "a real man." But these endings result again in a certain silencing of those who identify in a strong sense as gay and lesbian. There is a presumption in the preceding discussion, and perhaps in these alternative narratives, that assimilation is preferable to the pleasures and wisdom of marginalization. It is a presumption that might well be at the core of the entire project of attempting to operate in the interplay of sedimentation and innovation that constitutes tradition. This is a provocative thought, but as promised, I will stop in the middle of it, recognizing that endings are not always advised, but that one has an obligation to pose difficulties for one's own projects.

Closing, But Not Concluding

Even as this difficulty stands, it is well to remember that the tale that I have woven in this book does not root the impetus for speaking only or necessarily in the project of assimilation. Speaking can be a response to the face of the other, and one who speaks or refuses to do so can also be held accountable to the demand for justice that springs up through the recognition of multiple others. Concurrently, the power of language does not lie solely in what is spoken, but in the extent to which it can carry the creative potential of speaking along with it through its poetic dimension.

Indeed, Roof is right in exposing the dangers attending the collusion of heterosexist logic and narrative structure. But what I have found is that in some narratives crafted by those who are marginalized, the saying refuses to disappear in the said. Leslie Feinberg's *Stone Butch Blues,* for instance, follows the familiar narrative pattern of a coming-of-age story. But it is a tale that is possible, probable, and nonetheless incoherent from the standpoint of traditional heterosexist presumptions regarding gender and sexual identity. It is in this incoherence that both the power of saying is felt and the call to responsibility and justice are made. Jess is a stone dyke who from an early age simply *is* a he/she, a woman who is masculine but is not a transexual. Her/His sexual object choice is a femme, a category that would include lipstick lesbians, but would encompass both males and females. Jess even ends up in a relationship at the end of the book with a man who is a femme. But in being a he/she, Jess exposes the artificiality of gender constructions. S/he must continually produce her/himself as what s/he is. At another point, Jess reveals that being a he/she is not tantamount to being a dyke. S/he introduces us to two heterosexual he/shes. Finally, s/he challenges us to consider that it is not his/her identity as a lesbian, but her/his identity as a he/she that stands at the heart of what is commonly termed homophobia.

Even though this book incorporates in its conclusion a coupling of two people, can one really say that it simply reinforces heterosexual privilege because of its narrative structure? Can one really claim that this coupling between a butch and a femme, who happen to be biologically identified by society as female and male, and gender identified as male and female, leaves heterosexual privilege untouched because of the narrative logic it employs? To refuse to hear the saying in the said here seems to me to do violence to the text and to those who may well hear their voice in it. The text itself points to this by exploring the violence done to Jess and her friends through the rejection that they experience from lesbians who refuse to accept them because they reduce them to being nothing more than advocates of gender stereotypes.

Towards the end of the text, there is the following exchange between Jess and her friend, Frankie:

> "You know, Frankie," I whispered. "There's things that happened to me because I'm a he-she that I've never talked about to a femme. I've never had the words."
>
> Frankie nodded. "You don't need words with me, Jess, I know."
>
> I shook my head. "I do need words, Frankie. Sometimes I feel like I'm choking to death on what I'm feeling. I need to talk and I don't even know how. Femmes always tried to

teach me to talk about my feelings. But it was their words they used for their feelings. I needed my own words—butch words to talk about butch feelings."

Frankie pulled me tighter. Tears welled up in my eyes. "I feel like I'm clogged up with all this toxic goo, Frankie. But I can't hear my own voice say the words out loud. I've got no language."

Frankie opened her arms wider, took more of me in. I leaned my face against her arm. She offered me refuge, the way I held Butch Al years ago in a jail cell. "Frankie," I've got no words for feelings that are tearing me apart. What would our words sound like?" I looked up at the sky. "Like thunder, maybe."

Frankie pressed her lips against my hair. "Yeah, like thunder. And yearning."

I smiled and kissed the hard muscle of her biceps. "Yearning," I repeated softly. "What a beautiful word to hear a butch say out loud."[46]

To fail to hear the ways in which the content of this text works to undermine heterosexist logic even as it employs a very traditional narrative trope is to fail to recognize the saying in the said, to recognize the ways in which the text works poetically to refuse a reduction of the saying to the said. Ironically, all texts that are true to saying must fail saying. This text accomplishes it splendidly. Conversely, all listening which is to be true to the saying must refuse reducing the saying to the said. Dismissing *Stone Butch Blues* because of the narrative structure it employs constitutes one form of not being true to the saying.

In view of the tale that I have woven here and throughout the text, the question, then, for gays and lesbians who embrace these identities stands as follows: How can they meet their obligations to the other, whomever the other might be at a given time or in a given circumstance? In the discussion of one's responsibility to the other in the preceding chapter, I noted that it is not fitting for me to answer this question for all gays and lesbians. Each of us occupies a unique relation to the other and to others. Further, as I also suggested there, our response to the other must be a response to the concrete other, to the other realized through social and cultural identities but not reducible to them, to the other constituted through unique histories. It seems fitting, then, given the narrative that I have woven in this book, to close but not conclude by returning to this question of responsibility, initially broached in chapter 5, through an individual testimony, which can in principle be neither complete nor satisfactory, but can serve as a touchstone for gays and lesbians as they address the question of responsibility for themselves. I hope that it can be a touchstone for others as well, in particular, those caught in the currents of identity politics as they ebb and flow, such as bisexuals and transexuals who have felt both the liberatory potential and the exclusionary power pulsing in those currents.

At some point in my late twenties, I cannot remember when, it struck me that I was happy being gay. I was happy because I realized that, had I not found myself with this identity, I would never have viewed this society and its ideals critically; I would have lacked the imagination and the inclination, given the extent to which I was born to privilege. This happiness did not follow from a simple rejection of the culture and the possibilities for creating a meaningful life that it proposes, but from the new ways of seeing things that opened up through being placed in a seemingly impossible position. In short, my delight in being marginalized was tied inextricably to my quest for meaning.

From what has been said in chapters 1 and 3, I take it that the quest for meaning is tied to the quest for a narrative in terms of which one can make sense of who one is and what one is doing. It is the quest for a narrative that one takes to be true in the sense that it opens a possibility for being in the world that one deems worthy of pursuit. It is through narrative that one has an identity, which as we saw in chapter 3, is necessary for agency. Further, as I maintained in chapter 1, the articulation of some common vision, presumably through the articulation of a common narrative, is necessary if marginalized persons are to find ground for the establishment of a community capable of offering resistance to narratives that promote heterosexual privilege. Part of the pleasure that I found in assuming gay identity was the potential I sensed in it for re-visioning the predominant narrative underpinning American culture. Embracing gay and lesbian identity carries with it the potential for constituting a narrative of critical engagement of the culture, a narrative in which gays and lesbians are agents. But taking up this narrative responsibly means recognizing and facing the dangers of embracing totalizing visions, of silencing the other through the narratives that one accepts as one's own, of reducing the other to the same.

By being dislocated and by having privileged access to the postmodern intellectual landscape through my training as a philosopher, I have come to recognize that assuming an identity as gay or lesbian implies assuming responsibility for addressing the ways in which these identities are complicit in promoting a heterosexist logic that constrains those holding both the sites of privilege and of marginalization. It is important to note that these sites are not only held by straights and gays and lesbians respectively. I have come to recognize that assuming a gay or lesbian identity means taking responsibility for addressing the ways in which these identity categories serve to make invisible and silence those assuming identities such as bisexual and transexual. I have also come to recognize that it means taking responsibility for addressing the ways in which identity politics serves to dislocate and disempower people politically. At the same time, I have come to recognize that it implies assuming responsibility for speaking in a way that challenges the refusal of gay and lesbian identity. That is, it involves viewing with suspicion those narratives leading to the disappearance of gays and lesbians in the name of eliminating heterosexist privilege to the extent that such narratives reinstall gays and lesbians in an impossible position. To simply prohibit such identities is to create a new forbidden zone that works to perpetuate the very heterosexist logic that it seeks to undermine.

As a gay philosophy teacher in a Catholic college, I have wrestled with what it means to be responsible to the other through my engagements with students and members of the college community. Thus I return to that student whom we met in chapter 1. What are my responsibilities to him? What are my responsibilities to others in my interactions with him? I have chosen to speak myself as gay, to identify, be identified, and craft my identity as a gay man. I have the responsibilities of a gay man, but like all gays and lesbians, to reduce myself to this would be to perpetrate violence on myself. I have a responsibility to be other than this. I am this student's teacher; I am the teacher of others. I have the responsibility of challenging testimony even as I operate under the real power constraints at play in teacher/student relations. My student has chosen to speak and to speak differently than me. I have a responsibility to listen. I have a responsibility to respond. I have a responsibility to open myself to change. I have a responsibility to call my student to attend to his own words, to hear what he is testifying to in them, and to recognize that his testimony is to and before the other, a face that is not nameless or reducible to a name. I have a responsibility to craft curriculum recognizing that no curriculum is without its story. I have a responsibility to attend to the story that I tell, tell the best one that I can, and recognize the violences that I perpetrate if I take what is said as comprehensive. I have a responsibility to write this book, not in order to undermine my student's claims, but to respond to him. Of course, I recognize that he, and indeed most of my students, will never read it. But in writing it, I call myself to account as I teach, research, write, and design curriculum. As I proceed, I am responsible for recognizing that all articulations and actions must fall short. In the end, it is this falling short that provides the potential for recognizing in gay and lesbian articulations of identity their viability and value. This value lies in part in the fact that even as they provide a meaningful identity, they carry their own problematic character with them, thereby continually calling one to more, precluding the closure of an identity that claims to be adequate and that thereby does violence to the one so identified.

It is my responsibility to attend to and to testify to the speaking in what is said.

Chapter One

1. Frank Browning, *The Culture of Desire* (New York: Vintage Books, 1994), p. xii.

2. Cornel West, *Race Matters* (New York: Vintage Books, 1994), pp. 22–23.

3. Martin Heidegger, *Being and Time,* trans. John Macquarrie and Edward Robinson (San Francisco: Harper and Row, 1962), H. 59; the First and Second Introductions; I.1.9, 10, 12.

4. Hans-Georg Gadamer, *Truth and Method* (New York: Crossroad Publishing Company, 1988), third part, section 3; Joel C. Weinsheimer, *Gadamer's Hermeneutics* (New Haven: Yale University Press, 1985), p. 220.

5. Weinsheimer, *Gadamer's Hermeneutics,* p. 213.

6. Paul Ricoeur, *Freud and Philosophy: An Essay on Interpretation,* trans. Denis Savage (New Haven: Yale University Press, 1970), p. 528.

7. See Hubert L. Dreyfus and Paul Rabinow, *Michel Foucault: Beyond Structuralism and Hermeneutics* (Chicago: University of Chicago Press, 1982), viii, and David R. Hiley, "Foucault and the Analysis of Power: Political Engagement without Liberal Hope or Comfort," *Praxis International* 4:2 (July 1984), p. 198.

8. Michel Foucault, "Two Lectures," in *Power/Knowledge,* ed. Colin Gordon, trans. Colin Gordon, Leo Marshall, John Mepham, and Kate Soper (New York: Pantheon Books, 1980), p. 93. According to Foucault: "There can be no possible exercise of power without a certain economy of discourses of truth which operates through and on the basis of this association. We are subjected to the production of truth through power and we cannot exercise power except through the production of truth." See also, Michel Foucault, *Discipline and Punish*, trans. Alan Sheridan (New York: Vintage Books, 1979), pp. 27–28.

9. Compare, for instance, Foucault's "Two Lectures," p. 98 with Nietzsche's *Beyond Good and Evil*, trans. Walter Kaufmann (New York: Vintage Books, 1989), p. 24, and with Nietsche's *Thus Spoke Zarathustra: A Book for Everyone and No One,* trans. R. J. Hollingdale (Harmondsworth, England: Penguin Books, 1961), part IV, "Of the Higher Order of Man," sections 3, 5, 6.

10. Allan Megill, *Prophets of Extremity* (Berkeley: University of California Press, 1985), pp. 221–223.

11. The following passage from *The Archeology of Knowledge* is to the point:

> . . . I would like to show that "discourses," in the form in which they can be heard or read, are not, as one might expect, a mere intersection of things and words: an obscure web of things, and a manifest, visible, coloured chain of words; I would like to show that discourse is not a slender surface of contact, or confrontation, between a reality and a language *(langue),* the intrication of a lexicon and an experience; I would like to show with precise examples that in analysing discourses themselves, one sees the loosening of the embrace, apparently so tight, of words and things, and the emergence of a group of rules proper to discursive practice. These rules define not the dumb existence of a reality, nor the canonical use of a vocabulary, but the ordering of objects. "Words and things" is the entirely serious title of a problem; it is the ironic title of a work that modifies its own form, displaces its own data, and reveals, at the end of the day, a quite different task. A task that consists not—of no longer—treating discourses as groups of signs (signifying elements referring to contents or representations) but as practices that systematically form the objects of which they speak. Of course, discourses are composed of signs; but what they do is more than use these signs to designate things. It is this more that renders them irreducible to the language *(langue)* and to speech. It is this "more" that we must reveal and describe.

Michel Foucault, *The Archaeology of Knowledge*, trans. A. M. Sheridan Smith (New York: Pantheon Books, 1972), pp. 48–49.

12. According to Foucault, "If interpretation is a never-ending task, it is simply because there is nothing to interpret. There is nothing absolutely primary to interpret because, when all is said and done, underneath it all everything is already interpretation." From Michel Foucault's, "Nietzsche, Freud, Marx," in *Nietzsche* (Paris: Cahiers de Royaumont , 1967), p. 189. See also, Megill, *Prophets of Extremity*, p. 223.

13. Megill makes the following observation:

> Effectively, Foucault is viewing the world as if it were discourse. This is a significant move, for if the world is discursive, then the whole of the extant order is discursive; and if the whole of the extant order is discursive, then it is obviously susceptible to discursive attack. What prevents us from replacing the reigning discourse with another discourse? What privilege could the reigning discourse possibly have? For example, if the present mode of sexuality is a discursive product, why not discursively produce another mode of sexuality? In the reigning discourse, homosexuality is subjected to exclusion; Foucault's strategy is designed, among other things, to show the absolutely arbitrary character of that exclusion. The power of a subversive discourse is magnified by its defining as purely discursive that which it seeks to oppose. (*Prophets of Extremity*, p. 238)

14. Jana Sawicki, *Disciplining Foucault* (New York: Routledge, 1991), p. 20.

15. Ladelle McWhorter, "Foucault's Analytics of Power," in *Crises in Continental Philosophy*, ed. Arleen B. Dallery, Charles E. Scott, and P. Holley Roberts (Albany, N.Y.: State University of New York Press, 1990), pp. 122–126. See also, Sawicki, *Disciplining Foucault*, p. 53.

16. For a brief account of the distinction between the juridico-discursive model of power and the traditional model, see Sawicki, *Disciplining Foucault*, pp. 20–21. For an account of the central theses of a productive model of power such as the one put forward by Foucault, see McWhorter, "Focault's Analytics of Power," p. 120.

17. Foucault, "Two Lectures," p. 90.

18. Ibid., p. 95.

19. Ibid., p. 92. This same objection is developed more fully in Michel Foucault, *The History of Sexuality, Vol. I,* trans. Robert Hurley (New York: Vintage Books, 1980), pp. 88–89.

20. Michel Foucault, "Truth and Power," in *Power / Knowledge,* p. 119.

21. Foucault, *The History of Sexuality, Vol. I,* pp. 95, 97.

22. Foucault, "Two Lectures," p. 93. In *The History of Sexuality, Vol. I,* Foucault offers the following account of productive power:

> By power, I do not mean "Power" as a group of institutions and mechanisms that ensure the subservience of the citizens of a given state . . . The analysis, made in terms of power, must not assume that the sovereignty of the state, the form of the law, or the over-all unity of a domination are given at the outset; rather, these are only the terminal forms power takes. It seems to me that power must be understood in the first instance as the multiplicity of force relations immanent in the sphere in which they operate and which constitute their own organization; as the process which, through cease-less struggles and confrontations, transforms, strengthens, or reverses them; as the support which these force relations find in one another, thus forming a chain or a system or on the contrary, the disjunctions and contradictions which isolate them from one another; and lastly, as the strategies in which they take effect, whose general design or institutional crystallization is embodied in the state apparatus, in the formulation of the law, in the various social hegemonies. Power's condition of possibility, or in any case the viewpoint which permits one to understand its exercise, even in its more "peripheral" effects, and which also makes it possible to use its mechanisms as a grid of intelligibility of the social order, must not be sought in the primary existence of a central point, in a unique source of sovereignty from which secondary and descendent forms would emanate; it is the moving substrate of force relations which, by virtue of their inequality, constantly engender states of power, but the latter are always local and unstable. The omnipresence of power: not because it has the privilege of consolidating everything under its invincible unity, but because it is produced from one moment to the next, at every point, or rather in every relation from one point to another. Power is everywhere; not because it embraces everything, but because it comes from everywhere . . . one needs to be nominalistic, no doubt: power is not an institution, and not a structure; nei-

ther is it a certain strength we are endowed with; it is the name that one attributes to a complex strategical situation in a particular society. (Pp. 92–93)

23. The relation between power, knowledge and discourse is highlighted by Foucault in his discussion of the constitution of "sexuality" as an area of concern. See Foucault, *The History of Sexuality, Vol. I*, pp. 98, 100, 102, 105–106.

24. For an illuminating and tightly developed discussion of Foucault's account of the constructed character of sex, see Judith Butler, *Gender Trouble* (New York: Routledge, 1990), pp. 94–95.

25. Foucault, *The History of Sexuality, Vol. I,* p. 25.

26. Ibid., p. 105.

27. Ibid., pp. 42–43.

28. Ibid., pp. 23–25.

29. Ibid., pp. 9–11.

30. Ibid., pp. 33–34.

31. Ibid., pp. 12–13.

32. This equation of the proliferation of discourse on sexuality with the proliferation of sexuality, an example of which can be found on pp. 37–38 of *The History of Sexuality, Vol. I,* itself is open to some criticism, as Allan Megill suggests in *Prophets of Extremity,* p. 237.

33. Foucault, *The History of Sexuality, Vol. I*, pp. 23–24.

34. Ibid., p. 60.

35. For a discussion of the deployment of sexuality in the family and how it interacts with traditional relations of alliance, see Foucault, *The History of Sexuality, Vol. I,* pp. 108–111, 145–146.

36. Foucault, *The History of Sexuality, Vol. I,* p. 62.

37. Sawicki, *Disciplining Foucault,* p. 22.

38. Megill, *Prophets of Extremity,* pp. 197–198.

39. Butler, *Gender Trouble,* p. 2. The following passage from *Gender Trouble* is also instructive regarding this claim:

> Foucault explicitly takes a stand against emancipator or liberationist models of sexuality in *The History of Sexuality* because they subscribe to a juridical model that does not acknowledge the historical production of "sex" as a category, that is, as a mystifying "effect" of power relations. His ostensible problem with feminism seems also to emerge here: Where feminist analysis takes the category of sex and, thus, according to him, the binary restriction on gender, as its point of departure, Foucault understands his own project to be an inquiry into how the category of "sex" and sexual difference are constructed within discourse as necessary features of bodily identity. The juridical model of law which structures the feminist emancipator model presumes, in his view, that the subject of emancipation, "the sexed body," in some sense, is not itself in need of a critical deconstruction . . . (Pp. 95–96)

40. Butler, *Gender Trouble,* p. 148. See also, p. 2.

41. Ibid., p. 3.

42. Ibid., pp. 5, 16–17, 30–31, 33–34, 128, 137–138, 144–147.

In opposition to Wittig, Butler emphasizes that one cannot appeal to a reality outside of the system of significations which power deploys in order to subvert the productions of power. It is this recognition that engenders her interest in the potential uses of parody to redeploy power:

> For power to be withdrawn, power itself would have to be understood as the retractable operation of volition; indeed, the heterosexual contract would be understood to be sustained through a series of choices, just as the social contract in Locke and Rousseau is understood to presuppose the rational choice or deliberate will of those it is said to govern. If power is not reduced to volition, however, and the classical liberal and existential model of freedom is refused, then power relations can be understood, as I think they ought to be, as constraining and constituting the very possibilities of volition. Hence, power can be neither withdrawn nor refused, but only redeployed. Indeed, in my view, the normative focus for gay and lesbian practice ought to be on the subversive and parodic redeployment of power rather than on the impossible fantasy of its full-scale transcendence. (*Gender Trouble,* p. 124)

43. Ibid., p. 17.

44. Ibid., p. 20.

45. See, for instance, *Gender Trouble,* p. 37.

46. Butler in fact critiques even Foucault's treatment of sexuality as harboring what she calls an "emancipatory ideal" (*Gender Trouble,* pp. 93–94).

47. Ibid., p. 15.

48. bel hooks, *Feminist Theory from Margin to Center* (Boston: South End Press, 1984), p. 97.

49. Eve Kosofsky Sedgwick, *Epistemology of the Closet* (Berkeley: University of California Press, 1990), p. 42.

50. Ibid., pp. 43–44.

51. Michel Foucault, "The Subject and Power," afterword to *Michel Foucault: Beyond Structuralism and Hermeneutics,* pp. 231–232.

52. Butler, *Gender Trouble,* p. 141.

53. Sawicki, *Disciplining Foucault,* p. 32.

54. Ibid., p. 96.

55. Ibid., p. 97.

56. The following passage from Megill's *Prophets of Extremity* is instructive: "Foucault tells us that there is no such thing as a "genuine" rhetoric, that all rhetorics are subject to the play of power, that all rhetorics are coercive. But he does so in a rhetoric that by this very argument cannot be genuine. Why, then, should we believe Foucault? All Cretans are liars. Or are they?" (p. 251).

57. Judith Butler, *Bodies That Matter* (New York: Routledge, 1993), p. x.

58. Ibid., p. xi.

59. Ibid., p. 8.

60. Michel Foucault, "The Ethics of the Concern for Self as a Practice of Freedom," in *Foucault Live: Collected Interviews, 1961–1984,* ed. Sylvere

Lotringer, trans. Lysa Hochroth and John Johnston (New York: Semiotext(e), 1996), p. 433.

61. Ibid., pp. 433–444.

62. Michel Foucault, "Sexuality and Solitude," in *On Signs: A Semiotics Reader,* ed. M. Blonsky (Oxford: Basil Blackwell, 1985), p. 367. There has been discussion about the extent to which Foucault's later work contrasts with his earlier work. While maintaining that there is a continuity, Lois McNay argues that there is a significant shift from Foucault's earlier focus on "docile bodies," to his discussion of the self in later works as having the capacity for agency and self-determination. Others, such as Moya Lloyd, suggest that the later work is meant to complement the earlier. To see what is at stake in this, see Lois McNay, *Foucault and Feminism* (Boston: Northeastern University Press, 1992), p. 74, and Moya Lloyd, "A Feminist Mapping of Foucauldian Politics," in *Feminist Interpretations of Michel Foucault,* ed. Susan J. Hekman (University Park: Pennsylvania State University Press), 1996, pp. 249–250.

63. Michel Foucault, *The History of Sexuality, Vol. II: The Use of Pleasure,* trans. Robert Hurley (New York: Vintage Books, 1986), pp. 5–6.

64. Foucault, *The Use of Pleasure*, p. 11.

65. Ibid., p. 12.

66. Foucault, "Ethics of the Concern for Self," p. 436.

67. Michel Foucault, *The History of Sexuality, Vol. III: The Care of the Self,* trans. Robert Hurley (New York: Vintage Books, 1988), pp. 44–45.

68. Foucault, *The Use of Pleasure,* p. 24.

69. Ibid., pp. 26–27. See also McNay, *Foucault and Feminism,* p. 59.

70. For a discussion of this interpretation of Foucault's later work, see Nancy Fraser, "Michel Foucault: A 'Young Conservative'?" in *Feminist Interpretations of Michel Foucault,* pp. 30–31.

71. Ladelle McWhorter, "Asceticism/Askesis: Foucault's Thinking in Historical Subjectivity," in *Ethics and Danger*, ed. Arleen Dallery and Charles Scott (Albany, N.Y.: State University of New York Press, 1992), p. 251.

72. Lloyd, "A Feminist Mapping of Foucauldian Politics," p. 243

73. Michel Foucault, "What Is Enlightenment," p. 46, as quoted in Lloyd, "A Feminist Mapping of Foucauldian Politics," p. 244.

74. Foucault, "What Is Enlightenment?" and "Practicing Criticism," in *Michel Foucault: Politics, Philosophy, Culture: Interviews and Other Writings, 1977–1984,* ed. Lawrence D. Kritzman, trans. Alan Sheridan et al. (London: Routledge, 1988). See also, Lloyd, "A Feminist Mapping of Foucauldian Politics," pp. 244–245.

75. Foucault, "Ethics of the Concern for Self," p. 433.

76. Lloyd, "A Feminist Mapping of Foucauldian Politics," p. 246.

77. Audre Lourde, "Age, Race, Class, and Sex: Women Redefining Difference," in *Ethics: A Feminist Reader,* ed. Elizabeth Frazer, Jennifer Hornsby, and Sabina Lovibond (Oxford: Blackwell, 1992), pp. 212–222.

78. Foucault, "The Subject and Power," p. 212.

79. See, for instance, McNay, *Foucault and Feminism,* pp. 8, 141.

80. For a discussion of Foucault's view of history and its implications for hermeneutics, see McNay, *Foucault and Feminism,* pp. 14–15.

81. Butler, *Gender Trouble,* p. 141.

82. Martin Heidegger, "The Origin of the Work of Art," in *Poetry, Language, Thought,* trans. Albert Hofstadter (New York: Harper and Row, 1971), p. 17.

83. Ibid., pp. 17–18.

84. Ibid., p. 36.

85. Ibid., p. 42.

86. The following passage from "The Origin of the Work of Art" aptly illustrates Heidegger's position with respect to the ontogenetic character of art:

> In the work, the happening of truth is at work and, indeed, at work according to the manner of a work. Accordingly the nature of art was defined to begin with as the setting-into-work of truth. Yet this definition is intentionally ambiguous. It says on the one hand: art is the fixing in place of a self-establishing truth in the figure. This happens in creation as the bringing forth of the unconcealedness of what is. Setting-into-work, however, also means: the bringing of work-being into movement and happening. This happens as preservation. Thus art is: the creative preserving of truth in the work.

> *Art then is the becoming and happening of truth.* Does truth,
> then, arise out of nothing? It does indeed if by nothing is
> meant the mere not of that which is, and if we here think of
> that which *is* as an object present in the ordinary way, which
> thereafter comes to light and is challenged by the existence
> of the work as only presumptively a true being. Truth is
> never gathered from objects that are present and ordinary.
> Rather, the opening up of the open, and the clearing of what
> is, happens only as the openness is projected, sketched out,
> that makes its advent in thrownness. (P. 71)

For further discussion of the claim that Heidegger's view of art is "ontological," and ultimately, "ontogenetic," see Allan Megill, *Prophets of Extremity,* pp. 157–162.

87. Heidegger, "The Origin of the Work of Art," p. 8.

88. Weinsheimer, *Gadamer's Hermeneutics,* pp. 85–86, 96.

89. Paul Ricoeur, *Main Trends in Philosophy* (New York: Holmes and
Meier, 1979), p. 265. Also of interest is Ricoeur's discussion of the referential character of metaphor as consisting in its capacity to redescribe reality.
See Paul Ricoeur, *The Rule of Metaphor,* trans. Robert Czerny, Kathleen
McLaughlin, and John Costello, S. J. (Toronto: University of Toronto Press,
1975); Paul Ricoeur, "Creativity in Language," *Philosophy Today* 17 (summer 1973), pp. 97–111; John Van Den Hengel, *The Home of Meaning,* (Washington: University Press of America, 1982), pp. 80–81.

90. Weinsheimer, *Gadamer's Hermeneutics,* pp. 99–100.

91. It is important, however, to recognize that this bestowal of Being
does not provide the grounds for claims to legitimacy based upon an appeal
to knowledge of the absolute truth. This becomes clear if we attend closely to
Heidegger's account of the unconcealment of Being. To describe this unconcealment, Heidegger uses the metaphor of a clearing. Being constitutes the
clearing in which the particular beings that we encounter stand out. This
standing out of beings within Being entails disclosure and concealment:

> Thanks to this clearing, beings are unconcealed in certain
> changing degrees. And yet a being can be *concealed*, too, only
> within the sphere of what is lighted. Each being we en-
> counter and which encounters us keeps to this curious oppo-
> sition of presence in that it always withholds itself at the
> same time in a concealedness. The clearing in which beings
> stand is in itself at the same time concealment. ("The Origin
> of the Work of Art," p. 53)

Beings can conceal themselves through refusal to be unconcealed and through dissemblance. As beings who stand in Being, we can never make claims to definitive knowledge. (See "The Origin of the Work of Art," pp. 53–54)

92. Paul Ricoeur, *Interpretation Theory: Discourse and the Surplus of Meaning* (Fort Worth: Texas Christian University Press, 1976), p. 21.

93. Paul Ricoeur, *Hermeneutics and the Human Sciences,* ed. and trans. John B. Thompson (Cambridge: Cambridge University Press, 1981), pp. 147–148. See also Patrick Bourgeois, *Extension of Ricoeur's Hermeneutic* (Hague: Martinus Nijhoff, 1975), pp. 118–125; Van Den Hengel, *The Home of Meaning,* p. 24; Mary Gerhart, "The Extent and Limits of Metaphor: Reply to Gary Madison," *Philosophy Today* 11 (spring 1977), p. 432.

94. Ricoeur, *Interpretation Theory,* p. 36. See also, Paul Ricoeur, "What Is a Text? Explanation and Interpretation," in *Mythic-Symbolic Language and Philosophical Anthropology*, by David Rasmussen (Hague: Martinus Nijhoff, 1971), p. 138.

95. Paul Ricoeur, *The Symbolism of Evil*, trans. Emerson Buchanan (New York: Harper and Row, 1969), pp. 13–14, 21–22.

96. Ibid., p. 355.

97. Paul Ricoeur, *History and Truth*, trans. Charles A. Kelbley (Evanston, IL: Northwestern University Press, 1965), pp. 307, 327.

98. Weinsheimer, *Gadamer's Hermeneutics*, p. 94.

99. Ibid., p. 25.

100. Gadamer, *Truth and Method*, p. 269.

101. Michel Foucault, *The Birth of the Clinic*, trans. A. M. Sheridan Smith (New York: Vintage/Random House, 1975), pp. xvi–xvii.

Chapter Two

1. Hans-Georg Gadamer, *Truth and Method* (New York: Crossroad Publishing Company, 1988), p. 421.

2. Paul Ricoeur, *Lectures on Ideology and Utopia,* ed. George H. Taylor (New York: Columbia University Press, 1986), p. 261.

3. Paul Ricoeur, *The Symbolism of Evil,* trans. Emerson Buchanan (Boston: Beacon Press, 1967), pp. 161–162.

4. Ibid., p. 166.

5. A helpful article in this regard: Stuart C. Hackett, "Philosophical Objectivity and Existential Involvement in the Methodology of Paul Ricoeur," *International Philosophical Quarterly* 9 (March 1969): 20–21.

6. Vatican's Congregation for the Doctrine of the Faith, "Pastoral Care of Homosexual Persons," *Origins* (November 1986).

7. Charles Curran, "Homosexuality and Moral Theology: Methodological and Substantive Considerations," in *Homosexuality and Ethics*, ed. Edward Batchelor Jr. (New York: Pilgrim Press, 1980), p. 94.

8. John J. McNeill, S. J., *The Church and the Homosexual* (New York: Next Year Publications, 1985), pp. 40–48.

9. Ibid., pp. 132–133.

10. Arthur Evans, *The God of Ecstasy* (New York: St. Martins Press, 1986), pp. 85–86.

11. Ibid., pp. 86–87.

12. Ibid., pp. 175–176.

13. Ibid., p. 175.

14. Gabriel Marcel, *The Philosophy of Existentialism,* trans. Manya Harari (Secaucus, N.J.: Citadel Press, 1984), p. 94.

15. Ibid., p. 96.

16. Ibid., p. 97.

17. Ibid.

18. Gabriel Marcel, "De Rufus à l'Invocation," p. 123, quoted by Marcel in *The Philosophy of Existentialism,* pp. 98–99.

19. For an elucidation of this notion, see Paul Ricoeur, *Interpretation Theory: Discourse and the Surplus of Meaning* (Fort Worth: Texas Christian

University Press, 1976), pp. 1–25, 34–37. See also John Van Den Hengel, *The Home of Meaning* (Washington: University Press of America, 1982), p. 24.

20. Paul Ricoeur, *Hermeneutics and the Human Sciences,* ed. and trans. John B. Thompson (Cambridge: Cambridge University Press, 1982), pp. 147–148.

21. Ricoeur, *Interpretation Theory*, p. 21. Ricoeur later in *Interpretation Theory* makes the following supporting remark: "In the sacred universe the capacity to speak is founded upon the capacity of the cosmos to signify" (p. 62).

22. Ibid., p. 59.

23. Ibid., p. 37. See also, Peter Joseph Albano, *The Relationship of Philosophy and Religion in the Thouqht of Paul Ricoeur* (Michigan: Xerox University Microfilms, 1976), p. 186.

24. Ricoeur, *The Symbolism of Evil,* p. 18.

25. Ricoeur refers to the text as intending a Weltanschauung in Paul Ricoeur, *Main Trends in Philosophy* (New York: Holmes and Maier, 1979), p. 265.

26. Ricoeur, *Interpretation Theory,* p. 37.

27. Patrick Bourgeois, *Extension of Ricoeur's Hermeneutic* (Hague: Martinus Nijhoff, 1975), p. 137. See also, Ricoeur, *Hermeneutics and the Human Sciences,* p. 174.

28. Paul Ricoeur, *The Rule of Metaphor,* trans. Robert Czerney, Kathleen McLaughlin, and John Costello, S. J. (Toronto: University of Toronto Press, 1977), p. 319.

29. For an extended discussion of the notion of ideology as distortion, see Ricoeur's treatment of Marx's *The German Ideology* in *Ideology and Utopia,* chapters 2–6.

30. Ricoeur, *Ideology and Utopia,* pp. 13, 200–203.

31. It is possible to draw an analogy between the sort of suspicion that can be cast on the work of Evans and McNeill and the suspicion that one might have regarding the testimony of conscience. According to Hegel, conscience arises through the recognition "that when moral consciousness declares pure duty to be the essence of its action, this pure purpose is a

dissemblance of the actual fact. For the real fact is that pure duty consists in the empty abstraction of pure thought, and finds its reality and content solely in some definite actual existence, an actuality which is actuality of consciousness itself—not of consciousness in the sense of a thought-entity, but as an individual." See G.W.F. Hegel, *The Phenomenology of Mind*, trans. J. B. Baille (New York: Harper Torchbooks, 1967), p. 648. With this recognition, the self realizes that the only moral obligations placed upon it are those placed by itself. See Quentin Lauer, S. J., *A Reading of Hegel's Phenomenology of Spirit* (New York: Fordham University Press, 1982), p. 221. Not being born out of adherence to any authority, even the authority of reason, these obligations are rooted in the immediate certainty that constitutes the essence of conscience. That is, they are rooted in a private individual conviction (*The Phenomenology of Mind*, pp. 648–649). See also Merold Westphal's instructive account of the Hegelian notion of conscience in *History and Truth in Hegel's Phenomenology* (Atlantic Highlands, N.J.: Humanities Press International, 1990). To claim to act from conscience is to claim to act from conviction. But because of the immediacy attaching to conviction, this claim is always subject to doubt. One might suspect that what masks itself as an act born of conviction is really an act of selfishness (*The Phenomenology of Mind*, p. 669). Similarly, one might wonder whether McNeill's and Evans's works are the products of narrow self-interest or of genuine conviction and insight.

32. Ricoeur, *Hermeneutics and the Human Sciences*, p. 134.

33. Ibid., p. 137.

34. Ibid., p. 139.

35. Ibid.

36. Ibid., p. 140.

37. The following passage from Ricoeur's *Hermeneutics and the Human Sciences* is instructive:

> For what must be interpreted in a text is a *proposed world* which I could inhabit and wherein I could project one of my own most possibilities. That is what I call the world of the text, the world proper to *this* unique text. (P. 142)

38. The following passage from Merold Westphal's "The Hermeneutics of Suspicion," in *Phenomenology of the Truth Proper to Religion*, ed. Daniel Guerriere (Albany, N.Y.: State University of New York Press) states Heidegger's case well:

It is neither metaphor nor objective spirit but the as-structure of experience that lies at the basis of hermeneutics. The crucial transition occurs in paragraph 32 of *Being and Time*. Even at the level of ordinary sense perception and prior to any explicit assertion, there is no "mere seeing" but always the act that sees something as something. Long before we encounter symbols and social structures we are engaged in understanding and interpretation. The hermeneutical situation is constitutive of Dasein's being-in-the-world. (P. 111)

39. Gadamer, *Truth and Method,* pp. 225–234.

40. Ibid., p. 246.

41. Paul Ricoeur, *History and Truth*, trans. Charles A. Kelbley (Evanston, IL: Northwestern University Press, 1965), pp. 42, 166.

42. Ibid., p. 42.

43. Ibid., p. 43.

44. Ibid., pp. 43–44.

45. See Ricoeur's *History and Truth,* pp. 175–191, for a discussion of the manifestation of this violence in the clerical and political realms.

46. Ricoeur, *History and Truth,* pp. 44, 176.

47. Ibid., p. 61.

48. Ibid., p. 47.

49. Ibid., p. 48.

50. Ibid., pp. 49–50.

51. Ibid., p. 50.

52. Ibid., p. 51.

53. Ricoeur, *The Symbolism of Evil,* pp. 19–20.

54. Ibid., p. 308. See also Ricoeur's *Ideology and Utopia,* where this idea is echoed (p. 312).

55. The following remarks by Ricoeur in *Ideology and Utopia* regarding the appropriate function of utopian visions in society are apropos in this regard:

> The result of reading a utopia is that it puts into question what presently exists; it makes the actual world seem strange. Usually we are tempted to say that we cannot live in a way different from the way we presently do. The utopia, though, introduces a sense of doubt that shatters the obvious. It works like the epoche in Husserl, when he speaks in *Ideas I* of the hypothesis of the destruction of the world—a purely mental experiment. The epoche requires us to suspend our assumptions about reality . . . The order which has been taken for granted suddenly appears queer and contingent. There is an experience of the contingency of order. This, I think, is the main value of utopias. At a time when everything is blocked by systems which have failed but which cannot be beaten—this is my pessimistic appreciation of our time—utopia is our assurance. It may be an escape, but it is also the aim of critique. It may be that particular times call for utopias. I wonder whether our present period is not such a time, but I do not want to prophesy; that is something else. (Pp. 299–300)

56. Ricoeur, *Ideology and Utopia*, p. 258.

57. Robert N. Bellah, Richard Madsen, William M. Sullivan, Ann Swidler, and Steven M. Tipton, *Habits of the Heart* (New York: Harper and Row, 1986), pp. 20, 334.

58. Jurgen Habermas, *Moral Consciousness and Communicative Action* (Cambridge: MIT Press, 1990), p. 46.

59. Ibid., p. 65.

60. Ibid., pp. 82, 96–97. See also, Steven Hendley, "From Communicative Action to the Face of the Other: Habermas and Levinas on the Foundations of Moral Theory," *Philosophy Today* 40 (winter 1996), p. 505.

61. Habermas, *Moral Consciousness,* p. 97.

62. Ibid., p. 100.

63. Ibid., p. 103.

64. Ibid., p. 104.

65. Ibid.

66. Seyla Benhabib, *Situating the Self* (New York: Routledge, 1992), p. 8.

67. Benhabib draws support for this claim from Habermas and Apel (see *Situating the Self,* p. 28).

65. Ibid., p. 37.

69. Ibid., pp. 9–11. In the following passage, Benhabib makes clear the full extent of her disagreement with Habermas over the question of consent versus agreement as it effects the formulation of the universalization principle:

> The chief difference between my proposal and Habermas's is that for him "U" has the effect of guaranteeing consensus. As long as their interests are not violated, all could freely consent to some moral content. But the difficulty with consent theories is as old as Rousseau's dictum—"on les forcera d'etre libre." Consent alone can never be a criterion of anything, neither of truth nor of moral validity; rather, it is always the rationality of the procedure for attaining agreement which is of philosophical interest. We must interpret consent not as an end-goal, but as a process for the cooperative generation of truth or validity. The core intuition behind modern universalizability procedures is not that everybody could or would agree to the same set of principles, but that these principles have been adopted as a result of a procedure, whether of moral reasoning or of public debate, which we are ready to deem "reasonable and fair." It is not the result of the process of moral judgment alone that counts but the process for the attainment of such judgment which plays a role in its validity, and I would say, moral worth. Consent is a misleading term for capturing the core idea behind communicative ethics: namely the processual generation of reasonable agreement about moral principles *via an open-ended moral conversation.* It is my claim that this core intuition, together with an interpretation of the normative constraints of argument in light of the principle of universal respect and egalitarian reciprocity, are sufficient to accomplish what U was intended to accomplish, but only at the price of consequentialist confusion. (*Situating the Self,* p. 37)

70. Clearly distinguishing her account of communicative ethics from Habermas's account, Benhabib maintains the following:

In such a conversation of moral justification as envisaged by communicative ethics, individuals do not have to view themselves as "unencumbered" selves. It is not necessary for them to define themselves independently either of the ends they cherish or of the constitutive attachments which make them what they are. In entering practical discourses individuals are not entering an "original position." They are not being asked to define themselves in ways which are radically counterfactual to their everyday identities. This model of moral argumentation does not predefine the set of issues which can be legitimately raised in the conversation and neither does it proceed from an unencumbered concept of the self. In communicative ethics, individuals do not stand behind any "veil of ignorance." (*Situating the Self,* p. 73)

It is worth noting that Benhabib develops extended arguments to support the claims that communicative ethics cannot abstract from the concrete self and cannot limit moral conversation to questions of the right, leaving to the side questions of the good life. With respect to the former claim, she notes that genuine reciprocity is not possible if the subjects involved are viewed only from the perspective of the universal other (see *Situating the Self*, chapter 5). With respect to the latter claim, Benhabib notes that, "Since practical discourses do not theoretically predefine the domain of moral debate and since individuals do not have to abstract from their everyday attachments and beliefs when they begin argumentation, we cannot preclude that it will be not only matters of justice but those of the good life as well that will become thematized in practical discourses . . ." (ibid., p. 77). Further, though Benhabib does believe that the distinction between questions of right and questions of the good life is significant and that the right should place limits upon what courses can be followed in the name of the good life, she notes that attempts to demarcate questions of justice from those of the good life have typically maintained that the former belong to the public sphere while the latter belong to the private sphere. However, the distinction between the public and private spheres often incorporates uncritical suppositions. This implies that one cannot automatically assume which questions are issues of justice and which are issues of the good life (see ibid., pp. 74–76, 97–99; chapter 5). Much is owed to feminist scholarship in bringing these unexamined suppositions to light (see ibid., pp. 109–110).

71. Benhabib, *Situating the Self,* p. 30.

72. Ibid., p. 32.

73. Ibid., pp. 33, 40–41.

74. Ibid., p. 33.

75. An interesting discussion of the difficulties that arise for a Habermasean when confronted with claims regarding animal rights, or the rights of those who cannot present their legitimate interests in human discourse on their own terms, is offered by Stephen Connor, *Theory and Cultural Value* (Cambridge: Blackwell Publishers, 1992), pp. 109–110.

76. Marie Fleming "Working in the Philosophical Discourse of Modernity Habermas, Foucault, and Derrida," *Philosophy Today* 40 (spring 1996), p. 172.

77. Ibid., p. 173.

78. Ibid., pp. 41–42, 154.

79. Ibid., pp. 41–42.

80. Ibid., p. 43.

81. Ibid., p. 44.

82. It seems to me that Benhabib in the end must come close to the same conclusion. See Benhabib, *Situating the Self*, pp. 52–53.

Chapter Three

1. An excellent discussion of the dangers presented by presuming that sexual orientation is either culturally or biologically determined, lending strength to Foucault's claim that all positions are dangerous, is offered by Eve Kosofsky Sedgwick, *Epistemology of the Closet* (Berkeley: University of California Press, 1990), pp. 40–44. For Foucault's claim, see Michel Foucault, "The Subject and Power," afterword to Hubert L. Dreyfus and Paul Rabinow, *Michel Foucault: Beyond Structuralism and Hermeneutics* (Chicago: University of Chicago Press, 1982), p. 232.

2. John D'Emilio, "Capitalism and Gay Identity," in *Feminist Frontiers II* ed. Laurel Richardson and Verta Taylor (New York: Random House, 1989), p. 184.

3. This is not to suggest that everyone uses sexual identity labels in relation to themselves in this way, but rather that this is a claim that is common to many gays and lesbians, as found in the coming out stories that

they tell. For further discussion of this, see Judith Roof, *come as you are: sexuality and narrative* (New York: Columbia University Press, 1986), pp. 104–105.

4. Paul Ricoeur, *Lectures on Ideology and Utopia,* ed. George H. Taylor (New York: Columbia University Press, 1986), pp. 11–12.

5. Ibid., pp. 13–14, 257–259.

6. The corpus of Ricoeur's work is marked by a hermeneutic turn that occurs in *The Symbolism of Evil,* the third volume of *Freedom and Nature,* a turn that can be characterized in terms of Ricoeur's attempt to explore the disclosive power of symbols and myths (Paul Ricoeur, *The Symbolism of Evil,* trans. Emerson Buchanan [Boston: Beacon Press,1967]); of metaphor (Paul Ricoeur, *The Rule of Metaphor,* trans. Robert Czerny, Kathleen McLaughlin, and John Costello [Toronto: University of Toronto Press, 1975]); of narrative (Paul Ricoeur, *Time and Narrative, Vols. I, II, III,* trans. Kathleen McLaughlin and David Pellauer [Chicago: University of Chicago Press, 1984, 1985, 1988]). The germ of Ricoeur's fundamental insights regarding the disclosive power of symbol and myth can be found in the concluding chapter of *The Symbolism of Evil,* "The Symbol Gives Rise to Thought," pp. 347–357.

7. In this claim, Ricoeur is close to Heidegger's insight in "The Origin of the Work of Art," when he distinguishes between truth as correctness and truth as aletheia. Truth as correctness may be understood in terms of the correspondence theory of truth, while truth as aletheia depends on a more primordial disclosure which Heidegger describes as the "unconcealedness of beings." See Martin Heidegger, "The Origin of the Work of Art," in Martin Heidegger, *Poetry, Language, Thought,* trans. Albert Hofstadter (New York: Harper and Row, 1971), p. 52.

8. Butler makes a strong case for this when she agrees with Slavoj Zizek and Jacques Lacan that socially intelligible sexed positions are realized through identity formations relying upon the foreclosure of certain possibilities, but that, contrary to Zizek's view, these constitutive foreclosures are historically, culturally, and socially contingent. See Judith Butler, *Bodies That Matter* (New York: Routledge, 1993), pp. 206–207.

9. This is a central theme that Butler plays and develops in a variety of contexts in *Bodies That Matter.* See, in particular, *Bodies That Matter*, p. 6; chapters 3 and 7.

10. In *Gender Trouble,* Butler not only argues for the constructed character of gender identity realized in the body through normatively gov-

erned reiterative practices, but further maintains that attempts on the part of some feminist theorists to employ essentialist accounts of gender in counterhegemonic ways end by reinstituting "ideal orders" that set up new relations of domination and oppression. See Judith Butler, *Gender Trouble* (New York: Routledge, 1990), p. 20.

11. Ibid., pp. 6–7.

12. Richard Boothby, *Death and Desire* (New York: Routledge, 1991), p. 58. In his discussion of the Imaginary, Lacan makes the point that the emergence of the ego occurs through the incorporation of certain desires and the exclusion of others. See Jacques Lacan, *The Seminar of Jacques Lacan, Book I: Freud's Papers on Technique, 1953–1954,* ed. Jacques-Alain Miller, trans. John Forrester (New York: W.W. Norton Co., 1988).

13. In his discussion of the Symbolic in Lacan, Boothby highlights the fact that the function of the Symbolic is to give voice to desire that was excluded in the formation of the ego (*Death and Desire,* pp. 109–110). But the Symbolic never gives comprehensive voice to the Real, nor is its approach to the Real direct (*Death and Desire,* p. 113). Butler does not foreground this disruptive potential of the Symbolic, but instead focuses on its productive potential, suggesting that while the Symbolic carries within it the seeds of its own disruption, it nonetheless tends to support the congealing of social identities through citation and performance.

14. Butler, *Bodies That Matter*, pp. 187–188, 94. See also Jacques Lacan, "The function and field of speech and language," in *Ecrits: A Selection*, trans. Alan Sheridan (New York: W.W. Norton, 1977), p. 68.

15. Lacan is less sanguine regarding this possibility for contestation, as seen if one considers the primacy he gives to the name of the father as support for the symbolic function in "The function and field of speech," *Ecrits,* pp. 65–67.

16. The idea of sexual identities as political signifiers operating as performatives is treated by Butler in her discussion of Slavoj Zizek's use of the notion of "political signifier" in *Bodies That Matter*, chapter 7.

17. Note that Butler distances herself from Lacanians such as Slavoj Zizek who claim that the feminine must occupy the site of the Real, the unthinkable, unsymbolizable, the foreclosed identity which is the "outside," making the "inside" of the socially intelligible possible, and who place the masculine within discourse and the symbolic. See *Bodies That Matter,* pp. 73–74, 206–207.

18. Ibid, pp. 219–222.

19. Ibid., pp. 117–118.

20. Butler articulates both possibilities in *Bodies That Matter*, p. 115.

21. Ricoeur, *Time and Narrative, Vol. I*, p. 52.

22. Ibid., p. 46.

23. In "Ethics and Narrativity," Peter Kemp offers a cogent account of Ricoeur's three stages of mimesis, together with the suggestion that mimesis 1 should be understood as narratively configured, consisting of a number of "little stories," a suggestion which extends narrative to a domain that Ricoeur describes as containing within itself an "inchoate narrativity." See Peter Kemp, "Ethics and Narrativity," in *The Philosophy of Paul Ricoeur*, ed. Lewis Edwin Hahn (Chicago: Open Court, 1995), pp. 373, 377. Interestingly, David Carr develops a critique of Ricoeur's claim that life contains an "inchoate narrativity," arguing instead that life is lived narratively. See David Carr, *Time, Narrative and History* (Bloomington: Indiana University Press, 1991), p. 15.

24. Indeed, in *Time and Narrative,* a central aspect of the project is to address the aporia between phenomenological and scientific conceptions of time. Ricoeur turns to the mimetic activity of narrative in order to develop a third conception of time that spans the gap opened by this aporia (see *Time and Narrative, Vol. III,* p. 245).

25. Hayden White, "The Value of Narrativity in the Representation of Reality," in *On Narrative*, ed. W. J. T. Mitchell (Chicago: University of Chicago Press), 1981, p. 10.

26. Ricoeur, *Time and Narrative, Vol. I,* p. 54.

27. Kemp, "Ethics and Narrativity," p. 373.

28. Alasdair MacIntyre, *After Virtue* (South Bend, Ind.: University of Notre Dame Press, 1981), pp. 191–193.

29. Ricoeur, *Time and Narrative, Vol. III,* p. 246.

30. Paul Ricoeur, *Oneself as Another,* trans. Kathleen Blamey (Chicago: University of Chicago Press, 1992). See also, *Time and Narrative, Vol. III,* p. 246.

31. Ricoeur, *Oneself as Another,* p. 143.

32. Ibid., pp. 141–142.

33. Ibid., p. 148.

34. Ricoeur, *Time and Narrative, Vol. III,* p. 246.

35. Ricoeur, *Oneself as Another,* pp. 121–122.

36. Butler, *Bodies That Matter,* pp. 7–8. In her latest work on hate speech, Butler further insists that it is impossible for human subjects ever to escape being socially constituted as such through naming. See Judith Butler, *Excitable Speech* (New York: Routledge, 1997), pp. 4–5.] At the same time, she insists that this by no means precludes contesting and attempting a transformation of the names through which one is constituted as a subject (see *Excitable Speech,* pp. 33–34).

37. Heidegger, "The Origin of the Work of Art," pp. 66–68. Note that Heidegger develops the notion of gift more explicitly in *On Time and Being* by attempting to think Being and Time in terms of "It gives," the giving of a gift, the gift of presence (where "presence" is distinguished from "the now"), which nonetheless remains concealed in the giving. See Martin Heidegger, *On Time and Being,* trans. Joan Stambaugh (New York: Harper and Row, 1972), pp. 8–9.

38. Butler, *Excitable Speech,* p. 5.

39. Ibid., pp. 1–2.

40. Ricoeur, *Oneself as Another,* p. 22.

41. It is important to emphasize that such recognition serves merely as a propaedeutic to dialogue. The politics and logic of such dialogue are extremely large questions, each of which deserves separate treatment.

Chapter Four

1. Richard Rubenstein, *The Cunning of History* (New York: Harper and Row, 1978), p. 2.

2. Ibid., p. 26.

3. Bruce Bawer, *A Place at the Table* (New York: Poseidon Press, 1993).

4. David Kolb offers a perspicuous account of Lyotard's views regarding this. See David Kolb, *The Critique of Pure Modernity* (Chicago: University of Chicago Press, 1986), pp. 256–260.

5. Jean-Francois Lyotard, *The Postmodern Condition: A Report on Knowledge,* trans. Geoff Bennington and Brian Massumi (Minneapolis: University of Minnesota Press, 1984), pp. 23–25.

6. Jean-Francois Lyotard, *The Differend,* trans. Georges Van Den Abbeele (Minneapolis: University of Minnesota Press, 1988), p. 12.

7. It is important to recognize that Lyotard distinguishes between traditional narratives and the language game of modern science, noting that "... the modern scientist questions the validity of narrative statements and concludes that they are never subject to argumentation or proof" (*The Postmodern Condition*, p. 27). However, he goes on to show that science is unable to legitimate itself by appealing to its own criteria for justification, that narratives arise in terms of which scientific practice(s) are justified. This, in fact, causes a legitimation crisis of science, which is particularly noteworthy, as traditional narratives did not, in Lyotard's view, incorporate the demand for legitimation of the narrative itself: "There is, then, an incommensurability between popular narrative pragmatics, which provides immediate legitimation, and the language game known to the West as the question of legitimacy—or rather, legitimacy as a referent in the game of inquiry. Narratives, as we have seen, determine criteria of competence and/or illustrate how they are to be applied. They thus define what has the right to be said and done in the culture in question, and since they are themselves a part of that culture, they are legitimated by the simple fact that they do what they do" (*The Postmodern Condition*, p. 23).

8. In saying this, I do not mean to imply that instituting gay and lesbian marriage would in fact grant voice to gays and lesbians. While refusal of the right to marry has played a significant role in refusing voice and recognition to designated groups in our society, it does not follow that granting access to marriage should be equated with marginalized groups having access to, or recognition by, the larger society.

9. Lyotard offers the following enlightening critique of Habermas relevant at this juncture:

> Social pragmatics does not have the "simplicity" of scientific
> pragmatics. It is a monster formed by the interweaving of
> various networks of heteromorphous classes of utterances
> (denotative, prescriptive, technical, evaluative, etc.). There is
> no reason to think that it would be possible to determine
> metaprescriptives common to all of these language games or

that a revisable consensus like the one in force at a given moment in the scientific community could embrace the totality
of metaprescriptions regulating the totality of statements circulating in the social collectivity. As a matter of fact, the contemporary decline of narratives of legitimation—be they traditional or "modern" (the emancipation of humanity, the
realization of the Idea)—is tied to the abandonment of this
belief. It is its absence for which the ideology of the "system,"
with its pretensions to totality, tries to compensate and which
it expresses in the cynicism of its criterion of performance.

For this reason, it seems neither possible, or even pru-
dent, to follow Habermas in orienting our treatment of the
problem of legitimation in the direction of a search for universal consensus through what he calls *Diskurs,* in other
words, a dialogue of argumentation.

This would be to make two assumptions. The first is
that it is possible for all speakers to come to agreement on
which rules or metaprescriptives are universally valid for
language games, when it is clear that language games are
heteromorphous, subject to heterogeneous sets of pragmatic
rules.

The second assumption is that the goal of dialogue is
consensus. But as I have shown in the analysis of the pragmatics of science, consensus is only a particular state of discussion, not its end. Its end, on the contrary, is paralogy. This
double observation (the heterogeneity of the rules and the
search for dissent) destroys a belief that still underlies
Habermas's research, namely, that humanity as a collective
(universal) subject seeks its common emancipation through
the regularization of the "moves" permitted in all language
games and that the legitimacy of any statement resides in its
contributing to that emancipation. (*The Postmodern Condition*, pp. 66–67)

There are two ideas here that are particularly relevant to the concerns
of this chapter:

1. Science proceeds not by forming consensus, but through
   dissent, coming up with ideas, changing the rules of the
   game itself. At least in the scientific enterprise, reaching
   consensus is not necessarily key; dissent is valuable. So
   might it be for social discourse.

2. The master narrative of universal emancipation can itself
   become oppressive to the extent that it requires the construction of a set of conditions that all narrative visions

must meet in order to be allowed to circulate in society. Meeting such criteria can itself so transform the narrative vision that it ceases to exist; the requirement leads to an act of terror against such narrative visions, thereby undermining the emancipatory narrative that legitimates the requirement of such restrictions in the first place.

10. Lyotard, *The Postmodern Condition,* p. 10.

11. Emmanuel Levinas, *Totality and Infinity,* trans. Alphonso Lingis (Pittsburgh: Duquesne University Press, 1961), p. 66.

12. Lyotard, *The Postmodern Condition,* pp. 9–11.

13. For a discussion of this shift, see Honi Haber, *Beyond Postmodern Politics* (New York: Routledge, 1994), pp. 136–137, fn. 12.

14. Geoffrey Bennington, *Lyotard Writing the Event* (Manchester: Manchester University Press, 1988), p. 112.

15. It is interesting to note here Bill Readings's discussion of Lyotard's decision in *Instructions paiennes* to move away from the claim that "everything is narrative," and his replacement of the term "narrative" with that of "phrase." Readings offers two reasons for this: (1) the claim that everything is narrative leads to the temptation of indifference, to viewing all accounts of power, knowledge, etc., as nothing but telling stories; (2) narrative is but one of many options for making phrases. Readings argues that the substitution of "phrase" for "narrative" does not solve the problem of indifference, and offers the following provocative suggestion:

This doesn't solve the problem, because I still want to be able to talk about narrative, even as one genre among others. It is important to work out how Lyotard is doing more in talking about little narratives than saying that accounts of power, value and knowledge amount to nothing but "telling stories," producing narratives from a series of indifferently assumed positions.

I think it is possible to have our cake and eat it too if we rephrase the claim that "everything is narrative" as "the condition of narrative is unsurpassable." This shift is what preserves Lyotard's version of the postmodern condition from mere relativist despair. In Lyotard's account of postmodernity, the epistemological condition is marked by a resistance

to metalanguages. And it is to this end that he talks about
the expanded field of little narratives, about an impious or
pagan attitude to knowledge, about minoritarian politics,
about language games or phrases, about experimentation,
about judgment without criteria. All of these terms resist becoming metalanguages; so much so that the distinguishing
feature of postmodernity, according to Lyotard, is an "in-
credulity towards metanarratives."

Bill Readings, *Introducing Lyotard: Art and Politics* (New York: Routledge, 1991), pp. 65–66.

16. Lyotard, *The Differend*, pp. 69–70, no. 10.

17. Ibid., p. 11, no. 18. See also, *The Differend,* p. 11, no. 18, p. 70, no. 111.

18. Ibid., p. 14, no. 25.

19. Tim Jordan, "The Philosophical Politics of Jean-François Lyotard," *Philosophy and the Social Sciences,* p. 270.

20. Lyotard, *The Differend*, p. 70, no. 14. See also, p. xii.

21. Jordan, "Philosophical Politics," p. 270.

22. Horst Ruthrof offers a helpful account of the relation between
phrases, phrase regimens, and genres of discourse. See Horst Ruthrof, "Differend and Agonistics: A Transcendental Argument," *Philosophy Today* 36:4
(winter 1992), pp. 325–326. See also, *The Differend,* p. 28, no. 39.

23. It is worth noting the objection that, if phrase regimens are incommensurable, then logically, it is difficult to see how one can maintain
that they can conflict. In *The Differend*, Lyotard addresses this by saying
that the conflict arises because only one can link at a time (p. 29, no. 40),
but he also offers the following interesting suggestion, which may not be
fully convincing, but which is worth noting:

> But if phrases belonging to different regimens or genres,
> such as those of cognition and those of the Idea, encounter
> each other to the point of giving rise to differends, then they
> must have certain properties in common and their "en-
> counter" must take place within a single universe, otherwise
> there would be no encounter at all!—The universe you are
> thinking of would be a universe prior to the phrases and
> where they would encounter each other; but it is your phrase

that presents it as being there before all phrases. That is the paradox that in general signals reality as that which is, even when there is no validatable testimony through cognitive procedures (Nos. 37, 47).—No, I am not saying that this universe is reality, but only that it is the condition for the encounter of phrases, and therefore the condition for differends.—The condition of the encounter is not this universe, but the phrase in which you present it. It is a transcendental and not an empirical condition. Regarding this universe, it can just as easily be said that it is the effect of the encounter as its condition (the two expressions are equivalent). Similarly, the linguist's phrase is the transcendental condition of the language to which it refers. This does not prevent language from being the empirical condition of the linguist's phrase. *Transcendental* and *empirical* are terms which do no more than indicate two different phrase families: the critical (criticizing) philosophical phrase and the cognitive phrase. Finally: phrases from heterogeneous regimens or genres "encounter" each other in proper names, in worlds determined by networks of names (Nos. 80, 81, 60). (Pp. 28–29, no. 39)

24. Ibid., p. 29, no. 40.

25. Ibid., p. 128, no. 178.

26. Ibid., p. 29, no. 41.

27. Ibid., p. 29, no. 40.

28. Ibid., p. 138, no. 189.

29. Ibid., p. 136, no. 184.

30. The importance that Lyotard assigns to this claim can be seen particularly well in *The Differend*, pp. 137–138, no. 188.

31. See Jordan, "Philosophical Politics," p. 272, for a helpful formulation of this point.

32. Jean-Francois Lyotard with Jean-Loup Thebaud, *Just Gaming*, trans. Brian Massumi, afterward by Samuel Weber (Minneapolis: University of Minnesota Press, 1985). See Samuel Weber and Jean-Loup Thebaud for objections found in the same volume.

33. See *The Differend*, p. 5, no. 7, and p. 140, no. 196.

34. For a very helpful discussion of Lyotard's dealings with "the event," see Readings, *Introducing Lyotard,* chapters, 2, 3.

35. Readings, *Introducing Lyotard*, p. 57.

36. Ibid., p. 115.

37. Bill Readings develops an interesting contrast between Lyotard's account of the indeterminate judgment and a relativist refusal to judge. See *Introducing Lyotard*, pp. 125–126.

38. Lyotard, *The Differend,* p. 142, no. 202.

39. Ibid., p. 166, Kant Remark 4. No. 4.

40. Ibid., p. 179, no. 256.

41. Ibid., p. 140, no. 197.

42. To appreciate the use of "other" here, it is helpful to note the following from the beginning of Levinas's *Otherwise than Being:*

> If transcendence has meaning, it can only signify the fact that the *event of being,* the *esse*, the *essence*, passes over to what is other than being. But what is *Being's other*? . . . And what can the *fact* of passing over mean here, where the passing over, ending at being's other, can only undo its facticity during such a passage?
> Transcendence is passing over to being's *otherwise*, but *otherwise than being*. And not to not-be; passing over is not here equivalent to dying. Being and not-being illuminate one another, and unfold a speculative dialectic which is a determination of being. Or else the negativity which attempts to repel being is immediately submerged by being . . .
> To be or not to be is not the question where transcendence is concerned. The statement of being's *other*, of the otherwise than being, claims to state a difference over and beyond that which separates being from nothingness—the very difference of the *beyond*, the difference of transcendence.

Emmanuel Levinas, *Otherwise than Being or Beyond Essence,* trans. Alphonso Lingis (Hague: Martinus Nijhoff, 1978).

43. G. W. F. Hegel, *Introductory Lectures of Aesthetics,* ed. Michael Inwood, trans. Bernard Bosanquet (London: Penguin Books, 1993), pp. 70–71.

44. Ibid., p. 71.

45. Ibid., p. 71.

46. Ibid., p. 73.

47. Ibid., p. 72.

48. Ibid., p. 73.

49. A. T. Nuyen, "The Trouble with Tolerance," *American Catholic Philosophical Quarterly,* 71:1, (1997), p. 3.

50. Ibid., pp. 4–5.

51. Wendy Farley, "Ethics and Reality: Dialogue between Caputo and Levinas," *Philosophy Today* (fall 1992), p. 217.

52. Merold Westphal, "Levinas and the Immediacy of the Face," *Faith and Philosophy,* 10:4 (October 1993), p. 490.

53. Levinas, *Totality and Infinity,* pp. 22–23.

54. While I will not address this in detail, it is important likewise to note that in *Totality and Infinity,* Levinas distinguishes between ontology and metaphysics, aligning ontology with the attempt to develop a totalizing picture of being available to cognition, while metaphysics, ". . . is turned toward the 'elsewhere' and the 'otherwise' and the 'other' " (p. 33). With respect to the distinction between ontology and metaphysics, it is worth reviewing *Totality and Infinity*, pp. 33–53, 80. For a particularly perspicuous account of this shift in traditional prioritization, what it means and what it implies, see Fabio Ciaramelli, "Levinas's Ethical Discourse Between Individuation and Universality," in *Re-Reading Levinas*, ed. R. Bernasconi and S. Critchley, (Bloomington: Indiana University Press, 1991), pp. 83–101.

55. Levinas, *Totality and Infinity,* pp. 45, 89, 94, 134, 170.

56. Martin Heidegger *Being and Time,* trans. John Macquarrie and Edward Robinson (San Francisco: Harper and Row, 1962) p. 26, H. 38.

57. Robert John Sheffler Manning, *Interpreting Otherwise than Heidegger: Emmanuel Levinas's ethics as first philosophy,* (Pittsburgh: Duquesne University Press, 1993), p. 41.

58. Levinas, *Totality and Infinity,* pp. 64–65.

59. Alphonso Lingis, "The Sensuality and the Sensitivity," in *Face to Face with Levinas,* ed. Richard A. Coheren (Albany, N.Y.: State University of New York Press, 1986), p. 221.

60. Ibid., p. 220.

61. Ibid., p. 222.

62. For a moving description of this, see Lingis, "The Sensuality and Sensitivity," pp. 222–223.

63. Levinas, *Totality and Infinity,* p. 265.

64. Colin Davis, *Levinas* (South Bend, IN: University of Notre Dame Press, 1996), p. 23.

65. For further discussion of the development of Levinas's throught regarding these themes prior to *Totality and Infinity,* see Manning, *Interpreting Otherwise than Heidegger,* pp. 29–58, and Davis, *Levinas,* chapter 1.

66. In his introduction to *Totality and Infinity,* John Wild emphasizes the contrast between Heidegger and Levinas in this regard. See p. 12.

67. Levinas, *Totality and Infinity,* pp. 133–134, 143. See also Ciaramelli, "Levinas's Ethical Discourse," p. 89.

68. For an interesting discussion of the prioritization of this response to the attempt to cognitively grasp the Other in Levinas, see Manning, *Interpreting Otherwise than Heidegger,* pp. 180–188.

69. Levinas, *Totality and Infinity,* p. 47. See also Manning, *Interpreting Otherwise than Heidegger,* p. 184.

70. For an interesting discussion of this point, see Farley, "Ethics and Reality," p. 217.

71. Needs are satisfied through appropriation, through making the other one's own, while desire is marked by an unquenchable longing for the otherwise than oneself, for that which can never be appropriated. Desire is therefore that which calls one beyond oneself, foreclosing completeness, moving one beyond being to transcendence:

> The metaphysical desire does not long to return, for it is desire for a land not of our birth, for a land foreign to every nature, which has not been our fatherland and to which we

shall never betake ourselves. The metaphysical desire does not rest upon any prior kinship. It is a desire that can not be satisfied. For we speak lightly of desires satisfied, or of sexual needs, or even of moral and religious needs. Love itself is thus taken to be the satisfaction of a sublime hunger. If this language is possible it is because most of our desires and love too are not pure. The desires one can satisfy resemble metaphysical desire only in the deceptions of satisfaction or in the exasperation of non-satisfaction and desire which constitutes voluptuosity itself. The metaphysical desire has another intention; it desires beyond everything that can simply complete it. It is like goodness—the Desired does not fulfill it, but deepens it. (Levinas, *Totality and Infinity*, p. 34)

See also, *Totality and Infinity*, p. 117.

72. Tina Chanter's *ethics and eros* (New York: Routledge, 1995) provides the following helpful elaboration of this point:

To know is to bring something under a concept, to relate it back to me, to make it familiar, to objectify it, to incorporate it into my own identity. By understanding it, not only do I refer it back to me. I also relate it to the whole, to the system of knowledge in general. Otherness is consumed in my conceptualization of it. Knowing is a movement that reduces the object to me, leaving no room for difference. I am made whole, and the whole encompasses me. Levinas is suspicious of the totalization that he believes to be inherent in philosophical discourse, or in any attempt to think, to conceptualize, to systematize, to theorize. He sees in philosophy the tendency to reduce everything to the same—to categorize, to subsume, to unify. (P. 185)

73. Levinas, *Totality and Infinity*, p. 39. See also, *Totality and Infinity*, p. 101.

74. Ibid., pp. 39, 50, 96.

75. Chanter, *ethics and eros*, pp. 184–185.

76. It should be noted that this claim bypasses an important, necessary, but in this context ill-advised, discussion of free will and what becomes of it in Levinas's thought given that free will is typically considered a necessary supposition for ethical action, but that Levinas's account of subjectivity requires that it precede freedom. A helpful discussion of this can be found in Ciaramelli, "Levinas's Ethical Discourse," pp. 86–88.

77. Levinas, *Totality and Infinity*, p. 201. See also, *Otherwise than Being*, pp. 6–7.

78. Levinas, *Totality and Infinity*, p. 199.

79. The following passage is particularly helpful at this juncture:

> The conscience welcomes the Other. It is the revelation of a resistance to my powers that does not counter them as a greater force, but calls in question the naïve right of my powers, my glorious spontaneity as a living being. Morality begins when freedom, instead of being justified by itself, feels itself to be arbitrary and violent. (*Totality and Infinity*, p. 84)

See also, *Otherwise than Being*, pp. 116–117.

80. Chanter, *ethics and eros*, p. 79.

81. Ciaramelli, "Levinas's Ethical Discourse," pp. 87–88.

82. Lingis, "The Sensuality and the Sensitivity," p. 49.

83. Emmanuel Levinas, *Time and the Other*, trans. R. Cohen, (Pittsburg: Duquesne University Press, 1987), p. 55.

84. The asymmetry of this demand is founded upon what Levinas calls a metaphysical asymmetry. See *Totality and Infinity*, p. 53.

85. For a particularly instructive account of the face to face relation, see Chanter, *ethics and eros*, p. 181.

86. In "Levinas's Ethical Discourse," Fabio Ciaramelli discusses the difficulties surrounding the asymmetry of the ethical demand and its claim to universality as found in Levinas's work. See particularly, p. 85.

87. Levinas, *Otherwise than Being*, pp. 86, 89, 90. It is appropriate in this context to look at Ciaramelli's account of the shift from the discussion of the face to face relation in *Totality and Infinity* to the discussion of proximity in *Otherwise than Being*. In *Totality and Infinity*, in order to avoid the selfish contestation of totality made by the egocentric self, Levinas is forced to recognize ipseity in general, but this is at variance with his concern to highlight the fact that the relation to the other is that which constitutes one's own personal individuation. Ciaramelli notes that Levinas seeks to circumvent this in *Otherwise than Being* by leaving ontological language behind, and shifting its focus from the ego to me. It is in this context that

Ciaramelli describes Levinas's shift from the face to face relation to proximity. See Ciaramelli, "Levinas's Ethical Discourse," pp. 90–91.

88. Ciaramelli, "Levinas's Ethical Discourse," p. 92.

89. The following passage from Chanter's *ethics and eros* is particularly helpful in thinking about how, according to Levinas, language is founded on the face to face relation, and why, according to Levinas, the said in its universalizing tendency must always fall short of that relation:

> For Levinas, the face to face founds language. The I's confrontation with the other enables a subject to differentiate itself from all the others, and by the same token to begin to collect things under concepts. Through language the subject can gather together and represent the fruits of its labor. A transformation is thus effected. The things from which the I lives, the "elemental" in which it is submersed, become objects of exchange, subject to the designs of others. Henceforth, the products of my work take on values bestowed on them by commerce. To share a world in common with others is also to produce goods which are susceptible of meanings over which I have no control. The act of representation, a giving of my world to another, is at the same time the possibility of conceiving a world at all. The gift is offered only on the basis of oneself. In other words, it is through the other that the I both becomes an I—identifies itself as such—and is able to generate the categories of being, or to universalize. The other produces the I by putting it in question. To be put in question is to have the things I live off be contested by a subject who approaches me. Language is the movement through which these new events occur, the constitution of the subject as such, and the putting in common of a world. Expressed in language, things are at the disposal not only of the I, they are also exposed to the other. (P. 190)

90. Levinas, *Totality and Infinity,* p. 73.

91. Levinas, *Otherwise than Being,* pp. 6–9.

92. Alphonso Lingis, "Translator's Introduction" to *Otherwise than Being,* p. xxix.

93. Note passage from Chanter's *ethics and eros* in note 89 above.

94. Levinas, *Totality and Infinity,* p. 174.

95. For a useful formulation of this point, see Alphonso Lingis, "Translator's Introduction" to *Otherwise than Being,* p. 35.

96. Chanter, *ethics and eros*, p. 207.

97. Levinas, *Otherwise than Being,* pp. 151–152.

98. Lingis, "Translator's Introduction, *Otherwise than Being,*" p. xxxvi. While I am currently focusing upon the significance of the said, it is important to remember the context for this. To this end, Tina Chanter's instructive suggestion for thinking about Levinas's stance with respect to the universal in light of his concern with the origins of the said in saying is felicitous:

> . . . for Levinas, the ethical continually disrupts the equilibrium of being, repeatedly discloses meaning, constantly disturbs the complacency with which we establish universal maxims for what we benevolently imagine to be the good of the whole. This does not mean that Levinas doubts the necessity of universal laws, nor the legitimacy of observing ethical standards of behavior. It means that the moral laws by which we live bear a significance beyond their universality. The interruption they suffer in taking account of the face to face is precisely what renews their efficacy, and what justifies the moral codes we construct by which to live. (*ethics and eros,* p. 182)

99. Levinas, *Totality and Infinity,* p. 177. See also, pp. 181–182.

100. Paul Ricoeur, *Time and Narrative, Vol. I,* trans. Kathleen McLaughlin and David Pellauer (Chicago: University of Chicago Press, 1984), p. 74.

101. Ibid., pp. 74–75.

102. Ibid., pp. 65–66.

103. As Levinas says in *Totality and Infinity:*

> Language is a relation between separated terms. To the one the other can indeed present himself as a theme, but his presence is not reabsorbed in his status as a theme. The word that bears on the Other as a theme seems to contain the Other. But already it is said to the Other who, as interlocutor, has quit the theme that encompassed him, and upsurges

inevitably behind the said. Words are said, be it only by the silence kept, whose weight acknowledges this evasion of the Other. The knowledge that absorbs the Other is forthwith situated within the discourse I address to him. Speaking, rather than "letting be," solicits the Other . . . In discourse the divergence that inevitably opens between the Other as my theme and the Other as my interlocutory, emancipated from the theme that seemed a moment to hold him, forthwith contests the meaning I ascribe to my interlocutor. The formal structure of language thereby announces the ethical inviolability of the Other and, without any odor of the "numinous," his "holiness." (P. 195)

104. The following passage from *Totality and Infinity* is worth bearing in mind here:

The welcoming of the face is peaceable from the first, for it answers to the unquenchable Desire for Infinity. War itself is but a possibility and nowise a condition for it. The peaceable welcome is produced primordially in the gentleness of the feminine face, in which the separated being can recollect itself, because of which it *inhabits,* and in its dwelling accomplishes separation. Inhabitation and the intimacy of the dwelling which make the separation of the human being possible thus imply a first revelation of the Other.

Thus the idea of infinity, revealed in the face, does not only *require* a separated being; the light of the face is necessary for separation. But in founding the intimacy of the home the idea of infinity provokes separation not by some force of opposition and dialectical evocation, but by the feminine grace of its radiance. The force of opposition and of dialectical evocation would, in integrating it into a synthesis, destroy transcendence. (Pp. 150–151)

See also, *Totality and Infinity,* p. 172.

105. Levinas, *Otherwise than Being,* pp. 13–14. See also, p. 11.

106. Ricoeur, *Time and Narrative, Vol. I,* p. 159.

107. See in particular, Levinas, *Otherwise than Being,* p. 16.

108. Ibid., p. 6.

109. Ibid., pp. 17–18.

110. Recall that Ricoeur maintains that experience as such has "an inchoate narrativity that does not proceed from projecting, as some say, literature on life but that constitutes a genuine demand for narrative" (*Time and Narrative, Vol. I*, p. 74). Ricoeur characterizes this inchoate narrativity as the prenarrative quality of experience. Hence, one lives from what he likewise calls a quasi-narrative.

111. Ricoeur, *Time and Narrative, Vol. I*, p. 78.

112. Ibid., p. 78.

113. Ibid., pp. 68–70.

114. Ibid., p. 69.

115. Ibid., p. 69.

116. Ibid., p. 70.

117. Ibid., pp. 65, 207.

118. Ibid., p. 75.

119. Luce Irigaray, "Questions to Emmanuel Levinas," in *Writing the Future,* ed. David Wood (New York: Routledge, 1990), p. 109.

120. Levinas, *Otherwise than Being,* pp. 75–81. For an excellent discussion of these issues, see Morny Joy, "Levinas: Alterity, the Feminine, and Women—A Meditation," *Studies in Religion/Sciences Religieuses* 22:4 (1993), pp. 463–485.

121. Levinas, *Ethics and Infinity,* p. 60.

122. Levinas, *Totality and Infinity,* p. 111.

123. Chanter, "Feminism and the Other," in *The Provocation of Levinas: Rethinking the Other,* ed. Robert Bernasconi and David Wood (New York: Routledge, 1988), p. 42.

124. Levinas, *Totality and Infinity,* p. 262.

125. Ibid., pp. 257–258.

126. Ibid., p. 259.

127. Ibid., p. 260.

128. Ibid., p. 266.

129. Ibid., p. 255.

130. Ibid., pp. 267–269.

131. For interesting discussions in regard to this, see Alison Ainsley, "Amourous Discourses: 'The Phenomenology of Eros' and Love Stories," in *The Provocation of Levinas: Rethinking the Other*, ed. Robert Bernasconi and David Wood (New York: Routledge, 1988), pp. 70–81, and Morny Joy, "Levinas: Alterity, the Feminine, and Women."

132. Emmanuel Levinas, "Judaism and the Feminine Element," trans. E. Wyschogrod, *Judaism*, 18:2 (1969), p. 35.

133. Chanter, "Feminism and the Other," p. 50.

134. Ibid., p. 53.

135. Joy, "Levinas: Alterity, the Feminine, and Women," p. 476. See also Kate Ince, "Questions to Luce Irigaray," *Hypatia,* 11:2 (spring 1996), pp. 122–140, where Ince argues that there is in fact less distance between Irigaray's and Levinas's positions than Irigaray supposes.

136. Luce Irigaray, "The Fecundity of the Caress," in *An Ethics of Sexual Difference,* trans. Carolyn Burke and Gillian C. Gill (Ithaca: Cornell University Press, 1993), p. 190.

137. Jacques Derrida, "At This Very Moment in This Work Here I Am," in *A Derrida Reader: Between Blinds,* ed. Peggy Kamuf (New York: Columbia University Press, 1991), pp. 430–431.

138. Ibid., p. 430.

139. Irigaray, "Questions to Emmanuel Levinas," p. 111.

140. Jacques Derrida, "Violence and Metaphysics: An Essay on the Thought of Emmanuel Levinas," in *Writing and Difference,* trans. Alan Bass (Chicago: University of Chicago Press, 1978), pp. 125–127.

141. Ibid., pp. 91, 114.

142. See, for example, Colin Davis, *Levinas*, p. 63.

143. Levinas, *Totality and Infinity*, p. 199.

144. Derrida, "The Violence of Metaphysics," p. 116.

145. Peter Atterton, "Levinas and the Language of Peace: A Response to Derrida," *Philosophy Today* (spring, 1992), p. 60.

146. Levinas, *Totality and Infinity,* quoted in Atterton, "Levinas and the Language of Peace," p. 59.

147. Atterton, "Levinas and the Language of Peace," p. 61.

148. Levinas, *Totality and Infinity,*, p. 204, quoted in Atterton, "Levinas and the Language of Peace," p. 61 (emphasis Atterton's).

Chapter Five

1. Aristotle, *The Poetics* in *The Works of Aristotle*, ed. J. A. Smith and W. D. Ross (Oxford: Oxford University Press, 1908ff.), I, 1460a, pp. 26–27.

2. Sigmund Freud, *Three Essays on the History of Sexuality, Standard Edition,* 7.

3. In *Come As You Are: Sexuality and Narrative*, Judith Roof offers the following interesting reflection regarding the limitations of visibility politics that is worth considering in the context of this discussion of *Ellen:*

> Like lesbian authors who try to shift public perceptions by making lesbians protagonists, visibility politics tries to strong-arm opinion by changing the image of an identity within the same logic that produced that identity, instead of trying to identify and alter the process by which identities are produced and situated and by which visibility/invisibility itself becomes the problem. (P. 149)

From Judith Roof, *Come As You Are* (New York: Columbia University Press, 1986).

4. Here I have in mind Judith Roof's extension of Roland Barthes' account of ideology to narrative in *Come As You Are:*

> Roland Barthes' rendering of ideology is probably more descriptive of an ideology coextensive with narrative's broad context. In his examination of the cultural operation of myth, Barthes sees bourgeois ideology as a particular confusion of

nature and history, where the historical is rendered natural. While this confusion explains specific ways the bourgeoisie has rendered its interests universal, the model of an ideology that works through "signs which pass themselves off as natural, which offer themselves as the only conceivable way of viewing the world," which "convert culture into nature," which " 'naturalize' social reality" and "make it seem as innocent and unchangeable as Nature itself," resonates with both narrative's ubiquity and its seemingly mimetic logic. (P. xvi)

5. Roof, *Come As You Are,* p. xiv.

6. Ibid., p. xiv.

7. Ibid., pp. xiv–xv.

8. Ibid., p. xxxii. It is important to note at this point an important ambiguity in Roof's text that is reflected in this quote. At times, Roof seems to support what I would call the "strong thesis" that there is something about narrative structure, understood as a structure which is transcultural and transhistorical, that colludes with modern heterosexual ideology, while at other times, she seems to support the weaker thesis that "our" modern Western understanding of what counts as narrative is the focus of her concern. I shall tend to adopt the latter reading, though with some trepidation, as it threatens a certain incoherence and ambiguity with respect to the use of the term "narrative."

9. Ibid., chapter 2.

10. Ibid., p. xix.

11. Ibid., p. xxi.

12. Ibid., pp. 142–143.

13. Ibid., p. 139.

14. Paul Ricoeur, *Time and Narrative, Vol. I,* trans. Kathleen McLaughlin and David Pellauer, (Chicago: University of Chicago Press, 1984), p. 57.

15. Roof, *Come As You Are,* p. 72.

16. John Boswell, *Same-Sex Unions in Premodern Europe* (New York: Vintage Books, 1995), chapters 3 and 4. In chapter 3, Boswell details vari-

ous conceptions of heterosexual unions, and in chapter 4, he deals with their homosexual parallels. It is important to note that the various relationships do not purely and simply mirror one another. Still, it is interesting to note that the most significant form of legal union, marriage, was not at all times restricted to heterosexual couples, though it seems clear that same-sex union had its critics. See particularly, pp. 80–81.

17. Boswell, *Same-Sex Unions,* p. 37.

18. Ibid., p. 61.

19. Ibid., p. 75.

20. Ibid., p. 97.

21. Ibid., p. 111.

22. Paul. 1 Cor. 7:29–31, quoted in Boswell, *Same-Sex Unions*, p. 109.

23. Boswell, *Same-Sex Unions,* pp. 135–136.

24. Ibid., p. 139.

25. Ibid., p. 150.

26. Martha Nussbaum, *The Fragility of Goodness: Luck and Ethics in Greek Tragedy and Philosophy* (New York: Cambridge University Press, 1986), chapters 6 and 7.

27. Ibid., pp. 176–184.

28. Ibid., p. 186.

29. Ibid., p. 198.

30. Martha Nussbaum, "Love and the Individual: Romantic Rightness and Platonic Aspiration," in *Restructuring Individualism,* ed. Thomas C. Heller, Morton Sosna, and David Wellbery (Stanford: Stanford University Press, 1986), pp. 264, 275.

31. Plato, *The Symposium* in *The Collected Dialogues of Plato*, ed. Edith Hamilton and Huntington Cairns (Princeton: Princeton University Press, 1961), 206e.

32. Ibid., 209c-e.

33. Roof, *Come As You Are,* p. 35.

34. Henning Bech, *when men meet: Homosexuality and Modernity,* trans. Teresa Mesquit and Tim Davies (Chicago: University of Chicago Press, 1997), p. 31ff.

35. Ibid., p. 33.

36. Ibid., pp. 44–84.

37. Ibid., pp. 188–189.

38. Ibid., p. 102.

39. Ibid., p. 134.

40. Ibid., p. 96.

41. Ibid., p. 97.

42. Ibid., p. 141.

43. See particularly, *when men meet,* p. 178.

44. Ibid., pp. 178–180; chapter 6.

45. Ibid., pp. 216–217.

46. Leslie Feinberg, *Stone Butch Blues* (Ithaca: Firebrand Books), 1993, p. 275.

Bibliography

Ainsley, Alison. (1988) "Amourous Discourses: 'The Phenomenology of Eros' and Love Stories." In *The Provocation of Levinas: Rethinking the Other*. Ed. Robert Bernasconi and David Wood. New York: Routledge.

Albano, Peter Joseph. (1976) *The Relationship of Philosophy and Religion in the Thought of Paul Ricoeur*. Michigan: Xerox University Microfilms.

Aristotle. (1908) *The Poetics* in *The Works of Aristotle*. Ed. J. A. Smith and W. D. Ross. Oxford: Oxford University Press.

Atterton, Peter. (1992) "Levinas and the Language of Peace: A Response to Derrida." *Philosophy Today* (spring): 59–70.

Auden, W. H. (1991) "Leap Before You Look." In *Collected Poems*. Ed. Edward Mendelson. New York: Vintage Books.

Bawer, Bruce. (1993) *A Place at the Table*. New York: Poseidon Press.

Bech, Henning. (1997) *when men meet: Homosexuality and Modernity*. Trans. Teresa Mesquit and Tim Davies. Chicago: University of Chicago Press.

Bellah, Robert, Richard Madsen, William M. Sullivan, Ann Swidler, and Steven M. Tipton. (1986) *Habits of the Heart*. New York: Harper and Row.

Benhabib, Seyla. (1992) *Situating the Self.* New York: Routledge.

Bennington, Geoffrey. (1988) *Lyotard Writing the Event.* Manchester: Manchester University Press.

Boothby, Richard. (1991) *Death and Desire.* New York: Routledge.

Boswell, John. (1995) *Same-Sex Unions in Premodern Europe.* New York: Vintage Books.

Bourgeois, Patrick. (1975) *Extension of Ricoeur's Hermeneutic.* Hague: Martinus Nijhoff.

Browning, Frank. (1994) *The Culture of Desire.* New York: Vintage Books.

Butler, Judith. (1993) *Bodies That Matter.* New York: Routledge.

———. (1993) *Excitable Speech.* New York: Routledge.

———. (1990) *Gender Trouble.* New York: Routledge.

Carr, David. (1991) *Time, Narrative and History.* Bloomington: Indiana University Press.

Chanter, Tina. (1990) "The Alterity and Immodesty of Time: Death as Future and Eros as Feminine in Levinas." In *Writing the Future.* Ed. David Wood. New York: Routledge.

———. (1995) *ethics and eros.* New York: Routledge.

———. (1988) "Feminism and the Other." In *The Provocation of Levinas: Rethinking the Other* Ed. Robert Bernasconi and David Wood. New York: Routledge.

Ciaramelli, Fabio. (1991) "Levinas's Ethical Discourse between Individuation and Universality." In *Re-Reading Levinas.* Ed. R. Bernasconi and S. Critchley. Bloomington: Indiana University Press.

Connor, Stephen. (1992) *Theory and Cultural Value.* Cambridge: Blackwell Publishers.

Curran, Charles. (1980) "Homosexuality and Moral Theology: Methodological and Substantive Considerations." *Homosexuality and Ethics.* Ed. Edward Batchelor Jr. New York: Pilgrim Press.

Davis, Colin. (1996) *Levinas*. South Bend, Ind.: University of Notre Dame Press.

D'Emilio, John. (1989) "Capitalism and Gay Identity." In *Feminist Frontiers II*. Ed. Laurel Richardson and Verta Taylor. New York: Random House.

Derrida, Jacques. (1991) "At This Very Moment in This Work Here I Am." In *A Derrida Reader: Between Blinds*. Ed. Peggy Kamuf. New York: Columbia University Press.

————. (1978) "Violence and Metaphysics: An Essay on the Thought of Emmanuel Levinas." In *Writing and Difference*. Trans. Alan Bass. Chicago: University of Chicago Press.

Dreyfus, Hubert L. and Paul Rabinow. (1982) *Michel Foucault: Beyond Structuralism and Hermeneutics*. Chicago: University of Chicago Press.

Evans, Arthur. (1986) *The God of Ecstasy*. New York: St. Martin's Press.

Farley, Wendy. (1992) "Ethics and Reality: Dialogue between Caputo and Levinas." *Philosophy Today* (fall): 210–220.

Feinberg, Leslie. (1993) *Stone Butch Blues*. Ithaca, N.Y.: Firebrand Books.

Fleming, Marie. (1996) "Working in the Philosophical Discourse of Modernity: Habermas, Foucault, and Derrida." In *Philosophy Today* 40 (spring): 169–178.

Foucault, Michel. (1972) *The Archaeology of Knowledge*. Trans. A. M. Sheridan Smith. New York: Pantheon Books.

————. (1975) *The Birth of the Clinic*. Trans. A. M. Sheridan Smith. New York: Vintage/Random House.

————. (1979) *Discipline and Punish*. Trans. Alan Sheridan. New York: Vintage Books.

————. (1996) "The Ethics of the Concern for the Self as a Practice of Freedom." In *Foucault Live. Interviews: 1961–1984*. Ed. Sylvere Lotringer. Trans. Lysa Hochroth and John Johnston. New York: Semiotext(e).

————. (1980) *The History of Sexuality, Vol. I*. Trans. Robert Hurley. New York: Vintage Books.

———. (1986) *The History of Sexuality, Vol. II: The Use of Pleasure.* Trans. Robert Hurley. New York: Vintage Books.

———. (1988) *The History of Sexuality, Vol. III: The Care of the Self.* Trans. Robert Hurley. New York: Vintage Books.

———. (1967) "Nietzsche, Freud, Marx." In *Nietzsche.* Paris: Cahiers de Royaumont.

———. (1988) "Practicing Criticism." In *Michel Foucault: Politics, Philosophy, Culture: Interviews and Other Writings, 1977–1984.* Ed. Lawrence D. Kritzman. Trans. Alan Sheridan et al. London: Routledge.

———. (1985) "Sexuality and Solitude." In *On Signs: A Semiotics Reader.* Ed. M. Blonsky. Oxford: Basil Blackwell.

———. (1990) "The Subject and Power." Afterword to *Michel Faucault: Beyond Structuralism and Hermeneutics,* by Hubert L. Dreyfus and Paul Rabinow. Chicago: University of Chicago Press.

———. (1980) "Truth and Power." In *Power/Knowledge.* Ed. Colin Gordon. Trans. Colin Gordon, Leo Marshall, John Mepham, and Kate Soper. New York: Pantheon Books.

———. (1980) "Two Lectures." In *Power/Knowledge.* Ed. Colin Gordon. Trans. Colin Gordon, Leo Marshall, John Mepham, and Kate Soper. New York: Pantheon Books.

———. (1988) "What Is Enlightenment?" In *Michel Foucault: Politics, Philosophy, Culture: Interviews and Other Writings, 1977–1984.* Ed. Lawrence D. Kritzman. Trans. Alan Sheridan et al. London: Routledge.

Fraser, Nancy. (1996) "Michel Foucault: A 'Young Conservative'?" In *Feminist Interpretations of Michel Foucault.* Ed. Susan J. Hekman. University Park: Pennsylvania State University Press.

Freud, Sigmund. *Three Essays on the History of Sexuality, Standard Edition,* 7.

Gadamer, Hans-Georg. (1988) *Truth and Method.* New York: Crossroad Publishing.

Gerhart, Mary. (1977) "The Extent and Limits of Metaphor: Reply to Gary Madison." *Philosophy Today* 11 (spring): 431–436.

Grosz, Elizabeth. (1990) *Jacques Lacan: A Feminist Introduction*. New York: Routledge.

Guerriere, Daniel, ed. (1990) *Phenomenology of the Truth Proper to Religion*. Albany, N.Y.: State University of New York Press.

Haber, Honi. (1994) *Beyond Postmodern Politics*. New York: Routledge, 1994.

Habermas, Jurgen. (1990) *Moral Consciousness and Communicative Action*. Cambridge: MIT Press.

Hackett, Stuart C. (1969) "Philosophical Objectivity and Existential Involvement in the Methodology of Paul Ricoeur." *International Philosophical Quarterly* 9 (March): 11–39.

Hartsock, Nancy. (1990) "Foucault on Power: A Theory for Women?" In *Feminism / Postmodernism*. Ed. Linda Nicholson. New York: Routledge.

Hegel, G. W. F. (1993) *Introductory Lectures of Aesthetics*. Ed. Michael Inwood. Trans. Bernard Bosanquet. London: Penguin Books.

———. (1967) *The Phenomenology of Mind*. Trans. J. B. Baille. New York: Harper Torchbooks.

Heidegger, Martin. (1962) *Being and Time*. Trans. John Macquarrie and Edward Robinson. San Francisco: Harper and Row.

———. (1977) "Letter on Humanism." *Basic Writings*. Ed. David Krell. New York: Harper and Row.

———. (1972) *On Time and Being*. Trans. Joan Stambrough. New York: Harper and Row.

———. (1971) "The Origin of the Work of Art." In *Poetry, Language, Thought*. Trans. Albert Hofstadter. New York: Harper and Row.

Hendley, Steven. (1996) "From Communicative Action to the Face of the Other: Habermas and Levinas on the Foundations of Moral Theory." *Philosophy Today* 40 (winter): 504–531.

Hiley, David R. (1984) "Foucault and the Analysis of Power: Political Engagement without Liberal Hope or Comfort." *Praxis International* 4:2 (July): 192–207.

hooks, bel. (1984) *Feminist Theory from Margin to Center*. Boston: South End Press.

Ince, Kate. (1996) "Questions to Luce Irigaray." *Hypatia* 11:2 (Spring): 122–140.

Irigaray, Luce. (1993) *An Ethics of Sexual Difference*. Trans. Carolyn Burke and Gillian Gill. Ithaca: Cornell University Press.

———. (1993) "The Fecundity of the Caress." In *An Ethics of Sexual Difference*. Trans. Carolyn Burke and Gillian C. Gill. Ithaca: Cornell University Press.

———. (1990) "Questions to Emmanuel Levinas." In *Writing the Future*. Ed. David Wood. New York: Routledge.

Jordan, Tim. (1995) "The Philosophical Politics of Jean-Francois Lyotard." *Philosophy and the Social Sciences* 25:3 (September): 267–285.

Joy, Morny. (1993) "Levinas: Alterity, the Feminine, and Women—A Meditation." *Studies in Religion / Sciences Religieuses* 22:4: 463–485.

Kemp, Peter. (1995) "Ethics and Narrativity." In *The Philosophy of Paul Ricoeur*, Ed. Lewis Edwin Hahn. Chicago: Open Court.

———. "Ricoeur between Heidegger and Levinas: Original Affirmation between Ontological Attestation and Ethical Injunction." *Philosophy and Social Criticism* 21:5/6: 41–61.

Kolb, David. (1986) *The Critique of Pure Modernity*. Chicago: University of Chicago Press.

Lacan, Jacques. (1977) "The function and field of speech and language." In *Ecrits: A Selection*. Trans. Alan Sheridan. New York: W. W. Norton.

———. (1988) *The Seminar of Jacques Lacan. Book I: Freud's Papers on Technique, 1953–1954*. Ed. Jacques-Alain Miller. Trans. John Forrester. New York: W. W. Norton.

Lauer, Quentin. (1982) *A Reading of Hegel's Phenomenology of Spirit*. New York: Fordham University Press.

Levinas, Emmanuel. (1985) *Ethics and Infinity*. Pittsburgh: Duquesne University Press.

————. (1969) "Judaism and the Feminine Element." Trans. E. Wyschogrod. *Judaism* 18:2: 30–38.

————. (1980) *Otherwise than Being or Beyond Essence*. Trans. with an introduction by Alphonso Lingis. Hague: Martinus Nijhoff.

————. (1987) *Time and the Other*. Trans. R. Cohen. Pittsburg: Duquesne University Press.

————. (1961) *Totality and Infinity*. Trans. Alphonso Lingis. Introduction by John Wild. Pittsburgh: Duquesne University Press.

Lingis, Alphonso. (1986) "The Sensuality and the Sensitivity." In *Face to Face with Levinas*. Ed. Richard A. Coheren. Albany, N.Y.: State University of New York Press.

————. (1980) "Translator's Introduction" to *Otherwise than Being or Beyond Essence*, by Emmanuel Levinas. Hague: Martinus Nijhoff.

Lloyd, Moya. (1996) "A Feminist Mapping of Foucauldian Politics." In *Feminist Interpretations of Michel Foucault*. Ed. Susan J. Heckman. University Park: Pennsylvania State University Press.

Lourde, Audre. (1992) "Age, Race, Class, and Sex": Women Redefining Difference." In *Ethics: A Feminist Reader*. Ed. Elizabeth Frazer, Jennifer Hornsby, and Sabina Lovibond. Oxford: Blackwell.

Lyotard, Jean-Francois. (1988) *The Differend*. Trans. Georges Van Den Abbeele. Minneapolis: University of Minnesota Press.

————. (1984) *The Postmodern Condition: A Report on Knowledge*. Trans. Geoff Bennington and Brian Massumi. Minneapolis: University of Minnesota Press.

Lyotard, Jean-Francois with Jean-Loup Thebaud. (1985) *Just Gaming*. Trans. Brian Massumi. Afterword by Samuel Weber. Minneapolis: University of Minnesota Press.

MacIntyre, Alasdair. (1981) *After Virtue*. Notre Dame: University of Notre Dame Press.

————. (1988) *The Seminar of Jacques Lacan, Book I: Freud's Papers on Technique*. Ed. Jacques-Alain Miller. Trans. John Forrester. New York: W. W. Norton.

Manning, Robert John Sheffler. (1993) *Interpreting Otherwise than Heidegger: Emmanuel Levinas's ethics as first philosophy*. Pittsburgh: Duquesne University Press.

———. (1984) "De Rufus à l'Invocation." In *The Philosophy of Existentialism*. Trans. Manya Harari. Secaucus, N.J.: Citadel Press.

Marcel, Gabriel. (1984) *The Philosophy of Existentialism*. Trans. Manya Harari. Secaucus, N.J.: Citadel Press.

McNay, Lois. (1992) *Foucault and Feminism*. Boston: Northeastern University Press.

———. (1984) *The Philosophy of Existentialism*. Trans. Manya Harari. Secaucus, N.J.: Citadel Press.

McNeill, John J. S.J. (1985) *The Church and the Homosexual*. New York: Next Year Publications.

McWhorter, Ladelle. (1992) "Asceticism/Askesis: Foucault's Thinking in Historical Subjectivity." In *Ethics and Danger*. Ed. Arleen Dallery and Charles Scott. Albany, N.Y.: State University of New York Press.

———. (1990) "Foucault's Analytics of Power," in *Crises in Continental Philosophy*. Ed. Arleen B. Dallery, Charles E. Scott, and P. Holley Roberts. Albany, N.Y.: State University of New York Press.

Megill, Allan. (1985) *Prophets of Extremity*. Berkeley: University of California Press.

Nietzsche, Friedrich. (1989) *Beyond Good and Evil*. Trans. Walter Kaufmann. New York: Vintage Books.

———. (1961) *Thus Spoke Zarathustra: A Book for Everyone and No One*. Trans. R. J. Hollingdale. Harmondsworth, England: Penguin Books.

Nussbaum, Martha. (1986) *The Fragility of Goodness: Luck and Ethics in Greek Tragedy and Philosophy*. New York: Cambridge University Press.

———. (1986) "Love and the Individual: Romantic Rightness and Platonic Aspiration," in *Restructuring Individualism*, Ed. Thomas C. Heller, Morton Sosna, and David Wellbery. Stanford: Stanford University Press.

Nuyen, A. T. (1997) "The Trouble with Tolerance." *American Catholic Philosophical Quarterly* 71:1: 1–12.

Plato. (1961) *The Symposium* in *The Collected Dialogues of Plato*. Ed. Edith Hamilton and Huntington Cairns. Princeton: Princeton University Press.

Readings, Bill. (1991) *Introducing Lyotard: Art and Politics*. New York: Routledge.

Ricoeur, Paul. (1973) "Creativity in Language." *Philosophy Today* 17 (summer): 97–111.

———. (1970) *Freud and Philosophy: An Essay on Interpretation*. Trans. Denis Savage. New Haven: Yale University Press.

———. (1981) *Hermeneutics and the Human Sciences*. Ed. and trans. John B. Thompson. Cambridge: Cambridge University Press.

———. (1965) *History and Truth*. Trans. Charles A. Kelbley. Evanston, Il: Northwestern University Press.

———. (1976) *Interpretation Theory: Discourse and the Surplus of Meaning*. Fort Worth: Texas Christian University Press.

———. (1986) *Lectures on Ideology and Utopia*. Ed. George H. Taylor. New York: Columbia University Press.

———. (1979) *Main Trends in Philosophy*. New York: Holmes and Maier.

———. (1992) *Oneself as Another*. Trans. Kathleen Blamey. Chicago: University of Chicago Press.

———. (1975) *The Rule of Metaphor*. Trans. Robert Czerny, Kathleen McLaughlin, and John Costello, S. J. Toronto: University of Toronto Press.

———. (1967) *The Symbolism of Evil*. Trans. Emerson Buchanan. Boston: Beacon Press.

———. (1984) *Time and Narrative, Vol. I*. Trans. Kathleen McLaughlin and David Pellauer. Chicago: University of Chicago Press.

———. (1985) *Time and Narrative, Vol. II*. Trans. Kathleen McLaughlin and David Pellauer. Chicago: University of Chicago Press.

———. (1988) *Time and Narrative, Vol. III*. Trans. Kathleen McLaughlin and David Pellauer. Chicago: University of Chicago Press.

———. (1971) "What Is a Text? Explanation and Interpretation." In *Mythic-Symbolic Language and Philosophical Anthropology*. Ed. David Rasmussen. Hague: Martinus Nijhoff.

Roof, Judith. (1986) *Come As You Are: Sexuality and Narrative*. New York: Columbia University Press.

Rubenstein, Richard. (1978) *The Cunning of History*. New York: Harper and Row.

Ruthrof, Horst. (1992) "Differend and Agonistics: A Transcendental Argument." *Philosophy Today* 36:4 (winter): 324–335.

Sawicki, Jana. (1991) *Disciplining Foucault*. New York: Routledge.

Sedgwick, Eve Kosofsky. (1990) *Epistemology of the Closet*. Berkeley: University of California Press.

Vaid, Urvashi. (1995) *Virtual Equality: The Mainstreaming of Gay and Lesbian Liberation*. New York: Anchor Books.

Van Den Hengel, John (1982) *The Home of Meaning*. Washington: University Press of America.

Vatican's Congregation for the Doctrine of the Faith. (1986) "Pastoral Care of Homosexual Persons," *Origins*, (November).

Weinsheimer, Joel C. (1985) *Gadamer's Hermeneutics*. New Haven: Yale University Press.

West, Cornel. (1994) *Race Matters*. New York: Vintage Books.

Westphal, Merold. "The Hermeneutics of Suspicion." *Phenomenology of the Truth Proper to Religion*. Ed. Daniel Guerriene. Albany, N.Y.: State University of New York Press.

———. (1990) *History and Truth in Hegel's Phenomenology*. Atlantic Highlands, N.J.: Humanities Press International.

―――. (1993) "Levinas and the Immediacy of the Face." *Faith and Philosophy* 10:4 (October): 486–502.

White, Haden. (1981) "The Value of Narrativity in the Representation of Reality." In *On Narrative*. Ed. W. J. T. Mitchell. Chicago: University of Chicago Press.